Marine Tourism, Climate Change, and Resilience in the Caribbean, Volume II

Marine Tourism, Climate Change, and Resilience in the Caribbean, Volume II

Recreation, Yachts, and Cruise Ships

Edited by
Kreg Ettenger
Martha Honey
Samantha Hogenson
Center for Responsible Travel (CREST)

BEP BUSINESS EXPERT PRESS

CREST
Center for Responsible Travel

Marine Tourism, Climate Change, and Resilience in the Caribbean, Volume II; Recreation, Yachts, and Cruise Ships
Copyright © Business Expert Press, LLC, 2018.
Center for Responsible Travel (CREST), 2018.

First published in 2018 by
Business Expert Press, LLC
222 East 46th Street, New York, NY 10017
www.businessexpertpress.com

Center for Responsible Travel (CREST)
1225 Eye Street, NW, Suite 600
Washington, DC 20005

ISBN-13: 978-1-63157-753-6 (paperback)
ISBN-13: 978-1-63157-754-3 (e-book)

Business Expert Press Tourism and Hospitality Management Collection

Collection ISSN: 2375-9623 (print)
Collection ISSN: 2375-9631 (electronic)

Cover and interior design by S4Carlisle Publishing Services Private Ltd., Chennai, India

First edition: 2018

10 9 8 7 6 5 4 3 2 1

Printed in the United States of America.

Abstract

As the nations of the Caribbean respond to the emerging effects of climate change and prepare for those to come, tourism has the potential to either worsen or mitigate these impacts. In the four volumes of this collection, we look at the role of coastal and marine tourism in the Caribbean and similar regions, considering the impacts of the tourism sector on marine and coastal environments, and on the human communities that depend on them. We also explore the way the tourism industry is responding to climate change, and how various sectors are adapting and preparing for various types of impacts. Through essays and case studies by scientists, business leaders, government and NGO staff, and others, we show that tourism could lead the way in reducing human-induced climate impacts, protecting and restoring crucial ecosystems and habitats, and building sustainable futures for the people of the Caribbean and beyond.

In this book, the last of four total volumes on coastal tourism and marine tourism, we look specifically at marine recreation and how its various sectors—ranging from surfing, diving and sport fishing, to yachting and cruise ships—are coping with and preparing for climate change in the Caribbean. As with the other three volumes, we focus on examples that show how industry leaders are responding to climate change, using their power and resources to foster positive change in the Caribbean and other parts of the world.

Keywords

adaptation, Caribbean, climate change, cruise ships, marine protected areas, marine recreation, marine tourism, mitigation, resilience, responsible tourism, sustainable development, sustainable tourism, yachting

Contents

Foreword and Acknowledgments

The idea for this volume on marine tourism, and its three companion volumes, grew out of the 2015 "Innovators Think Tank: Climate Change and Coastal & Marine Tourism," held in Punta Cana, Dominican Republic, July 22–24, 2015. Organized and hosted by the Center for Responsible Travel (CREST) and the Grupo Puntacana Foundation, the Think Tank brought together some 35 sustainable tourism practitioners and climate change experts to take stock of how coastal and marine tourism in the Caribbean are dealing with climate change and its impacts, and to identify priorities that need to be addressed. Our discussions, ably facilitated by Roger-Mark De Souza of the Woodrow Wilson Center, were organized around a single critical theme: *How coastal and marine tourism must be planned, built, and operated in this era of climate change.*

One outcome of the Think Tank was the unanimous decision to put together a publication on the same theme as a tool for public education. We are grateful that many of the Think Tank participants agreed to contribute essays and case studies for these four volumes. Additional authors were identified during the years that we have worked on the books. All generously contributed their expertise to this common project.

Early in the process, Kreg Ettenger, associate professor in the Department of Anthropology at the University of Maine, agreed to come on board as editor of the marine tourism volumes. His contributions have been enormous and have added greatly to the quality of the books. Indispensable as well to this project has been Samantha Hogenson, CREST's managing director, who not only contributed to the concept and content, but also, with her usual efficiency, oversaw the final copyediting and assembling of the manuscript.

She also oversaw the CREST researchers who have worked diligently on numerous essential, but often tedious, details. Patricia Nuñez Garcia, who was part of the CREST team at the Think Tank, transcribed a number of presentations that have been reshaped into contributions for the manuscript. Ashley Newson and Helena Servé organized many of the photos and graphics, including successfully securing permissions for each of them. Helena also stepped in to assist with numerous research tasks, as well as some copyediting. Finally, six other CREST researchers—Gabriela Aguerrevere Yanez, Angela Borrero, Emily Simmons, Noora Laukkanen, Jessica McCommon, and Eugene Kim—contributed to tracking down information, researching topics, and identifying potential authors. We are grateful to this entire team!

We would like to thank Scott Isenberg and Business Expert Press for taking an early interest in our proposal and agreeing to publish these volumes. We were fortunate to make contact just as BEP was launching its Tourism and Hospitality Management Collection, and to find that, like CREST, BEP focuses on reaching academic and business audiences. We are also grateful to the collection editor, Dr. Betsy Stringam of New Mexico State University, for her helpful comments and enthusiastic reception of our manuscripts.

We thank these contributors and collaborators one and all, and hope that they will be as pleased with the final product as we are at CREST.

—Martha Honey
CREST Executive Director

Key Definitions

Adaptation: The adjustment in natural or human systems in response to actual or expected climatic stimuli or their effects, which moderates harm or exploits beneficial opportunities.[1]

Caribbean: According to the United Nations, the Caribbean region consists of: Anguilla, Antigua and Barbuda, Aruba, The Bahamas, Barbados, Bonaire, Saint Eustatius and Saba, British Virgin Islands, Cayman Islands, Cuba, Curaçao, Dominica, Dominican Republic, Grenada, Guadeloupe, Haiti, Jamaica, Martinique, Montserrat, Puerto Rico, Saint-Barthélemy, Saint Kitts and Nevis, Saint Lucia, Saint Vincent and the Grenadines, Saint Martin (French) and Sint Maarten (Dutch), Trinidad and Tobago, Turks and Caicos Islands, and United States Virgin Islands.[2]

Marine Protected Area: The International Union for the Conservation of Nature and Natural Resources (IUCN) defines a protected area as "A clearly defined geographical space, recognised, dedicated and managed, through legal or other effective means, to achieve the long-term conservation of nature with associated ecosystem services and cultural values." Marine protected areas come under a variety of names and with a wide range of purposes and levels of protection, as described in the IUCN's 2012 guidelines on the subject.[3] The Convention on Biological Diversity, in its COP 7 Decisions in 2004, expanded the term to "Marine and Coastal Protected Areas" (MCPAs) to include adjacent coastal areas, which are often important components of critical marine ecosystems.[4]

Marine Tourism: Those recreational activities that involve travel away from one's place of residence and which have as their host or focus the marine environment.[5]

Mitigation: The lessening or limitation of the adverse impacts of hazards and related disasters.[6]

Resilience: The ability to prepare and plan for, absorb, recover from, and more successfully adapt to adverse events.[7]

Responsible Tourism: Tourism that maximizes the benefits to local communities, minimizes negative social or environmental impacts, and helps local people conserve fragile cultures and habitats or species.[8]

Sustainable Development: Development that meets the needs of the present without compromising the ability of future generations to meet their own needs.[9]

Sustainable Tourism: Tourism that leads to the management of all resources in such a way that economic, social, and aesthetic needs can be fulfilled while maintaining cultural integrity, essential ecological processes, biological diversity, and life support systems.[10]

List of Acronyms

APPS—Act to Prevent Pollution from Ships
AWTS—Advanced Wastewater Treatment Systems
BREA—Business Research and Economic Advisors
CCMU—Climate Change Management Unit
CDC—Carriacou Development Corporation
CLIA—Cruise Lines International Association
CO_2e—carbon dioxide equivalent
CRPA—Florida Coral Reef Protection Act
CTO—Caribbean Tourism Organization
CZMU—Coastal Zone Management Unit
EAF—Ecosystem Approach to Fisheries
ECA—North American Emission Control Area
ECLAC—Economic Commission for Latin America and
    the Caribbean
EGCS—exhaust gas cleaning systems
EIA—Environmental Impact Assessment
EPA – United States Environmental Protection Agency
ESD—epizootic shell disease
FCCA—Florida-Caribbean Cruise Association
FDEP—Florida Department of Environmental Protection
FEE—Foundation for Environmental Education
FOE—Friends of the Earth
GDP—gross domestic product
GHG—greenhouse gas
GIDC—Grenada Investment Development Corporation
GIZ—German Agency for International Cooperation
GSTC—Global Sustainable Tourism Council
IMO—International Maritime Organization
ITF—International Transport Workers Federation
kWh—kilowatt-hours
LED—light emitting diode

LMMAs—Locally Managed Marine Areas

LNG—liquid natural gas

MARPOL—International Convention for the Prevention of Pollution from Ships

MAYAG—Marine and Yachting Association of Grenada

MMAs—Marine Managed Areas

MOBPC—Mangrove Oyster Bed Protection Community

MPAs—marine protected areas

MSDs—Marine Sanitation Devices

MW—megawatts

NABU—Nature and Biodiversity Conservation Union

NCL—Norwegian Cruise Lines

NDC—National Democratic Congress (Grenada)

NGO—nongovernmental organization

NOx—nitrogen oxides

NPS—United States National Park Service

OAS—Organization of American States

OECD—Organization for Economic Cooperation and Development

PADF—Pan American Development Foundation

PIANC—World Association for Waterborne Transport Infrastructure

PPM—parts per million

PV—photovoltaic

RCL—Royal Caribbean Cruises, Ltd.

SEMARNAT—Environmental and Natural Resources Ministry

SIOBMPA—Sandy Island Oyster Bed Marine

SLR—sea level rise

SOLAS—International Convention for the Safety of Life at Sea

SOx—sulfur oxides

SRM—Shark Reef Marine Reserve

STI—Sustainable Travel International

TBT—tributyltin

UNAM—National Autonomous University of Mexico

UNDP—United Nations Development Programme

UNEP—United Nations Environment Programme

UNESCO—United Nations Educational, Scientific and Cultural Organisation

UNWTO—United Nations World Tourism Organization
WWF—World Wildlife Fund
WwN—Working with Nature
ZOFEMAT—Federal Terrestrial Marine Zone (Mexico)

Notes

1. The United Nations Office for Disaster Risk Reduction. (2009). *Terminology.* https://www.unisdr.org/we/inform/terminology

2. United Nations Department of Economic and Social Affairs. *Composition of Macro Geographical (Continental) Regions, Geographical Sub-Regions, and Selected Economic and Other Groupings.* UN Statistics Division. http://unstats.un.org/unsd/methods/m49/m49regin.htm

3. Jon Day, et al. (2012). *Guidelines for Applying the IUCN Protected Area Management Categories to Marine Protected Areas.* Gland, Switzerland: IUCN. https://portals.iucn.org/library/node/10201

4. Convention on Biological Diversity. (2004). *Seventh Ordinary Meeting of the Conference of the Parties to the Convention on Biological Diversity, February 9-20, 2004, Kuala Lumpur, Malaysia.* https://www.cbd.int/decisions/cop/?m=cop-07

5. Mark Orams. (1999). *Marine Tourism: Development, Impacts and Management.* London: Routledge.

6. United Nations Office for Disaster Risk Reduction. (2009).

7. Urban Land Institute Center for Sustainability. (2015). *Returns on Resilience: The Business Case.* Washington, D.C.: The Urban Land Institute. http://uli.org/wp-content/uploads/ULI-Documents/Returns-on-Resilience-The-Business-Case.pdf

8. City of Cape Town. (August 2002). *Cape Town Declaration.* Cape Town Conference on Responsible Tourism in Destinations. https://www.capetown.gov.za/en/tourism/Documents/Responsible%20Tourism/Toruism_RT_2002_Cape_Town_Declaration.pdf

9. World Commission on Environment and Development. (1987). *Our Common Future.* Oxford: Oxford University Press. http://www.un-documents.net/our-common-future.pdf

10. United Nations Sustainable Development Knowledge Platform, (2016). *Sustainable Tourism.* https://sustainabledevelopment.un.org/topics/sustainabletourism

Map of the Caribbean

Map of the Caribbean Sea and its islands.

Image Source: Karl Musser, Creative Commons

CHAPTER 1

Introduction

Kreg Ettenger

Tourism is a major economic activity in the Caribbean, generating US$56.4 billion in total annual revenue and contributing 13.4 percent of total regional employment in 2016.[1] A heavy reliance on marine-based tourism means that the region is especially susceptible to the types of impacts that climate change will have, and is already having, on ecosystems and the physical environment throughout the Caribbean and across the globe. Specifically, damage to coral reefs, beaches, mangroves, seagrass beds, and other critical habitats are impacting the types of activities in which marine tourists engage, namely fishing, snorkeling and diving, surfing, and sailing. In addition, the physical and economic infrastructures that support these activities—including harbors and marinas, coastal resorts, airports, and the human communities that make tourism possible—are all facing threats of various types and scales as a result of climate change. In short, the industries that make up the marine tourism sector in the Caribbean, as in other parts of the oceanic world, have a direct and significant stake in understanding, responding to, and preparing for how climate change will affect them now and in the future.

These industries also contribute, to varying degrees, to environmental and other stressors that exacerbate the effects of climate change on this region. From the carbon emissions of cruise ships and pleasure boats (not to mention the planes that carry most marine tourists to and from the region), to the direct physical impacts of divers and other recreationists on coral reefs and other fragile marine ecosystems, to the added stress on local resources and waste management systems, marine tourism plays a part in degrading the very environments that are critical to the future of the industry. For this reason, an increasing number of marine tourists and advocacy groups are looking for more sustainable ways to enjoy the marine environment, while a growing number of marine tourism businesses are trying to make their practices more sustainable in response to this demand.

In the first volume of this two-volume marine tourism set, we looked at the threats that marine environments in the Caribbean are facing as a result of climate change and other human-induced factors. Authors looked specifically at coral reefs and how these are in jeopardy as a result of both climate change and a host of other factors; other case studies looked at mangroves and the growing problem of encroaching sargassum seaweed. The volume then considered the state of fisheries in the Caribbean and in two other regions, looking at how non-governmental organizations (NGOs) are playing a role in helping local fishing communities develop more sustainable harvesting strategies. Volume I also looked at the role of marine protected areas, or MPAs, in conservation efforts throughout the region and how their importance will be even greater in the era of climate change. And finally, authors showed how marine tourists can be incorporated into marine conservation efforts through such innovative programs as participating in the care of coral reef nurseries.

Here, in Volume II, we turn toward a discussion of the various sectors of the marine tourism industry in the Caribbean, considering the impacts these sectors are having on the region's environment and what steps individual companies or advocacy groups are taking to minimize these impacts. Industries considered include individual sports such as surfing, diving, and sport fishing; the thriving, yet vulnerable, yachting and marina sector; and the juggernaut of Caribbean marine tourism, the cruise ship industry. Each of these sectors has impacts that can exacerbate the negative effects of climate change, and each is already being impacted by climate change, some significantly. However, as we have shown in the other volumes, each of these sectors also has examples of individual companies that are taking steps to lessen their impacts on the environment, while also adapting to the "new normal" in the region. These examples, often the result of innovative partnerships with NGOs, national or international agencies, and local communities, are what we choose to focus on in this book. The following are short synopses of the three chapters in this volume, including overview essays and case studies.

Chapter 2: Marine Recreation

All types of marine recreation depend on healthy oceans, diverse and plentiful marine life, attractive and accessible coastlines, safe and vibrant coastal communities, and adequate coastal infrastructure, including hospitality facilities and workers. As Mark Spalding and Luke Elder point out in their overview essay, all of these factors can be threatened by climate change. Sea level rise is wiping out beaches and affecting famous surfing areas; large ocean storms are affecting coastlines, communities, and recreation infrastructure; ocean warming and acidification are damaging coral reefs and their associated biota; and declines in fish stocks are impacting both sport and commercial fishing. These and other changes threaten the future of marine recreation in many parts of the world, including the Caribbean. In response, some in the marine recreation industry are taking steps to protect their own interests as well as the world's oceans, beaches, and coastal communities. A growing number of organizations are getting involved in advocacy at the local and global levels, helping members of their own communities change their behaviors, while lobbying for more government and international action on climate change and marine preservation. Surfers, divers, sport fishers, and others are all coming to realize that only concerted action to mitigate, reverse, and prepare for the effects of climate change will save their treasured sports and the places they love.

The two case studies in this chapter reinforce these ideas. The first, written by Travis Bays and Shengxiao Yu, describes Bodhi Surf & Yoga, a small business located on the Pacific coast of Costa Rica. Bodhi's responses to climate change and other environmental threats include restoring vegetation around local beaches, ensuring proper wastewater management, implementing community education programs, and promoting good practices among guests, both while they are at Bodhi and after they return home. Tools such as their Travelers' Philanthropy Program and the Ocean Guardian Pledge reinforce the idea that surfers can, and should, help play a role in mitigating climate change, in part through steps they take in their everyday lives.

The second case study is written from the perspective of an experienced diver and marine scientist who has explored coral reefs around the world, including in the Caribbean. The author, Rick MacPherson, laments the drastic decline of coral reefs over the past few decades, the result of overfishing, rapid coastal development, invasive species, climate change, and in some cases, dive tourism itself. MacPherson ends with a description of a shark diving business in Fiji that ultimately led to the creation of a marine reserve and the partial restoration of the local fishing economy, both side benefits to this tourism-led project.

Chapter 3: Caribbean Yachting and Marinas in an Era of Climate Change

Chapter 3 begins with an in-depth essay on the rise of yachting in the Caribbean, from its roots as an occasional activity of wealthy Americans in the early twentieth century, to yet another form of mass tourism today. As it has risen in popularity, its economic influence in the Caribbean has also grown, to the extent that it today vies with cruise tourism in terms of its overall contribution to the region's tourism revenue. As author Martha Honey points out, however, it does so with fewer than one-tenth the number of visitors as the cruise ship industry, showing the relative importance of this activity and its continued growth potential. At the same time, the yachting sector is perhaps one of the most vulnerable to the effects of climate change, with several large marinas already devastated by major hurricanes in the past two decades. As Honey points out, there is a clear need for better design and construction techniques in this sector, as well as a need to protect the reefs, coastlines, mangroves, clean harbors, and other resources on which the sector depends. There must also be a focus on sustainable growth, rather than the type of rapid and ill-advised development that is now occurring in many places as Caribbean destinations vie with one another to attract more yachting business, including the massive *megayachts* and *superyachts* that have become the new playthings of the super-rich.

In the first case study in this chapter, Esteban Biondi looks in more depth at the environmental impacts of marina construction and operation, and considers some of the design tools that are available to reduce these impacts. Among the guidelines he describes are *Working with Nature* (WwN) and the *Clean and Resilient Marina Initiative*, both of which offer guidance to planners and developers seeking to minimize the impacts of new or expanded marinas while also preparing for the impacts of climate change. Biondi also considers the social impacts of marinas and describes how some are working with local fishing communities to offer more benefits and fewer drawbacks.

In the second case study, Robin Swaisland looks at the yachting sector in Grenada, at one time among the Caribbean's most popular boating destinations. In the early 2000s, this sector was devastated by three successive hurricanes, Lenny, Ivan, and Emily, causing billions of dollars in damages, damaging hundreds of yachts, and forcing the permanent closure or relocation of several marinas. As the marina sector in Grenada works to rebuild, it now faces competition from many other regional yachting destinations, as well as the looming threat of more damage from an increasing number of large tropical storms, and the likely impact of sea level rise on marine tourism infrastructure. Swaisland concludes by looking at some of the steps industry leaders in Grenada are taking to reduce their own impacts on climate change.

In the final case study, Martha Honey returns to look at one marina complex in Grenada, the Tyrell Bay Marina on the island of Carriacou. According to Honey, this is a prime example of how not to do marina resort development, with massive facilities that are inappropriate to the region in economic, social, and environmental terms. As she describes, the development has already had negative impacts on coastal ecosystems, including the fragile Mangrove Oyster Beds area, while bringing few local economic benefits. As this case study illustrates, while some areas are making strides to reduce the negative impacts of marinas and yachting, and to better prepare for the coming effects of climate change, this is far from universal in the Caribbean region.

Chapter 4: Cruise Tourism

The final chapter in this volume looks at a behemoth of Caribbean tourism, the cruise ship industry. Like the yachting sector, the cruise industry has grown far beyond its humble roots to become one of the true tourism power players in the region. However, it has done so much faster, to a much larger extent, and with considerably greater environmental and social impacts than the yachting industry. As Martha Honey points out in her overview essay, cruise ships also bring fewer economic benefits to the Caribbean than other forms of marine and land-based tourism, due in part to the short stays of visitors in each destination, but also because of the very economic structure of the cruise industry. Cruise passengers are really buying a destination package in the ship itself, with ports of call being minor diversions with little onshore spending, according to Honey. This leaves most Caribbean nations paying a large price in environmental and other terms as they cope with huge numbers of short-term visitors, but seeing little payoff in return. In terms of climate change, the cruise industry has multiple impacts, ranging from carbon dioxide (CO_2) and other greenhouse gas (GHG) emissions from their massive engines, to the release of sewage and other effluents that impact marine ecosystems and cause additional GHG production. In short, this is an industry that needs serious oversight and regulation if they are to become responsible members of the Caribbean tourism industry. As Honey points out, this would be in their own best interest, as they need well-preserved marine environments and coastal destinations for their passengers. They are also already seeing the effects of climate change cut into their bottom line, through cancelled and diverted cruises, unhappy passengers, and damaged infrastructure from a growing number of major hurricanes in the region.

The three case studies for this chapter further elaborate on the environmental impacts of the cruise industry, but also describe some steps currently being taken by industry leaders. In the first case study, Julia Lewis describes in some detail the various environmental impacts of the cruise industry, including its effects on global climate. She describes, for example, the rather disgusting—but perfectly legal—practice of dumping raw sewage at sea. When one considers that each of the dozens of cruise ships sailing in the Caribbean is essentially a floating town with as many as 9,000 residents (passengers and crew), it is not surprising that millions of gallons of *black water* and *gray water* are dumped into the sea every day. In addition, ships regularly dump ballast water, oily bilge water, and various hazardous wastes into the ocean, whether legally or illegally. In addition, they dump macerated food waste into the ocean, emit pollutants from onboard garbage incinerators, and of course, generate large amounts of GHGs from their ship engines and generators. These and other environmental impacts, such as reef destruction, sedimentation from harbor dredging, and sunscreen pollution, are all described by Lewis.

The next case study paints a somewhat more positive picture, focusing on one cruise line and the steps it has taken to be more environmentally sustainable. Samantha Hogenson looks at Royal Caribbean Cruises, Ltd. (RCL), widely acknowledged as a cruise industry leader in terms of reducing various environmental impacts, including carbon emissions. According to Hogenson, RCL has been working on sustainability issues for more than two decades, with its innovative *Save the Waves* program addressing multiple types of environmental impacts, from solid waste disposal to sewage treatment to fuel consumption and emissions. RCL is also working with organizations such as World Wildlife Fund (WWF) to create guidelines for more sustainable actions in individual destinations, something that has been a clear weakness of the cruise industry. While not perfect, and admitting the difficulty of monitoring and enforcing company guidelines on individual ships, the actions that Royal Caribbean has taken are certainly steps in the right direction.

The final case study, by Kennedy Magio and Elisa Arguelles, looks at climate change and cruise tourism in Cozumel, México. According to the authors, the island currently vies with The Bahamas as the world's leading international cruise tourism destination. Of Cozumel's 4.3 million visitors in 2016, some 3.7 million (or 86 percent) were cruise ship passengers, disembarking from about 1,600 ships. Despite these numbers, however, stay-over tourists actually generated more revenue for the island than cruise passengers, because they each spent, on average, five times as much. This is the type of math that makes it difficult to justify cruise ship tourism as an economic generator for many Caribbean nations. As the authors point out, there are also environmental and climate impacts of cruise tourism in Cozumel, as well as other places in the Caribbean. Ironically, cruise lines have the advantage of being able to move their ships out of harm's way in the face of severe storms, while local communities such as Cozumel bear the brunt of cleanup and rebuilding costs. Cozumel suffered some US$400 million worth of damage in 2005 alone from hurricanes Wilma, Emily, and Stan, which devastated the island's hotels, resorts, and marine tourism infrastructure. As the authors conclude, more needs to be done to reduce the negative impacts of cruise tourism and to better prepare places such as Cozumel for future climate-related threats.

Conclusion

Our goal in this volume, as with Volume I, is to demonstrate that far from being simply culprits in the demise of the region, the marine tourism industry is largely aware of the impacts of its activities on the Caribbean's marine environments and is taking at least some steps to reduce these effects. It is in their own interest to do so, for if the delicate marine environments of the Caribbean cannot be protected, there will be no marine tourism industry to speak of. Climate change already threatens many of the region's most important and (from a tourism perspective) attractive features, including beaches, seagrass beds, mangroves, coral reefs, and the diverse species that call these habitats home. Without drastic action, many of these ecosystems could be gone within our lifetimes, and certainly within the lifetimes of our children. A collapse of the marine tourism industry in the Caribbean would be an economic loss in and of itself, but more importantly, would likely coincide with a devastating loss of food and other marine resources and employment for the people of the region. This is a future that no conscientious traveler would ever want to imagine. We hope that the essays and case studies that follow, therefore, give some ideas as to how such a future can be avoided.

Notes

1. World Travel & Tourism Council. (2017). *Travel and Tourism. Economic Impact 2017. Caribbean.* https://www.wttc.org/-/media/files/reports/economic-impact-research/regions-2017/caribbean2017.pdf

CHAPTER 2

Marine Recreation

Overview—Major Types of Marine Recreation: Climate Change Impacts and Responses

Mark J. Spalding and Luke Elder

Marine Tourism and Climate Change

The marine environment has long been considered one of the most appealing settings for tourism and recreation. Generally, marine tourism includes "those recreational activities that involve travel away from one's place of residence and which have as their host or focus the marine environment."[1] Marine tourism and recreation include a variety of activities from swimming, scenic boat trips, cruise ships and ferries, sailing, fishing, and wildlife watching, to jet skiing, ocean kayaking, surfing, rowing, and snorkeling. This list is by no means exhaustive, and only catalogues a few examples of the multitude of active and passive marine recreational activities relished by both tourists and coastal residents alike.

Coastal and marine tourism industries depend on agreeable climate and weather, as well as on clean oceans and healthy marine ecosystems. Tourism businesses, along with sectors they support such as agriculture, construction, and artisanal crafts, are affected by tourist demand, which in turn is affected by climate. Weather factors, safety concerns, and recreational opportunities all influence vacation and travel decisions. Extreme weather events, for example, can significantly affect ocean activities and the coastal and island communities to which marine tourists travel. In small island states and developing countries, the changing climate can significantly reduce the number of tourists, impacting one of the main drivers of the economy. Climate change is also driving fundamental changes in the ocean, including sea level rise, storm surges, coastal alteration and erosion, ocean warming, oxygen depletion, and ocean acidification. These conditions are affecting the beaches, coral reefs, fisheries, and other attractions that lure tourists to coastal and marine destinations. At the same time, the tourism industry contributes to greenhouse gas (GHG) emissions and climate change through the transport of tourists across the world to their favorite coastal and marine habitats, in addition to their consumption patterns upon arrival.

Surfing, sport fishing, diving, and snorkeling (see Image 2.0.1) are all iconic forms of marine recreation that have been affected by climate change, or whose future could be impacted by predicted change. Yet, all have the potential for adaptation to, and even mitigation of, climate change impacts with the proper strategies. In some cases, individuals, businesses, and organizations with interests in these activities have already recognized and are beginning to respond to emerging threats. The following sections describe briefly how these recreational activities are being affected by climate change, and what steps each sector is taking, or could take, to address these impacts. The case studies that follow provide some concrete examples of positive steps already being taken.

Image 2.0.1 Snorkelers swim in a biodiverse coral reef[2]

Surfing

Surfing is one of the oldest marine sports, dating back hundreds of years to western Polynesia, where fishermen rode waves back to shore with their daily catch.[3] Modern practitioners of this quintessential coastal pastime (see Image 2.0.2) rely on healthy oceans and coasts to give them consistent and predictable waves. However, most surfers today agree that climate change has already started to alter their favorite sport in a variety of ways. Chad Nelsen, CEO of the Surfrider Foundation, sums up the issue this way: "The impacts associated with climate change are the biggest issues [facing surfers]. . . [W]arming oceans, sea level rise and ocean acidification are threats. . .that are going to affect all of us at the local level and at our favorite surf spots around the globe. We not only need to start reducing emissions, but also plan to adapt to the changes that are already underway."[4]

Melting glaciers and ice sheets, along with thermal expansion of the ocean, are causing sea level rise, which changes where and how waves break on reefs and shorelines. Extreme beach erosion, coastal alteration, rising high tides, coral reef decline, and *permanent high tides* are all causing wave patterns to shift.[5] Increased nuisance flooding, as well as shrinking beaches and higher tides, may reduce beach access, temporarily or permanently.[6] The sizes and styles of waves are changing, with some shrinking and others growing.[7] In short, climate change threatens many aspects of surfing, from where and when it can take place to the tourism industry that it supports.[8]

Specific Threats from Climate Change

All major surf swells in the world, including those in Hawaii, Fiji, Tahiti, and numerous other places, are located over shallow coral reefs. These create *reef breaks*, fast and hollow swells that surfers tout as the most consistently flawless waves. Big wave breaks rely on healthy and functioning coral, and more generally, on a healthy and functioning ocean.

A major driver of change to surfing is ocean *acidification*, caused by the ocean's uptake of excess carbon dioxide (CO_2) from the atmosphere. Acidification is fundamentally changing the chemistry of the ocean.[10] Seawater has become 30 percent more acidic on average, forcing many

Image 2.0.2 A surfer enjoys a day in the water[9]

calcareous (calcium carbonate) marine organisms, including corals, to struggle to maintain their normal physiology.[11] As the formation of new coral declines, the impacts of storms and other events that erode and damage reefs will be more pronounced. While the devastating impacts of coral reef decline on global fisheries and biodiversity have been discussed in Volume I, from a recreational perspective, the decline of reefs could have major impacts on surfing, as many important reef breaks, such as Hawaii's Pipeline, become a thing of the past.

A second major threat is the increased frequency and intensity of coastal storms, especially when combined with rising sea levels. Storm surges, flooding, and erosion can permanently alter the coastlines and communities on which surfers depend. Storms cause sand displacement and shift wave patterns, making them less predictable. An extreme storm event can result in permanent change to an iconic surf spot, causing losses to the surf community, the local residents who rely on the surfing industry, and the marine habitat. And while larger ocean storms can mean "epic swells" for surfers, they can also change beaches and wave patterns to the extent that classic surf spots are no longer usable, or become too dangerous for recreational surfing. At the other end of the spectrum, some parts of the planet might actually see fewer storms and big wave events.[12] Meanwhile, sea level rise could make certain beaches, including famous low tide surfing areas such as California's Rincon and Pleasure Point, essentially useless for surfing.[13]

Mitigation and Adaptation

Most traditional responses to the effects of climate change on the ocean do not help surfers, and in fact, can diminish beaches and coastlines. Beach filling, storm walls, and beach armoring often destroy beach function, and do not always increase long-term coastal resilience. There are some successful mitigation and adaptation solutions, however, to problems affecting the surfing community. Seagrass and mangrove protection and restoration can mitigate the impacts of storm surges and help naturally increase coastal resilience while not harming surfing conditions. "Low impact" surf contests and camps are designed to minimize environmental impacts, including climate change, through carbon offsets and other tools.[14] Even biodegradable "green" surfboards help by lessening the impact of surfing on the climate in general.[15]

Multiple NGOs and the surfing community are taking action to tackle these issues. The Surfrider Foundation, an international network of surfer activists, works diligently on these problems; currently, there are over 100 outreach and advocacy campaigns, including over 30 on coastal and ocean protection.[16] Sustainable Surf, a nonprofit founded by social entrepreneurs, uses surfing as an on-ramp to discussing these complex, and politically charged, issues. Their Deep Blue Surfing Events help "reduce direct threats to the sport of surfing from global climate change (such as sea level rise, ocean acidification, and loss of coral reefs)."[17] Save the Waves is a nonprofit dedicated to protecting coastal ecosystems through innovative strategies, often in partnership with local communities, for the benefit of surfers as well as all coastal recreational tourists.[18] In addition to grassroots surf organizations such as these, professional surfing athletes can, and do, serve as spokespeople for action on climate change and ocean acidification.

Diving and Snorkeling

Diving and snorkeling represent major tourist activities in the Caribbean and other coastal and island locations around the world. An important ingredient is coral reefs, with their colorful assemblages of corals, sponges, anemones, fish, and other marine life (see Image 2.0.3). In a recent story on the Frommer's travel website touting the Caribbean's ten best snorkeling sites, for example, nine of those sites were noted for their reef habitats.[19] Coral reefs contribute directly to the roughly US$2.1 billion per year that the dive industry contributes to the Caribbean economy.[20] In fact, this industry, and the jobs created, would be virtually nonexistent without reefs to attract divers and snorkelers.

Healthy coral reefs draw divers, snorkelers, and other tourists from all over the world. But decreased reef diversity due to overfishing, ocean warming, and decalcification threatens this type of tourism. Ironically, as tourists travel across the world via car, plane, and boat to visit famous coral reef dive sites, they contribute to climate change and add to the impacts that are destroying these spectacular habitats. As no one wants to see a dying or dead reef devoid of fish, tourism rates in many coastal communities could decline along with local reefs, and livelihoods dependent on dive tourism will be affected.

Specific Threats from Climate Change

Rising sea levels, increasing water temperatures, and ocean acidification all threaten the future of coral reefs. As with seagrass habitats, some reefs

Image 2.0.3 A SCUBA diver explores a colorful coral reef[21]

will become too deep to receive sufficient sunlight to survive and thrive. Increased sea surface temperatures contribute to coral bleaching, a stress response that prompts corals to expel their essential symbiotic algae. This causes corals to turn white, lose their major food source, and become more susceptible to diseases (see Case Study 2.1 in Volume I). Ocean acidification, meanwhile, prevents corals from forming strong skeletons due to a decrease in available calcium carbonate. One study estimates that reef-building corals will calcify up to 50 percent less, relative to pre-industrial rates, by the middle of this century.[22]

Ocean acidification also affects the sea life around coral reefs. In a study off Papua New Guinea, scientists found that when pH dropped to 7.8, coral reef diversity declined by as much as 40 percent.[23] A loss of reef-building organisms not only threatens both the geological and biological identities of coral reef ecosystems, but also their attraction as popular tourist destinations. Unhealthy reefs are less productive, have fewer fish, and are less biodiverse, all of which discourage tourists to dive, snorkel, and recreate in them.

Mitigation and Adaptation

General strategies such as continuing research, reducing water pollution, and monitoring coral reef health could help safeguard healthy and vibrant dive sites for the next generation. Sustainable Travel International (STI) has launched a climate-friendly scuba dive program, including the world's first custom carbon dive calculator, to address dive industry impacts on climate change.[24] The calculator determines the carbon footprint from a dive trip, including air travel and diving activities, and compensates for these emissions by funding carbon offset programs.[25]

The Ocean Foundation has developed an innovative carbon offset program, SeaGrass Grow, which employs the first-ever verified seagrass offset methodology.[26] SeaGrass Grow is designed to restore seagrass meadows along our coastlines. Its main objectives are to restore habitat, educate the public, support coastal community resilience and economic stability, and offset carbon emissions. SeaGrass Grow launched its voluntary offset Blue Carbon Calculator in 2008, and since then, has offset emissions for corporations, nonprofits, restaurants, and event coordinators. These efforts acknowledge that everyone, including tourists, is responsible for climate change and can be part of the solution.

Recreational Fishing

Drive down any coastline and you are likely to see local residents or tourists with fishing rods in their hands and lines in the water. Recreational fishing supports more than 828,000 jobs in the United States, with an estimated 33 million people spending US$48 billion annually on the sport.[27] In the Caribbean, recreational saltwater fishing is a major part of the economy for many islands and communities, as well as an important component of the tourism industry. While no regional figures are readily available, a study of Costa Rica estimated that the direct and indirect economic impacts of American and Canadian sport fishers is over US$1 billion each year.[28] This suggests that the annual contribution of this sector to the Caribbean economy is in the tens of billions of dollars.

Specific Threats from Climate Change

The greatest single threat to saltwater sport fishing might be the impacts of climate change on fish populations. Rising sea levels contribute to the loss of valuable habitats that provide protection and food resources for juvenile fish. For mangroves, a critical coastal habitat for fish and other marine life, sea level rise causes sediment erosion, inundation stress, and increased salinity, all of which pose problems. For seagrass meadows, another important ecosystem, increased water depth restricts the amount of light reaching grasses, reducing their photosynthesis, productivity, and geographic range. Changes in tides, water currents, and turbidity can impact the growth, reproduction, and propagation of seagrass. Loss of this essential habitat for juvenile fish will undoubtedly impact recreational fishing for the worse. Warmer waters can also damage coral reefs, yet another critical habitat for fish.

Changes in ocean temperatures can also affect fish health, reproduction, and survival. In the past century, sea surface temperatures rose at an average rate of 0.13°F per decade.[29] Along with other changes, this warming significantly influences fish metabolism, growth rate, productivity, seasonal reproduction, and susceptibility to diseases and toxins. In addition, changes in ocean temperatures can force species to change locations, or open new areas to predators including invasive species, disrupting food chains and ecosystems. Fish stocks already in decline due to overfishing and habitat destruction must also face the threat of ocean acidification. Pteropods, the base of the food chain on which bigger fish feed, are having difficulty forming calcium carbonate shells due to more acidic waters.[30] Ocean acidification has also reduced the ability of fish larvae to find suitable habitat, orient themselves, and find their way home.[31] Fish eggs are much more sensitive to acidity changes than adult fish and may dwindle with decreasing pH.[32] All of these changes make it harder for fish to survive and grow big enough, or in large enough numbers, to be useful for recreational angling.

Mitigation and Adaption

Various mitigation strategies can help to protect the recreational fishing industry and the fish populations on which the industry relies. Marine Protected Areas (MPAs) can protect fisheries and ecosystems while also promoting tourism as part of their management planning (see Volume I, Essay 4.1). In well-managed MPAs, tourists can see endangered species, coral reefs, and beautiful beaches, all of which broaden coastal communities' economic options and revenue streams. Tourists can pay fees to support conservation and the livelihoods of local residents, and in turn, are able to fish in pristine and protected marine environments. MPAs can help to ensure sustainable fisheries by protecting certain types of fish, allowing them to grow to a large size and reproduce before being caught, thereby increasing the value of the reserve and of fishing and tourism in the waters around it. Protected areas can also improve the ability of local communities to obtain fish for food, especially if wild populations are supplemented with sustainable aquaculture.

Another strategy is to create programs that help diversify livelihoods, including investing in marine tourism and aquaculture. Programs can improve communication, collaboration, and information sharing on climate change and fisheries adaptation. The *ecosystem approach to fisheries* (EAF) management, which encompasses the marine environment and targets commercial fish stocks through adaptive management, is an example of this strategy. Access to larger, more sophisticated vessels with multi-fisheries capabilities allows recreational fishermen to travel farther and move to different locations that offer better fishing opportunities, diversified fishing activities, and a wider range of species and stocks to fish.

Conclusion

Surfers, sailors, divers, ecotourism companies, eco-resorts, and all those who enjoy the ocean have the responsibility and power to bring this issue to the forefront and demand action so we can go on enjoying our ocean. We need to improve climate research, monitoring, and forecasting, and to support sustainable tourism, fishing, and development. These actions, combined with stewardship of our invaluable coastal and marine natural resources, can help ensure that people will continue to be awed and entertained by a day at the beach or on the water.[33]

Notes

1. Mark Orams. (1999). *Marine Tourism Development, Impacts and Management.* London: Routledge.
2. Image Source: Chris Guinness. Used with permission from The Ocean Foundation.
3. Matt Warshaw. (2010). *The History of Surfing.* San Francisco: Chronicle Books. (It should be noted that the first wave-riders remains a contested title, with claims from ancient Peru, Hawaii, and Polynesia, among others.)
4. Pat Fallon (Interviewer) and Chad Nelsen. (Interviewee). (2015). "Surfonomics with Surfrider CEO Chad Nelsen" [Interview transcript]. *Whalebone Magazine.* http://whalebonemag.com/two-coasts-one -ocean-surfonomics-with-surfrider-ceo-chad-nelsen/
5. MoStoke.com. (2017). "How Will Rising Sea Levels Change our Breaks?" http://homesolarus.com/gridfreedom/read/tag/permanent-high-tide/
6. Holly Bamford. (2015.) "Nuisance Flooding: Communities Working to Overcome this Worsening Symptom of Sea Level Rise." *Medium.* https://medium.com/@NOAA/nuisance-flooding-7cea715ab8f6
7. James Urton. (2015). "Climate Change May Flatten Famed Surfing Waves." *San Jose Mercury News.* http://phys.org/news/2015-02 -climate-flatten-famed-surfing.html

8. Brian Merchant. (2013). "Global Warming is Going to Ruin Surfing for 25% of the Planet." *Motherboard.* http://motherboard.vice.com/blog/global-warming-is-going-to-ruin-surfing

9. Image Source: Martin Garrido. Used with permission from The Ocean Foundation.

10. Jeremy T. Mathis, Jessica N. Cross, Wiley Evans, and Scott C. Doney. (2015). "Ocean Acidification in the Surface Waters of the Pacific-Arctic Boundary Regions." *Oceanography* 28(2), 122–135. http://dx.doi.org/10.5670/oceanog.2015.36

11. Jeremy T. Mathis, Jessica N. Cross, Wiley Evans, and Scott C. Doney. (2015).Op cit.

12. Andrew J. Dowdy, Graham A. Mills, Bertrand Timbal, and Yang Wang. (2014). "Fewer Large Waves Projected for Eastern Australia Due to Decreasing Storminess." *Nature Climate Change* 4, 283–286. doi: 10.1038/nclimate2142.

13. Sam Kornell. (2012). "Will Climate Change Wipe Out Surfing?" *Pacific Standard.* http://www.psmag.com/books-and-culture/will-climate-change-wipe-out-surfing-44209

14. Beachapedia. "Low Impact Surf Contests." http://www.beachapedia.org/Low_Impact_Surf_Contests

15. Pat Fallon. Surfonomics with Surfrider CEO Chad Nelsen [Interview, 2015]. *Whalebone.* http://whalebonemag.com/two-coasts-one-ocean-surfonomics-with-surfrider-ceo-chad-nelsen/

16. Surfrider Foundation. "Campaigns." http://www.surfrider.org/campaigns

17. Sustainable Surf. "Current Projects." http://sustainablesurf.org/projects/

18. Save the Waves Coalition. "Programs." http://www.savethewaves.org/programs/

19. Frommers. "The 10 Best Caribbean Snorkeling Spots." http://www.frommers.com/slideshows/847912-the-10-best-caribbean-snorkeling-spots#slide848061

20. Lauretta Burke and Jon Maidens. (2004). *Reefs at Risk in the Caribbean.* Washington, DC: World Resources Institute (WRI). http://www.wri.org/publication/reefs-risk-caribbean

21. Image Source: NOAA. Used with permission from The Ocean Foundation.

22. Joan A. Kleypas and Chris Langdon. (2006). "Coral Reefs and Changing Seawater Chemistry." In *Coral Reefs and Climate Change: Science and Management,* eds. Jonathan T. Phinney, William Skirving, Joanie Kleypas, and Ove Hoegh-Guldberg, 73–110. Washington, DC: American Geophysical Union.

23. Katharina E. Fabricius, Chris Langdon, Sven Uthicke, Craig Humphrey, Sam Noonan, Glenn De'ath, Remy Okazaki, Nancy Muehllehner, Martin S. Glas, and Janice M. Lough. (2011). "Losers and Winners in Coral Reefs Acclimatized to Elevated Carbon Dioxide Concentrations." *Nature Climate Change,* 1, 165–69. doi:10.1038/nclimate1122.

24. Sustainable Travel International. (April 2007). "Scuba Dive Industry Addresses Global Warming and Climate Friendly Diving." *Responsible Travel Report.* http://www.responsibletravelreport.com/sti-news/news/2241-scuba-dive-industry-addresses-global-warming-and-climate-friendly-diving

25. Carbon offsets pay for reforestation programs and other methods that help "offset" the CO_2 emissions of travel and other human activities, thereby reducing global carbon levels.

26. The Ocean Foundation. "SeaGrass Grow." http://www.seagrassgrow.org/index.php?ht=a/GetDocumentAction/i/3571

27. American Sportfishing Association. (January 2013). *Sportfishing in America: An Economic Force for Conservation,* 2. http://asafishing.org/uploads/2011_ASASportfishing_in_America_Report_January_2013.pdf

28. Max Alberto Soto Jimenez, Marlon Yong Chacon, Alejandro Gutierrez Li, Carolina Fernandez Garcia, Rudolf Lucke Bolanos, Freddy Rojas, and Gabriela Gonzalez. (May 30, 2010). *Analysis of the Economic Contribution of Recreational and Commercial Fisheries to the Costa Rican Economy.* San Jose: Instituto de Investigaciones en Ciencias Economicas of Universidad de Costa Rica, Sponsored by The Billfish Foundation. https://www.igfa.org/images/uploads/files/costaricamarinefisherieseconomics5-30-10.pdf

29. NOAA (National Oceanic and Atmospheric Administration). 2015 update to data originally published in: NOAA. (2009). *Sea Level Variations of the United States 1854–2006.* NOAA Technical Report

NOS CO-OPS 053. www.tidesandcurrents.noaa.gov/publications/
Tech_rpt_53.pdf

30. James C. Orr and Victoria J. Fabry, et al. (2005). "Anthropogenic Ocean Acidification Over the Twenty-First Century and Its Impact on Calcifying Organisms." *Nature,* 437, 681–86.

31. Philip L. Munday, Danielle L. Dixson, Jennifer M. Donelson, Geoffrey P. Jones, Morgan S. Pratchett, Galina V. Devitsina, and Kjell B. Doving. (2009). "Ocean Acidification Impairs Olfactory Discrimination and Homing Ability of a Marine Fish." *Proceedings of the National Academies of Sciences,* 106(6), 1848–52. doi:10.1072/pnas.0809996106.

32. Andrea Y. Frommel, Rommel Maneja, David Lowe, Arne M. Malzahn, Audrey J. Geffen, Arild Folkvord, Uwe Piatkowski, Thorsten B. H. Reusch, and Catriona Clemmesen. (2011). "Severe Tissue Damage in Atlantic Cod Larvae Under Increasing Ocean Acidification." *Nature Climate Change.* 2, 42–46. doi:10.1038/nclimate1324

Case Study 2.1

Connecting with Nature and Community to Create Lasting Change: The Bodhi Surf + Yoga School, Costa Rica

by Travis Bays and Shengxiao Yu

Located on the Southern Pacific coast of Costa Rica, Bodhi Surf + Yoga is a tourism business that is purpose-driven at its core. Bodhi (which means "awareness" in Sanskrit) shies away from providing an all-inclusive experience to its guests. Bodhi staff see fostering a relationship between guests and locals as integral to the mission and want guests to explore the community on their own.[1]

Bodhi Surf + Yoga is run by two couples and longtime friends who are committed to providing personalized and intimate experiences for guests. As coastal business owners and surfers, Bodhi staff spend a lot of time in the ocean and see it as their second home. They also see firsthand the impact of human activities on the ocean ecosystem. Bodhi staff share this love of and commitment to the ocean with guests by giving them an up-close experience with the ocean, and then, encouraging them to become committed to its protection. Staff members are involved in every part of the guest experience, including trip planning, in-country support, community engagement, hosting the guests at the Bodhi Lodge, and providing surf and yoga instruction.

Addressing Climate Change Through Partnerships

Corporate social responsibility has become the bandwagon of the day, with many businesses looking at *impact investment* and the *triple bottom line* (people, planet, profit). While some of these efforts have made changes in communities, they are largely based on what corporate social responsibility teams design *for* communities, sometimes in isolation *from* communities. In contrast, Bodhi Surf is a small business with staff who are residents of and immersed in the community, and who work in partnership with local NGOs. They listen to the voices of other residents and address the effects of climate change in context.

Partnerships grounded in the local community

Bodhi Surf + Yoga is located between the villages of Uvita and Bahia Ballena, often referred to together as Bahia-Uvita (see Image 2.1.1). Similar
to coastal communities around the world, Bahia-Uvita is experiencing the
distressing effects of climate change. Nearby reefs have a high sensitivity
and low adaptability to increased temperatures and decreased precipita-
tion, and declining reef health has negatively impacted coastal communities. Bahia Ballena is also vulnerable to coastal erosion, coral bleaching,
increased storms, and other impacts of climate change. Bodhi Surf + Yoga
participated in a recent climate change diagnostic and uses the recommendations to focus its work on climate change, which include promoting biodiversity, maintaining and restoring vegetation around beaches,
ensuring proper wastewater management, implementing community
education programs, and analyzing visitors' impacts on the community.

Due to Bodhi Surf +Yoga's deep connection to Bahia Ballena-Uvita, it
has always made investing in the community the core of its mission. Since
its inception, Bodhi has donated time, energy, and resources, both human
and financial, to the community. Bodhi works principally with two local
NGOs, Geoporter and Forjando Alas. Geoporter provides geospatial

*Image 2.1.1 The symbolic Whale Tail of the Marino Ballena
National Park, Bahia Ballena-Uvita, Osa²*

technology education to improve the community's understanding of its environment,[3] while Forjando Alas is an after-school program aimed at creating a safe space for kids to learn life skills (see Image 2.1.2).[4] Geoporter has conducted several GPS data collection activities to map the locations of trash in the streets of Uvita. These activities were carried out by Forjando Alas students, who learn about geospatial technology by applying it to their own community. The students have analyzed the data to map the greatest concentrations of trash in order to engage in targeted public awareness campaigns. Geoporter also conducts other sessions where students explore different physical landforms around the world and study conservation efforts to protect various animal species.

Every month, Bodhi Surf + Yoga also hosts Surf and Service Saturdays to give free surf instruction to local youth in the Forjando Alas program, in exchange for community service hours to address a climate-related issue (see Image 2.1.3). By donating a few staff hours to more than ten kids each week, Bodhi amplifies its impact by addressing urgent environmental needs and raising environmental consciousness among the youth. Geoporter and Forjando Alas staff have also participated in the Surf and Service Saturdays program.

Image 2.1.2 Students in the Forjando Alas after-school program learn how their actions can affect the world[5]

Image 2.1.3 Local youth in Bahia Ballena-Uvita, Osa, take part in a neighborhood cleanup program as part of "Surf and Service Saturdays"[6]

Partnerships with Global Impacts

Beyond local partnerships, Bodhi uses its position as a tourism company to extend its impact to the global level. It does this in two main ways: through a travelers' philanthropy program that seeks to change tourists' behavior over the long term, and through partnerships with educational institutions and international NGOs.

Travelers' philanthropy program

In July 2014, Bodhi Surf + Yoga launched its travelers' philanthropy program,[7] in collaboration with the Costa Rica-USA Foundation for Cooperation and its affiliate, Amigos of Costa Rica.[8] Bodhi broke away from the traditional model of soliciting funds from guests, and instead, decided to donate 2 percent of its profits from vacation packages to its local NGO partners, Geoporter and Forjando Alas. Guests are informed of this gift in their thank-you email. They are also invited to match or give more than the gift card amount, and to share the story of Bodhi and its local NGO partners with their families and friends. This model allows for a deeper (and longer-lasting) engagement with travelers. It says thank you for investing in the community by choosing Bodhi Surf + Yoga; it fosters reflection from the travelers once they leave Bahia Ballena-Uvita; and it amplifies Bodhi's community impact to a global audience.

Ocean Guardian pledge

Tourists often experience transformative thoughts while traveling, especially when they intimately experience the environment. Many people, however, let that transformation fade once they arrive back at their normal life. Bodhi Surf + Yoga attempts to capture that transformation to foster "ocean guardians" who will translate mental realizations into actions that are woven into the travelers' normal lives to make sustained impact. Through its Ocean Guardian Journey program, Bodhi uses its personal relationships with guests to create sustained behavioral changes that protect the ocean.

Before guests leave Bodhi, they are encouraged to sign the Ocean Guardian Pledge[9] to commit to actions that protect the ocean in their daily lives. Travelers who sign the pledge receive monthly e-mails with concrete actions to reduce their environmental impacts, such as using reusable shopping bags, learning about responsible travel, organizing a carpool, and performing a home energy audit. By making such simple changes, people can make their lives more sustainable. Former guests also receive gift cards that they can redeem at Amigos of Costa Rica, an NGO that raises funds to support sustainable change in Costa Rica through education, capacity building, conservation, and science and technology (see Image 2.1.4).[10]

THANKS FOR YOUR SUPPORT
Redeem your gift card at:
http://amigosofcostarica.org/projects/ocean-guardian-journey

Image 2.1.4 The Ocean Guardian Travelers' Philanthropy Gift Card reminds visitors of their pledge to help protect the world's oceans[11]

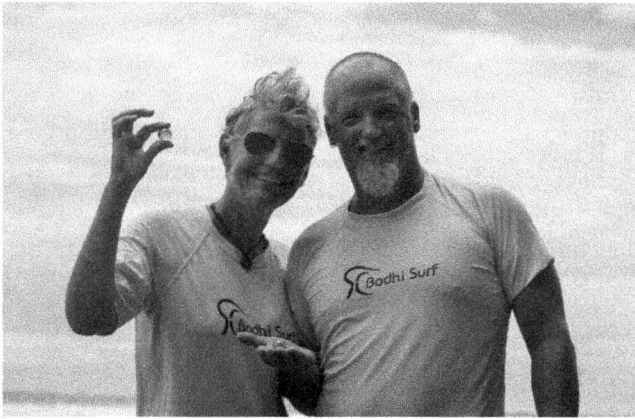

Image 2.1.5 Spreading the Blue Gratitude one marble at a time[13]

By experiencing the ocean through Bodhi Surf + Yoga, travelers are inspired through the Ocean Guardian Journey program to remember their connection to the ocean and implement changes in their daily lives. One former guest of Bodhi, Lisa Burton, wrote on TripAdvisor that "despite coming from the landlocked state of Minnesota, our 10,000 lakes allow us to take this pledge and take responsibility for our local waterways as well as the oceans to our east and west. Upon our departure, the Bodhi owners gave us a blue marble to signify the ocean and serve as a reminder of our greater responsibility to the environment (see Image 2.1.5)."[12]

Educational partnerships

Bodhi Surf + Yoga partners with various educational organizations, including universities and colleges, as well as NGOs, to spread its message and inspire action among students and youth. Bodhi often hosts students from Global Leadership Adventures (GLA), a service learning organization that provides opportunities to high school students to work with community-based businesses and organizations.[14] Every year, Bodhi hosts five groups of approximately 20 students each for GLA's Costa Rica: Protecting the Pacific program, with each group working with a local NGO partner.[15] Members of the Bahia Ballena-Uvita community appreciate the opportunity to engage with GLA students, as it deepens their exposure to people from other places. The personal relationships fostered are paramount to doing effective work grounded in the local community and amplified to the global stage.

Recently, researchers from Skidmore College in New York State (USA) conducted a study to understand how participation in the GLA program at Bodhi affected students' commitment to volunteerism, environmental attitudes and behaviors, and involvement in environmental issues. Preliminary results from this study showed significant increases in environmental knowledge and positive changes in attitudes among the GLA participants with Bodhi Surf + Yoga. Prior to their GLA trip, 65 percent of students could not describe environmental issues facing Costa Rica. After the trip, the majority of students showed a deeper understanding of the impacts of hotel and resort development, consumer habits, and plastic usage on the coastal environment.

Using Bodhi Surf + Yoga as a case study, researchers from The Pennsylvania State University in the United States are conducting a long-term study to see how a nature-based tourism experience can impact a traveler's pro-environment behavior.[16] The study will assess how behavioral changes, advocacy, and activism in favor of environmental conservation can be inspired by a travel experience. The study examines the influences of both the onsite experience at Bodhi and the Ocean Guardian Journey campaign.[17] This research will provide concrete data on Bodhi's impact on visitors, as well as a deeper understanding of its role in confronting climate change and promoting a more sustainable environment.

Conclusions

At Bodhi Surf + Yoga, surfing and yoga are not just physical activities, but lifestyles that are aligned with conservation and environmentalism (see Image 2.1.6). Surfers spend more time in the ocean than most people and are very aware of the state of their favorite surf spots and the ocean in general. Learning to surf at Bodhi means learning pro-environmental behaviors, which are at least as important as standing up on a surfboard. Yoga, which helps provide physical and spiritual awareness, allows *prana*—the vital life force of all living things—to enter the yoga practitioner. This allows for the development of consciousness and respect for all living things, also known as *awakening*.

Image 2.1.6 A fundamental assumption of Bodhi Surf + Yoga, and other tourism experiences grounded in natural and human connections, is that you will protect what you love[18]

Bodhi Surf + Yoga is directly dependent on the well-being of the surrounding community as well as on local terrestrial and marine ecosystems. After all, the beauty of the local environment and the cultural richness of the community are what attract visitors in the first place! For that reason, Bodhi has a vested interest in ensuring the health and well-being of these entities and encouraging others to do the same. Through these efforts, and those of the community and global partners, Bodhi not only provides a world-class nature tourism experience, but educates patrons about climate change and other environmental issues, and inspires them to take more responsible actions at home.

Notes

1. Bodhi Surf School. "Why Choose Bodhi Surf School." http://www.bodhisurfschool.com/why-bodhi-surf
2. Image Source: Andres Madrigal.
3. Geoporter. "Welcome to Geoporter." http://geoporter.net/
4. Forjando Alas. http://forjandoalas.org/
5. Image Source: Shengxiao Yu.

6. Image Source: Melissa Rejeb.

7. For more on Travelers' Philanthropy, see www.responsibletravel.org

8. Amigos of Costa Rica. (2017). "Ocean Guardian Journey: A Travelers' Philanthropy Program." https://www.amigosofcostarica.org/projects/ocean-guardian-journey

9. Bodhi Surf School. "Ocean Guardian Pledge." http://www.bodhisurfschool.com/ocean-guardians/pledge

10. https://amigosofcostarica.org/

11. Image Source: Amigos of Costa Rica.

12. TripAdvisor. "Bodhi Surf School (Uvita, Costa Rica) - Reviews." http://www.tripadvisor.com/Attraction_Review-g635755-d1918722-Reviews-or20-Bodhi_Surf_School-Uvita_Province_of_Puntarenas.html#REVIEWS

13. Image Source: Melissa Rejeb.

14. Global Leadership Adventures. (2016). "Costa Rica - Protecting the Pacific." https://www.experiencegla.com/destinations/teen-programs-latin-america/costa-rica/costa-rica-protecting-pacific/

15. Global Leadership Adventures. (2016).

16. Carter Hunt, William Durham, Laura Driscoll, and Martha Honey. (2015). "Can Ecotourism Deliver Real Economic, Social and Environmental Benefits? A Study of the Osa Peninsula, Costa Rica." *Journal of Sustainable Tourism,* 23(3), 339–357.

17. Mele Wheaton, Nicole Ardoin, Carter Hunt, Janel Schuh, Matthew Kresse, Claire Menke, and William Durham. (2016). "Using Web and Mobile Technology to Motivate Pro-Environmental Action After a Nature-Based Tour." *Journal of Sustainable Tourism,* 24(4), 594–615.

18. Image Source: Melissa Rejeb.

Case Study 2.2

Linking Marine Recreation and Marine Protected Areas: A Marine Scientist and Lifelong Diver's Point of View[1]

by Rick MacPherson with Kreg Ettenger

I am a coral reef scientist, and now find myself at the intersection of science and policy reform. It is an interesting place to be. After spending a lifetime counting parrotfish, I am now counting votes and policymakers. It has brought me into a different aspect of the work that I do, which, over my lifetime, has focused on the intersection between marine protected area (MPA) effectiveness and marine tourism. I believe there is a strong overlap.

I was born in 1963, on another planet. At that time, the atmospheric CO_2 concentrations were about 321 parts per million (ppm). They are now over 400 ppm. In 1963, we had devastating hurricanes occurring at a frequency of roughly one every hundred years. We now have them every other year, or so it seems. Caribbean live coral cover in 1963 was near 60 percent, on average. Our live coral cover average right now is between 15 and 18 percent (see Image 2.2.1). You could see sharks on 100 percent of dives in 1963. I challenge you to see sharks in most Caribbean destinations now. Around the world, coastal fishing communities were thriving in 1963. Now, many are just tourist attractions or ghost towns. So, it really is a different planet than just five decades ago.

I learned to dive when I was 10, so for over 40 years now, I have been diving. I have a personal data set of seeing coral reefs for those four decades. That's why, when I come up from a typical dive today and hear all of the folks on the boat exclaiming, "Wow, that was a great dive," I wonder, did we dive the same reef? Because I didn't see any fish, the water was turbid, and the reef had less than 10 percent live coral cover. The baseline has shifted, as Jeremy Jackson and others have pointed out.[2] If we have no benchmark for what it used to look like, we begin to think that what we are seeing today is normal.

Coral reefs are in serious trouble. I want to emphasize, however, that MPAs work; that reef resilience can be strengthened over time; that

Image 2.2.1 A dead coral reef[3]

marine recreation providers are ideal partners for MPAs; and that there are tools for marine recreation and MPAs to build resilience. Even though it might seem grim, there is hope.

Tourist Expectations and Marine Protected Areas

Studies have shown that when tourists select a dive destination, they want to see large fish, sharks, rays, and turtles; they want diverse, colorful, healthy coral; and they want good water quality and visibility.[4] So tourists are looking for the very things that many coral reefs have lost. Researchers have also looked at what tourists think about protection measures, including limiting tourist activities within certain areas. They have found that tourists are willing to accept restrictions on their access and conduct if those restrictions are part of a conservation effort. So when I hear things such as, "Well, you know, the tourists don't want to be told what to do or where to go," that does not hold up, according to the evidence.

As a response, the conservation community has explored the concept of marine protected areas (MPAs). These are not new. Terrestrial protected areas, such as national parks, have existed for a long time, and MPAs have been employed for at least a few decades. They go by many names: marine managed areas (MMAs), locally managed marine areas

(LMMAs), marine parks, sanctuaries, monuments, reserves, and so on. Whatever you call them, the science says MPAs work. They do not work just by legislative protection, however. They take management, which is labor, and they take resources to pay people, as well as for materials. So just stamping something as an MPA is not a solution; it also takes work.

There is a spectrum of how much government is involved in an MPA. If you do not want too much government involvement, then an LMMA might fit your need. If you think you need strong government buy-in and support, a legislated MPA might be what you want. There is also a continuum in terms of protection. MPAs can be mixed use, limited take, no take, or no access. The Galapagos have examples of the last category; you just cannot go to some of the islands. Palau also has a set of islands that are off-limits completely. Most protected areas try to at least restrict extractive practices, including commercial fishing and even sport or subsistence fishing.

MPAs used to be created based on what we might consider *normal tourism criteria*. For instance, is the site accessible? Is there clear water? Is it scenic and safe? Are there lots of pretty fish for people to see? If those are your criteria, then you draw lines on a map that enclose an area and you create your MPA, and we are all happy. But what happens if criteria have to change in response to climate change threats? Then, we start looking at a different set of criteria. Is there good water quality? Are there many different types of coral? Does the coral have particular resistance to bleaching? Is there good survival and strong recovery after events? Is there local capacity for good management? Again, MPAs do not manage themselves.

MPAs, Climate Change, and Resilience

Coral reef *resilience* refers to their ability to resist stresses brought on by climate change or other factors, and also the quickness with which they can recover. There are different kinds of resilience. There's *biological resilience*, meaning does the system recover, does it have life, does it have high coral cover, high biodiversity, low disease, and broad size range? Can it last through a bleaching event (see Image 2.2.2) or a thermal stress event? Then, there is *social resilience*, which is as important to consider as biological resilience. Do the communities that rely upon reefs

Image 2.2.2 **A NOAA *diver examines a reef after a coral bleaching event in St. Croix, U.S. Virgin Islands*[5]**

have a diversity of local resources? Are they getting protein from places other than the ocean? Can they generate revenue from something other than coral reefs? Are they able to self-organize and self-govern? Does the community have the capacity to learn and adapt, and to achieve financial sustainability? We need to factor all these things into our understanding of resilience.

Over the past decade, we have begun to reevaluate our existing suite of MPAs throughout the Caribbean, and the world, to include more climate change resilience criteria. One example from the Caribbean is Roatán, an island in the Bay of Honduras between Útila and Guanaja. Roatán has a zoned no-take MPA. Interestingly, about a decade ago, we discovered a strand of healthy *Acropora cervicornis,* an endangered species of staghorn coral, thriving in an area it should not have been. This was outside the MPA, in a place where cruise ships dock on the island. We built a case that this reef should be included within the protected area, and an effort was launched to reevaluate the MPA's boundaries. Eventually, the lines got extended to include this new area, called Cordelia Bank, within the no-take zone. That is just one example of adaptation—being able to reevaluate lines on the map—because we cannot just assume that protected areas remain static in a changing situation.

Partnerships with the Marine Tourism Industry

Management needs, labor costs, and materials often make it difficult to achieve MPA goals. Where can we find more hands, more eyes, more support? Marine recreation and tourism providers can make great partners. Tourism providers, particularly the diving community, often have detailed knowledge of high-priority areas, unique features, and even rare species. Divers have been shown to be able to perceive low levels of reef damage even before the scientific community characterizes it. Providers also have relationships with local communities, who can assist in biophysical work, including monitoring. And recreation providers host a captive and interested audience who can then spread the word about climate change. For marine recreation providers, healthy reefs mean healthy businesses.

One of the best examples of a marriage between a protected area, a tourism business, and a local community is the Shark Reef Marine Reserve (SRMR) in Fiji. SRMR was created in 2004 as a protected shark sanctuary.[6] The reefs were dying, and the local community was not deriving protein from them anymore. So an operator came in to help establish this MPA. He began feeding sharks to be able to create an attracted dive, meaning that you dive with sharks and the sharks are fed to aggregate them (see Image 2.2.3). Revenue generated from this shark dive was used to pay fishermen not to fish in a no-take zone of the reef. It gave a decade of recovery to the MPA, which allowed live coral cover to come back and the fish to get larger. It also had a reserve effect, which means fish were able to reproduce without being caught, and the surplus started to spill over outside of the MPA. Fishermen were, perhaps not surprisingly, finding greater catch in the areas where they continued to fish. In addition, scientific research is now showing a strong link between healthy shark populations and healthy coral reefs. Protecting sharks apparently protects reefs by controlling populations of herbivorous fish that can damage reefs by overgrazing.[7]

Following these successes, the SRMR dive operator began working on a mangrove replantation effort with the village that benefited traditional resource owners. In addition to their considerable value as wildlife habitat and shoreline protectors, mangroves act as a carbon sink, absorbing CO_2 from the environment. As a result, local businesses that are partnering with SRMR are not just carbon neutral, they are carbon negative. All in all, the

Image 2.2.3 Shark monitoring, NOAA[8]

Shark Reef Marine Reserve is one of the best success stories in marine conservation, with tourism providers and local fishing communities working together to protect coral reefs and marine and coastal ecosystems.

Conclusion

Even though the perils of our time might be unprecedented, so are the opportunities in front of us. There is great potential for linking MPAs and marine tourism to protect vital resources such as coral reefs in the face of climate change. The recreational diving industry, including our largest lobbying organization, the Diving Equipment & Marketing Association, must speak with one voice on this issue. We must all work to forge alliances with local communities, conservation organizations, and marine scientists to respond to the growing threats posed by climate change. And we must support MPAs as a way of helping coral reefs to be more resilient, ensuring that they can provide food for communities and attractions for divers for generations to come.

Notes

1. This case study was prepared by the second listed author from a presentation given by the lead author at the session "Marine Recreation & MPAs: Fishing, Diving, Surfing," at CREST's *Innovators*

Think Tank on Climate Change & Coastal Tourism, July 22–24, 2015, Punta Cana, Dominican Republic. The original presentation, with extensive photos, is available at: http://www.innovators2015.com/presentations/MacPhersonDRinnovators.pdf

2. Nancy Knowlton and Jeremy B. Jackson. (2008). "Shifting Baselines, Local Impacts, and Global Change on Coral Reefs." *PLOS Biology.* http://dx.doi.org/10.1371/journal.pbio.0060054

3. Image Source: David Burdick, NOAA. Creative Commons.

4. Linwood H. Pendleton. (1994). "Environmental Quality and Recreation Demand in a Caribbean Coral Reef." *Coastal Management,* 22(4). http://dx.doi.org.prxy4.ursus.maine.edu/10.1080/08920759409362246

5. Image Source: NOAA. Creative Commons.

6. Juerg M. Brunnschweiler. (2010). "The Shark Reef Marine Reserve: A Marine Tourism Project in Fiji Involving Local Communities." *Journal of Sustainable Tourism,* 18(1), 29–42. http://www.tandfonline.com/doi/abs/10.1080/09669580903071987

7. Jonathan L. Ruppert, Michael J. Travers, Luke L. Smith, Marie-Josée Fortin, and Mark G. Meekan. (2013). "Caught in the Middle: Combined Impacts of Shark Removal and Coral Loss on the Fish Communities of Coral Reefs." *PLOS One.* http://dx.doi.org/10.1371/journal.pone.0074648

8. Image Source: Kevin Lino, NOAA/NMFS/PIFSC/ESD. Creative Commons.

Case Study 2.3

Sport Fishing and Diving at Turneffe Atoll, Belize: Sustaining Resources through Marine Recreation[1]

by Martha Honey and Kreg Ettenger

Introduction

Sport fishing in marine environments is sometimes viewed as an extractive activity with negative effects on local marine life and habitats. Done improperly, with poor management practices and a lack of control over where fishers go and what they do, it can be just that. But if measures are taken to protect the fisheries themselves, as well as the critical habitats that support them, sport fishing can generate substantial local and regional tourism revenue, create awareness about climate change and other environmental issues, and motivate local residents to protect and manage resources in more sustainable ways.

At Turneffe Atoll, one of Belize's three offshore atolls,[2] sport fishing is an important component in marine tourism and recreation activities. Currently, it ranks second only to diving and snorkeling in terms of its overall contribution to Turneffe's tourism economy, generating millions of dollars each year and helping to employ many local residents. Rather than leading to the overuse and exploitation of local fisheries, the careful catch-and-release methods used at Turneffe Atoll actually help to protect these resources by providing a significant international demand for the tarpon, bonefish, permit, and other finfish that populate the atoll's reefs, flats,[3] and lagoons. This demand helps drive a tourism industry that supports hundreds of local residents who work not only as guides, but also in local resorts and other tourism businesses.

In this case study, we consider how sport fishing can be a component of sustainable marine tourism in places such as Turneffe Atoll and elsewhere in the Caribbean. Drawing upon a larger study that was done by the Center for Responsible Travel for the Turneffe Atoll Trust, we use data from site visits, interviews, and previous studies to show how important this activity is economically, and to argue that it is also highly sustainable from a biological perspective, especially when compared to commercial fishing and other extractive activities.

An Overview of Turneffe Atoll

Located 25 miles (40 km) east of Belize City, Turneffe Atoll is a discrete group of cayes[4] surrounded by its own living coral reef. Approximately 30 miles (48 km) long and 10 miles (16 km) wide, Turneffe is the largest and most biologically diverse coral atoll in this hemisphere (see Image 2.3.1). The atoll's land and seascape consist of a network of highly productive flats, creeks, and lagoons dotted by mangroves and seagrass beds. Its shallows serve as important breeding areas for a wide range of fish species, crocodiles, lobster, conch, and other invertebrates. It also includes at least three significant fish spawning aggregation sites. As the largest of the offshore atolls lying to the east of Belize's coastal shelf, Turneffe is considered to be an integral part of Belize's reef system, as well as a global ecological hotspot for marine biodiversity. It supports a number of threatened and endangered species, including the American saltwater crocodile, Antillean manatee, and several species of sea turtles. The atoll also supports some of the last remaining littoral forests (those occurring along coastlines or on islands) in Belize.

In addition to its wealth of biodiversity, Turneffe Atoll has significant economic value to Belize.[6] Using 2010 data, Turneffe's economic contribution to Belize was estimated to be around US$62 million per year, including US$38 million in shoreline protection from tropical storms; US$23.5 million in tourism revenue; and US$500,000 for commercial fishing. It has historically been a substantial contributor to the commercial harvest of conch, lobster, and finfish in Belize. Turneffe's commercial fishing experienced a sharp decline over the decade prior to 2010, however, leading to increased pressure to develop other economic activities. Between 2004 and 2009, sales of Turneffe lobster tails to Belize's fishing cooperatives declined by over 70 percent, while the number of conch sold through cooperatives declined over 60 percent. According to local fishermen, a number of things have contributed to these declines, including illegal harvesting practices.[7]

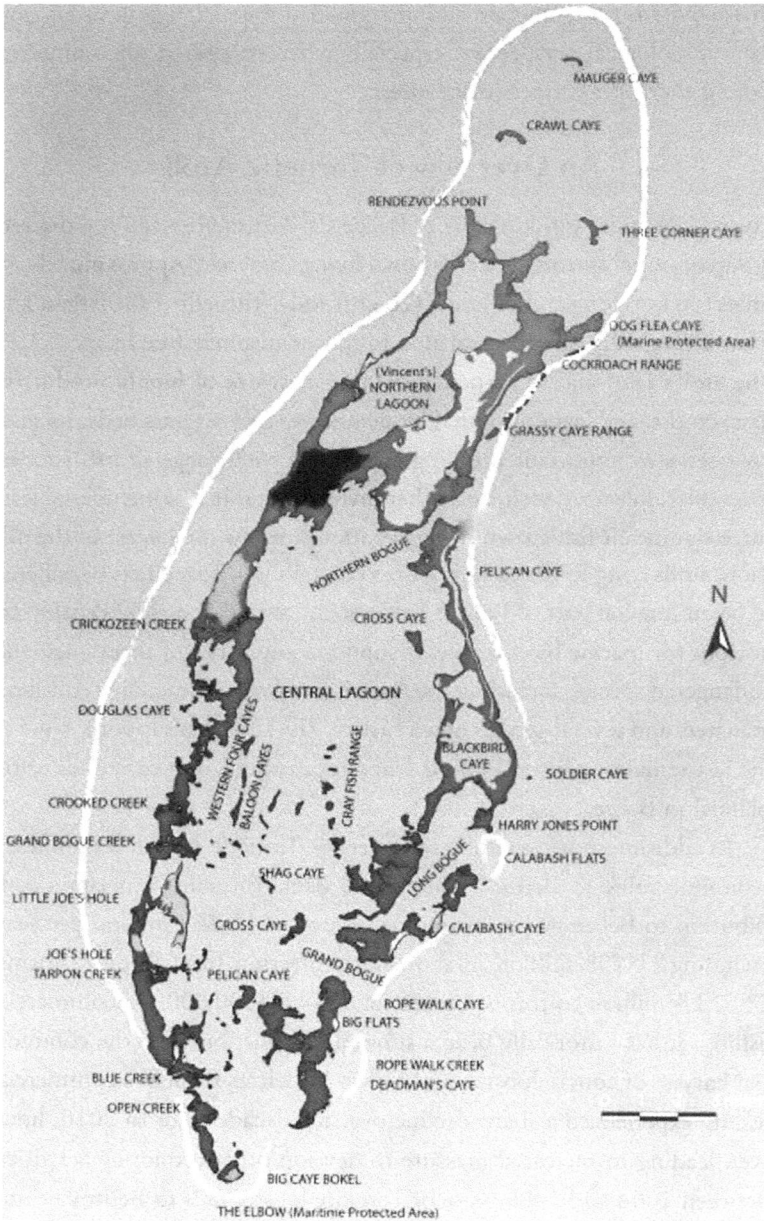

Image 2.3.1 Map of Turneffe Atoll[5]

Tourism and Development Pressure

With the decline of commercial fishing, tourism has offered an important alternative source of income for local fishermen, who work mainly as guides with tourism businesses (see Image 2.3.2). The atoll is known worldwide as a premier sport fishing and scuba diving destination, as well as a growing center for marine research. Tourism is now the leading economic activity on Turneffe Atoll, generating an estimated US$19 million annually in total direct expenditures.[8] When value added or multiplier effects are used, the total economic effect of tourism in Turneffe is close to US$23.5 million per year. Turneffe's tax revenue from tourists averages US$3.4 million annually. One study found that tourism at Turneffe Atoll supported 1,220 full-time jobs, generating US$14.6 million in personal income to workers employed in tourism and associated industries.[9]

With the growth in tourism at Turneffe, development pressure is now increasing, threatening the atoll's ecosystems and marine and coastal resources. Over the last decade, land ownership on Turneffe has shifted dramatically. In 2000, nearly all land at Turneffe was government-owned; by 2011, 23 percent was privately owned. Only a small percentage of the 190 privately owned parcels have been cleared or

Image 2.3.2 Turneffe Flats Resort Atoll Adventure Guide Abel Coe teaches visitors about local marine life[10]

developed to date. Six sites, totaling around 200 acres, have been developed for tourism: three all-inclusive sport fishing and dive resorts, two educational research stations, and one restaurant and resort. Another four properties, totaling 25 acres, have been fully or partially cleared for residential development.

Distance and inaccessibility have helped to protect Turneffe from the fast-paced and often chaotic overdevelopment that has occurred elsewhere in Belize's coastal areas. Nevertheless, Turneffe has already experienced some destructive and inappropriate development, and this is likely to increase as more of its land becomes privately owned, and as access is increased with more airstrips and faster boat linkages to the mainland. As the Turneffe Atoll Coastal Advisory Committee's 2011 *Development Guidelines* state, in order to "sustain Turneffe Atoll's sensitive and valuable terrestrial and marine environments," its tourism industry must be "managed sustainably by facilitating low-impact, nature-based tourism capitalizing on its unique natural assets."[11]

In 2012, partly in response to increased pressure from tourism activities, the Belize government created the Turneffe Atoll Marine Reserve. Until then, Turneffe Atoll had been the only atoll in the Belize Barrier Reef System with no significant protection or directed management. Studies at Turneffe, including the one on which this case study is based, have shown that diving, sport fishing, and other forms of marine-based tourism benefit from successful marine reserves and can help to protect them. In contrast, large-scale commercial fishing and large-scale or poorly planned resort development tend to damage fragile atoll environments, including corals, mangroves, and other marine habitats.

In addition to threats from overdevelopment and resource exploitation, Turneffe Atoll is at risk from the various effects of climate change in this region. It also plays a key role in helping to mitigate these effects, as the Turneffe Flats Resorts website explains:

Approximately 90 percent of Turneffe is low lying land covered by mangroves, making it particularly sensitive to sea [level] rise. At the same time, Turneffe's ecosystems mitigate many of the dire effects of climate change. A major economic function of Turneffe Atoll, for instance, is the protection of Belize City from hurricanes, which economists value at more than 90 million dollars annually. Additionally, mangroves produce significant carbon offsets and essential fisheries habitat. Turneffe is, therefore, threatened by climate change but also offers environmental assets to help our planet adapt to these changes.[12]

Diving, Sport Fishing, and Ecotourism

Turneffe Atoll has become a world-renowned destination for marine tourism, including scuba diving and sport fishing, as well as wildlife viewing and other forms of ecotourism. Two main types of tourism businesses are found on Turneffe Atoll: all-inclusive resorts, which provide tourism activities as part of a package price, and businesses not based at Turneffe that provide daily excursions to the atoll. Tourists stay at one of the three resorts currently operating on the atoll, or come on day trips from Belize City, San Pedro, Caye Caulker, and Placentia, or from cruise ships in port. In a detailed study, Anthony Fedler identified 68 businesses, including hotels, resorts, dive shops, live-aboard boats, research facilities, and tour operators, that offered tourism services at Turneffe. Based on data from 49 businesses that completed his survey, Fedler calculated the economic value of some 11,500 tourists who visited Turneffe in 2010 for diving, sport fishing, and other ecotourism activities.[13] Table 2.1 summarizes these results.

As evident from these statistics, diving and snorkeling are the predominant marine tourism activities on Turneffe Atoll, contributing more than US$9 million to the local economy in 2010. Sport fishing is second, contributing over US$4 million per year to Turneffe's economy. Importantly, recreational fishing generates more revenue per tourist than diving due to the fact that most sport fishers stay at local resorts for multiple days. Other ecotourism activities, such as wildlife viewing and nature tourism, contributed another US$2.7 million. These three activities combined generated nearly US$10 million in direct expenditures, and almost US$16 million in total economic value, in 2010. This means that roughly two-thirds of the total tourism revenue at Turneffe Atoll comes from tourists who engage in these three primary activities, and in particular, from those who come to the atoll for diving, snorkeling, and sport fishing.

Table 2.1 Tourist numbers & expenditures at Turneffe Atoll, 2010 (in US$)[14]

Type of tourism	No. of tourists per activity	Ave. days in Turneffe	Ave. daily expenditure	Turneffe-related expenditures	Total economic value to Turneffe[15]
Resorts on Turneffe					
Diving/Snorkeling	1,387	7	$232	$2,252,488	$3,466,695
Sport fishing	1,250	7	$327	$2,861,250	$3,937,500
Ecotourism	1,221	7	$179	$1,529,913	$2,581,194
Subtotals				$6,643,651	$9,985,389
Daily excursions					
Diving/Snorkeling	6,894	2.43	$182	$3,048,940	$5,595,308
Sport fishing	267	2	$150	$80,100	$163,404
Ecotourism	512	1	$85	$43,520	$123,392
Subtotals				$3,172,560	$5,882,104
Total				$9,816,211	$15,867,493

Turneffe offers catch-and-release sport fishing for bonefish (*Albula spp.*), Atlantic tarpon (*Megalops atlanticus*), and permit (*Trachinotus falcatus*) (see Image 2.3.3). It has been recognized by experts as one of the world's seven best bonefish destinations, and one of the 10 best permit fishing destinations.[16] Catch-and-release fishing (where captured fish are immediately returned alive to the sea) plays an essential role in ensuring the sustainability of this activity, as well as in preserving local fish stocks. In 2009, Belize passed landmark sport fishing legislation, becoming the first country in the world to mandate that all bonefish, tarpon, and permit be released.[17] As Alex Anderson and Craig Hayes explain, however, this type of sustainable fishing has actually been practiced at Turneffe for much longer:

Catch-and-release sport fishing has been the standard practice at Turneffe Atoll for three decades. Over this period, the health of Turneffe's sport fishery has not only been sustained, it has improved. Sport fish stocks have increased, as has average fish size. This would appear to substantiate that catch-and-release, as it is practiced in Belize, has successfully established a sustainable sport fishery.[18]

Image 2.3.3 A permit fish is released during a Turneffe Flats sport fishing trip[19]

Relative Impacts of Resorts, Day Trips, and Cruise Ships

Turneffe attracts a relatively small number of high-value visitors. The most economically beneficial are those tourists who stay at one of the atoll's three lodges, and whose visits last a week or more on average. These are followed by tourists who visit Turneffe with tour boats and spend, on average, just over two days diving or fishing at sites within the atoll. Least beneficial are cruise ship passengers, who spend less than half a day diving or snorkeling at Turneffe, and whose contribution to the local economy is minimal. Turneffe's best option in terms of economic benefits, therefore, as well as for environmental and social sustainability, is to carefully expand both the overnight capacity of the atoll and the number of day visitors brought in from elsewhere in Belize.

The majority of sport fishing and ecotourism at Turneffe is done by guests at resorts on the atoll, rather than through day visits from other locations. In contrast, for diving and snorkeling, nearly five times more tourists participate in such activities via daily excursions than from resorts. Our findings show that for all three types of activities—diving, sport fishing, and ecotourism—tourists staying in a Turneffe-based resort generate more money for Belize's economy than do those on day excursions. Thus, tourism proponents should explore ways to sustainably increase Turneffe-based accommodations while insuring protection of the atoll's environment. The atoll's carrying capacity is limited, and tourism needs to be done in ways that do not overwhelm the atoll's fragile environment.

In comparison to the significant economic value of sport fishing and diving to the Turneffe economy, cruise tourism contributes rather little, even when cruise ship passengers engage in marine recreation activities. Fedler estimated that in 2010, 1,300 cruise ship passengers took part in diving and snorkeling tours on Turneffe Atoll. Based on our own calculations, and considering the economic leakage that occurs when cruise ship passengers book activities directly through cruise lines, the revenue generated for the Belize economy was somewhere between US$110,000 and US$120,000; the amount actually flowing into Turneffe's economy was likely a fraction of this. In contrast, scuba diving offered by resorts in

Turneffe generated US$3.5 million in 2010, or roughly 29 times as much revenue, for virtually the same number of divers.

In terms of environmental impacts, all forms of marine tourism at Turneffe, whether based on resorts, day trips, or cruise ships, have their share. The impacts of cruise ships on local, regional, and global environments are described in Chapter 4 of this volume. Day trips, while having fewer direct environmental impacts on local communities and resources, can have significant impacts in terms of their carbon footprint; fishing boats from the Belizean mainland have to travel 25 miles (40 km) or more to reach Turneffe. Resorts, for their part, can be sustainably built and operated, but can also do significant damage to mangroves, dunes, and other coastal habitats, and can place enormous burdens on fresh water and other limited resources. At Turneffe Atoll, there are examples of both sustainably managed resorts and those that are doing serious harm to the environment.

One example of the latter is a new resort called the *Belize Dive Haven Resort and Marina by Sir Hakimi*—by far, the largest resort to date at Turneffe (see Image 2.3.4). Promotional material for the resort states, "This exclusive, private island already boasts a 300-foot pier with a 60' × 70' restaurant overlooking the clear, blue Caribbean Sea, and a 500' dock and dredged bay to accommodate large yachts."[20] Nearly everything about the project seems inappropriate for an environmentally fragile atoll. When completed, the facility will include a 96-room hotel, an airstrip, condos, and a supermarket. An April 2012 visit to the construction site revealed not only extensive dredging of sand from the shallow waters around the caye, but an enormous (200 foot) swimming pool. The concrete shells of two buildings containing a total of 48 rooms had already been built, and foundations for two more were in place. By December 2016, while the infrastructure had expanded considerably, the resort was still not open.[21]

Some resorts, including Turneffe Flats Resort and Turneffe Island Resort, are designed on a much more appropriate scale and are run using sustainable management practices, showing that not all resorts on Turneffe need to destroy the environments on which they depend. Based on CREST researchers' observations and interviews, there appears to be a need for improved environmental assessment prior to building tourism facilities and more oversight of construction activities once they begin.

Image 2.3.4 Sir Hakimi's Belize Dive Haven under construction in 2012[22]

Ensuring Sustainable, High-Value Tourism at Turneffe Atoll

The future of tourism in Turneffe is being shaped by government policy, Belize's international tourism image, and the realities of the atoll itself, as well as by trends in international tourism. Turneffe has a successful and largely sustainable tourism industry based on three non-extractive activities: catch-and-release sport fishing, diving, and ecotourism. There is potential for each of these activities, including fishing, to be gradually and carefully expanded. However, the atoll faces threats from a lack of control over tourism construction and other development. Creation of the new marine reserve is a major step toward sustainable development, but it must be accompanied with clear enforcement of Belize's regulations for tourism development, as well as adherence to internationally recognized best practices for sustainable tourism.

Equally important is determining how much Turneffe's tourism sector can expand and still be sustainable. Based on our own analysis and the opinions of local experts, the total number of operating resorts should probably not exceed half a dozen. Several all-inclusive resorts could be complemented with a small number of more basic overnight guesthouses. According to the

2011 *Management Guidelines*, "Some traditional fishermen have expressed a desire to develop their fishing camps into small guest houses offering the eco-cultural experience of the fishermen." The guidelines go on to recommend that zoning should provide local fishers with the option of developing such guest houses, thereby "promoting opportunities for traditional users to benefit from tourism."[23] This will be increasingly important if commercial fishing resources, mainly lobster and conch, continue to decline.

The most suitable types of tourism for fragile island and atoll ecosystems such as Turneffe are small-scale, low-impact resorts that specialize in non-consumptive fishing, diving, snorkeling, and other marine and land-based activities. These ecolodges can, and should, be built in accordance with sustainability guidelines, such as those created by leading certifying organizations. Another opportunity for low-impact economic development on the atoll is educational and volunteer tourism run through the atoll's current research centers or in conjunction with ecolodges. Larger, more mass-market-oriented hotels and resorts are wholly inappropriate for Turneffe Atoll.

Clearly, the establishment of the new Turneffe Atoll Marine Reserve is a critical step in the right direction in terms of ensuring the sustainable development and longevity of both commercial fishing and marine-based tourism. The marine reserve will attract the types of environmentally and socially conscious tourists that are most appropriate for Turneffe (see Image 2.3.5). The marine reserve by itself, however, will not "save"

Image 2.3.5 Divers at Turneffe Atoll view a barracuda[24]

Turneffe. It must be accompanied by stronger standards for sustainable construction and operation of resorts, research facilities, private homes, and other developments to conform to existing regulations in Belize and the growing knowledge of international best practices. Only through protecting the atoll's marine and terrestrial ecosystems will Turneffe continue to grow as an attractive destination for high-value tourism.

Conclusion

Turneffe Atoll's non-extractive, small-scale marine tourism has demonstrated its compatibility with sustainable management of local fisheries and other marine resources. This type of tourism, which includes sport fishing, diving, and snorkeling, depends on a healthy marine environment. Turneffe's world-renowned catch-and-release sport fishing is causing negligible mortality and has led to an increase in stocks of bone, tarpon, and permit. These species are not of commercial value, and in the main, sport fishing takes places in different locations than commercial fishing. This has enabled sport and commercial fishing to coexist, rather than compete with each another. In addition, with the decline of commercial fish stocks, tourism has provided alternative employment for dozens of commercial fishermen.

To respond to climate change, the decline of commercial fishing, and other pressures, Turneffe needs to gradually grow its market for high-value tourism that emphasizes environmental stewardship, good jobs, and sustainable use of local resources, all based on relatively modest numbers of visitors. The emphasis should be on controlled and sustainable growth, and on strengthening existing facilities to improve their environmental and social practices. Adoption of an internationally recognized, national certification program for accommodations (as well as for other tourism facilities, including boats and beaches) is important in ensuring long-term protection of the atoll. In terms of day visitors, emphasis should be on increasing the numbers of visitors from Belize City and other parts of the country, rather than from cruise tourism, which provides the least economic benefit to Turneffe.

Fortunately, the type of tourism that is most suitable for and beneficial to Turneffe Atoll constitutes a significant and growing sector of the traveling public. Broadly stated, these are *experiential* or *conscientious* travelers who seek vacations that are both enjoyable and educational, who want to connect with nature and have authentic experiences, and who are concerned about the impacts of their travels on the environment and host communities. The new MPA enhances Turneffe Atoll's appeal to these discerning travelers and helps ensure the longevity and sustainability of the destination and its main economic sector, marine-based tourism.

Notes

1. This case study is largely based on the report, *Turneffe Atoll, Belize: Balancing Sustainable Tourism & Commercial Fishing in a Marine Protected Area (MPA)*, prepared by the Center for Responsible Travel (CREST) for the Turneffe Atoll Trust, January 2013. The primary author of that report was CREST Co-Director Martha Honey, with assistance from staff members Catherine Ardagh, Kyle Hook, and Naomi Garner. Findings were based on a site visit and interviews in Belize City and at Turneffe Atoll, along with a review of multiple primary documents, academic studies, published articles, and web-sites. CREST would like to thank the Turneffe Atoll Trust for com-missioning and financing this study. Craig Hayes, the Trust's Board Chairman and owner of Turneffe Flats Resort, provided background materials, organized the site visit and interviews in April 2012, and reviewed the final draft. The report was also reviewed by CREST Co-Director William H. Durham at Stanford University.

2. An atoll is "a ring-shaped coral reef, island, or series of islets [often surrounding] a body of water called a lagoon." National Geographic Society. http://nationalgeographic.org/encyclopedia/atoll/

3. Reef "flats" have been described as "expansive shallow areas with adjacent tidal creeks [forming] a complex habitat mosaic comprised of mangroves, sea grass, benthic algae, sand, coral rubble, limestone, and mud bottom that supports an inherently diverse community" of marine life. J. Aaron Adams and Steven Cooke. (2015). "Advancing the Science and Management of Flats Fisheries for Bonefish, Tarpon, and Permit." *Environmental Biology of Fishes*, 98(11), 2123–31.

4. A cay or caye is a small, low-elevation, sandy island on the surface of a coral reef. They occur in tropical environments throughout the

Caribbean, Pacific, Atlantic, and Indian Oceans. "Cay." *Wikipedia.* https://en.wikipedia.org/wiki/Cay

5. Image Source: Turneffe Atoll Coastal Advisory Committee. Used with permission by the Center for Responsible Travel (CREST) from the report, *Turneffe Atoll, Belize: Balancing Sustainable Tourism & Commercial Fishing in a Marine Protected Area (MPA),* prepared by the Center for Responsible Travel (CREST) for the Turneffe Atoll Trust. (January 2013).

6. Anthony Fedler. (2011). *The Economic Value of Turneffe Atoll: Full Report.* Human Dimensions Consulting.

7. Ibid, 15–16.

8. Martha Honey, Catherine Ardagh, Kyle Hook, Naomi Garner. (January 2013). *Turneffe Atoll, Belize: Balancing Sustainable Tourism & Commercial Fishing in a Marine Protected Area (MPA).* Prepared by the Center for Responsible Travel (CREST) for the Turneffe Atoll Trust. http://responsibletravel.org/docs/Turneffe%20Atoll%20Full%20Report.pdf

9. Anthony Fedler. (2011). Op cit.

10. Image Source: Turneffe Flats Resort. Photo credit Pablo Negri.

11. Turneffe Atoll Coastal Advisory Committee. (2011). *Turneffe Atoll Coastal Zone Management Guidelines 2011.* Belize City, Belize: Coastal Zone Management Authority and Institute.

12. Turneffe Flats. (2016). "Threats." http://www.tflats.com/threats/

13. No attempt was made to estimate tourism revenue from non-responding businesses; therefore, these statistics underestimate the full extent of tourism benefits from Turneffe Atoll.

14. Table Source: Center for Responsible Travel (CREST) from the report, *Turneffe Atoll, Belize: Balancing Sustainable Tourism & Commercial Fishing in a Marine Protected Area (MPA),* prepared by the Center for Responsible Travel (CREST) for the Turneffe Atoll Trust. (January 2013).

15. *Total economic value* includes the spinoff effects from spending by those employed in the tourism industry, the value of ancillary businesses, and other indirect economic benefits.

16. Turneffe Atoll Coastal Advisory Committee. (2011). Op cit., 1.

17. *Ambergris Today.* (February 12, 2009). "Belize Passes Landmark Catch and Release Fishing Legislation." Press Release. Belize City, Belize.

http://ambergriscaye.com/forum/ubbthreads.php/topics/324468/belize-passes-landmark-catch-and-release-law.html

18. Alex Anderson and Craig Hayes, (2011). "Analysis of Fish Mortality Related to Catch and Release Sport Fishing in Belize." Unpublished research report. http://www.turneffeatoll.org/tat-action-plan/most-catch-release-mortality-at-turneffe

19. Image Source: Turneffe Flats Resort. Photo credit Terry Gunn.

20. Belize Dive Haven Resort & Marina. http://belizedivehaven.com/

21. As of December 12, 2016, the resort's website was not yet accepting bookings, but visitors could sign up to receive email updates on its grand opening. http://belizedivehaven.com/

22. Image Source: Center for Responsible Travel (CREST).

23. Turneffe Atoll Coastal Advisory Committee. (2011). *Turneffe Atoll Coastal Zone Management Guidelines 2011.* Coastal Zone Management Authority and Institute: Belize City.

24. Image source: Turneffe Flats Resort.

CHAPTER 3

Caribbean Yachting and Marinas in an Era of Climate Change

Overview—Battening Down the Hatches: Yachting, Marinas, and Sustainability

Martha Honey

The Caribbean is one of the world's outstanding regions for yacht cruising. While yachting and marinas are spread throughout the Caribbean, the most important concentrations are in the Northwest region (Puerto Rico, British Virgin Islands, and U.S. Virgin Islands), Leeward Islands (St. Maarten/St. Martin, St. Barts, Antigua/Barbuda, and Guadeloupe), Southern region (Grenada, Trinidad and Tobago), and Windward Islands (Martinique, St. Lucia, St. Vincent and the Grenadines, and Barbados).[1] Unlike many other sectors of the tourism industry, yachting offers both accommodations (onboard) and recreation (sailing, pleasure cruising, fishing, diving, etc.). Similarly, its economic benefits to local communities come from two streams: recreation and services. Most Caribbean islands tend to focus on one or the other, while few countries take advantage of both streams (although Grenada appears positioned to do so).[2] Trinidad and Tobago, for instance, have established themselves as service centers, while St. Vincent and the Grenadines focus on marine recreation.

Expansion of yachting and marinas in the Caribbean is closely tied to two factors: the U.S. economy and hurricanes. In terms of the first, boat ownership and new marina construction in the Americas has followed the flow of U.S. vacationers, and more recently, North American and European retirees to the Caribbean, as well as to Mexico and Central America. A second key factor is the threat posed by hurricanes and other natural hazards, many linked to climate change. Most Caribbean islands are within the Caribbean Hurricane Belt, where the majority of Atlantic tropical storms are likely to occur.[3] Between 1989 and 1999, three of the Caribbean's major yachting destinations, Antigua/Barbuda, St. Martin/St. Maarten, and Puerto Rico, all suffered repeated damage and loss of business from hurricanes, as did the British Virgin Islands (BVI), the region's most popular yacht charter destination.[4] These islands were also hit hard by Hurricanes Irma and Maria, some of the strongest storms ever recorded in the Atlantic, causing an estimated US$200 billion in damage to the region,[5] including severe impacts to many resorts, hotels and marinas.[6] The traditional hurricane season lasts from June 1 to November 30, but storms outside this range are increasingly likely due to the extension of warm ocean temperatures into the winter months. In addition, as hurricanes become increasingly frequent, fierce, and erratic, even islands outside the Hurricane Belt are not totally secure. Grenada, for instance, which has a growing number of marinas, was badly hit by hurricanes in 1999, 2004, and 2005.

While yachting is a marine activity, its facilities—namely, marinas and boatyards—must be constructed on shorelines and nearshore areas, making it also a component of coastal tourism.[7] Marinas are necessary for the development of recreational boating and nautical tourism.[8] These activities can provide significant positive impacts on coastal tourism businesses, as well as on commercial boating, technical services, and other industries. They can also benefit local communities, including supporting traditional subsistence activities such as fishing, as well as tourism-related small businesses.

History of Marinas in the Caribbean

Marinas developed slowly during the first half of the twentieth century. In the early 1900s, only the wealthy in the United States had pleasure boats and they built private harbors to dock them. After World War II, the U.S. middle class also began buying recreational boats, and demand for marinas increased. During the long economic expansion of the 1990s and most of the first decade of the twenty-first century, sales of motorboats and sailboats increased steadily, and in recent years, powerboats have been more popular among U.S. boat owners than sailboats.[9] As pleasure boat sales increased, so did the demand for marinas. However, with the deep economic depression in the late 2000s, boat sales in the United States plummeted, many marinas closed, and new marina construction in the Caribbean slowed.

As the Caribbean has gradually recovered from this financial crisis, the number of yacht charters, production of large luxury yachts, and growth of marinas are once again increasing. In fact, marinas are viewed by some experts as a bellwether of economic recovery and the overall health of the Caribbean region. By 2013, new marina construction linked to high-end residential tourism development was a sign that the severe economic downturn was over. As Caribbean real estate executive James Burdess stated in 2013, "Over the last three years we have seen an increase in marinas being built and a large increase in the number of super yachts coming to the Caribbean."[10] In September 2013, *Vacation News* reported that "Rising demand for marina berths in the Caribbean [was] fueling new residential projects."[11] Indeed, in recent years, there has been a growing relationship between marinas and coastal resorts. Desire to live near the water has caused incredible demand for waterfront property. In many areas, developers have been buying up existing freestanding marinas and converting the land into more profitable luxury housing developments.[12] Boat owners, in turn, are increasingly seeking *destination marinas* that offer more than simply fishing and cruising. Destination marinas typically include a mix of hotels and resorts, condo and vacation home developments, restaurants, retail shops, and sometimes, golf courses.

By 2013, the Caribbean had 113 marinas with a total of 13,469 berths, and another 8 marinas were under development. One new marina was Port Ferdinand on the northwest coast of Barbados, which opened in December 2013 with 120 berths, plus the first of 83 luxury apartment condos, each with price tags from US$2.1 million to $6.5 million (see Image 3.0.1). The apartments have waterside views overlooking the

Image 3.0.1 Each home at Port Ferdinand includes access to a 50-plus foot yacht berth close by with duty-free yacht concessions[14]

marina and come with their own berths. "Basically, a boat slip is like a hotel room," says the Florida marina firm Richard Graves & Associates. "One accommodates the guest's boat and the other accommodates the guest."[13]

The upshot of these trends may be that leisure boat ownership and private, rather than public, marinas are again becoming an attraction, primarily for wealthy elite, as was the case in the early and mid-twentieth century. This includes well-off retirees, many of them American. According to Richard Graves & Associates, "Marinas near upscale retirement locations fare particularly well."[15] Like golf courses that allow vacation homes to sell for more because they are on green space, vacation homes next to marinas command higher prices because they offer "blue views." As elaborated below, expansion of marinas (much like golf courses) appears to be based, at least in part, on real estate speculation, rather than on realistic assessments of consumer demand for recreational boating.

Profile of Yachts and Marinas in the Caribbean

The Caribbean yachting sector today is far from homogeneous. A recent study in Grenada identified several main market segments of yachts:

charters, short-term visitors (ranging from day cruises up to six-month stays), long-term visitors (including live aboards and second-home owners), and luxury yachts. Each segment has its own distinct customer behavior and spending patterns (see Case Study 3.2). One trend is the rapidly growing category of luxury yachts, including *super- and megayachts*. While definitions vary, superyachts are generally over 24 meters (about 79 feet) in length, while megayachts are typically over 30 meters (100 feet) and can be up to 100 meters (330 feet) or more, with a handful measuring between 500 and 600 feet.[16] Such ships require professional crews to operate, and their price tags range from US$10 million to $100 million or more. By 2013, there were 4,600 superyachts, an increase of 25 percent in the previous five years, according to the UK-based Marina Projects.[17] About 1,500 of these were available for charter, generally in the Mediterranean in the summer and the Caribbean in the winter. Their owners are an eclectic global mix of tycoons from the United States, Russia, South Africa, the Middle East, Europe, and Asia.

Megayachts and superyachts typically have no real home port and are often registered, like cruise ships, with *flags of convenience* (see the Chapter 4 Overview) from countries they may never have visited. Popular flag of convenience countries for large yachts are the Cayman Islands, Marshall Islands, Isle of Man, and the British Virgin Islands. Docking rates for megayachts are two to four times higher than for normal size pleasure boats, and there is "a critical shortage throughout the world" of marinas with docks large enough to accommodate these giant pleasure boats.[18] While recreational boating tends to be subject to fluctuations in the economy, wealthy owners of megayachts appear not to be seriously affected by economic downturns.[19] Today, most new marinas, including those in the Caribbean, include slips and services for megayachts.

Marinas themselves vary considerably in terms of size and services. They can include a range of boating infrastructure for leisure activities and tourism, all under one management. A central component is *wet slips* (commonly called simply slips), which are berthing spaces designed for mooring individual boats. Berthing is usually provided by a fixed or floating dock connected to land, in a body of water that is sufficiently deep and provides adequate protection. Marinas can also include *dry storage*, onshore facilities for storing watercraft, including *dry stacks* that holds boats vertically in racks. Dry dock storage has become increasingly popular because it allows an operator to handle hundreds of boats on less waterfront property than a conventional wet slip marina. Dockage is a marina's main profit center, and docking rates are charged on a daily, monthly, seasonal, or annual basis, with rates calculated by the length of the boat and the length of their stay.

Marinas operate in a competitive landscape. Because their construction and fixed operating costs are considerable, high occupancy rates are crucial to financial success. Most marinas cater to both annual and seasonal slip holders, and to casual or transient boaters. The profitability of individual marinas depends on their location, marketing, and sales of amenities and customized services. Today's marinas offer a wide range of amenities, including electricity and water; television, phone, and internet hookups; bilge and sewage pump outs; maintenance and repair services; fuel, groceries, and supplies; bars and restaurants; laundry services; and chandleries selling nautical supplies and even boats. Marinas may also house government services, such as customs and police. And, as stated earlier, they are often part of larger resort or vacation home complexes.

The Economic Importance of the Caribbean Yachting Sector

While the yachting sector is less studied than either stay-over tourism in coastal resorts or ocean-based tourism via cruise ships, its contribution to local economies in the Caribbean is clearly significant. For instance, a 1999 study comparing stay-over, cruise, and yacht tourism in Antigua-Barbuda found that yachting contributed roughly 50 percent more to the local economy than cruise ships, even though 11 times more visitors arrived via cruise ships than yachts. Table 3.1 shows the length of visitor stays, expenditure per day, and total overall expenditure for the three groups in 1999. The biggest difference between cruise tourists and yacht tourists is not in their daily expenditure, but in their average length of stay: one day for the former versus nearly 11 days for the latter. As the report's author states, "Despite the significantly larger investments made by governments in cruise tourism infrastructure and the higher profile of the cruise tourism sector, the contribution from yachting in visitor

Table 3.1 Economic impacts of stay-over, cruise ship, and yachting visitors to Antigua-Barbuda in 1999[20]

Type of visitor	Total number of visitors	Percentage of total visitors	Avg. length of stay (days)	Average daily expenditure (US$)	Total expenditure (US$ millions)	Contribution toward overall tourism revenue
Yachting	29,114	5.2%	10.8	42.71	13.43	4.5%
Stay-Over	207,662	36.8%	7.8	169.67	274.83	92.4%
Cruise Ship	328,038	58.1%	1.0	27.95	9.17	3.1%
Total	564,814	100%	4.0	240.59	297.43	100%

spending to Antigua's economy was higher than cruise tourism." He concludes that "already, the sector's contribution compared to cruise tourism is commendable," and that there is potential for further growth of the yacht sector.[21]

A 2013 study in Grenada similarly found that the marine and yachting sector "is a major contributor to the economy of Grenada." "It is almost certain," the report continues, "that it outstrips the international cruise segment, and it is quite possible that it is comparable with the resort tourism segment" (also see Case Study 3.2). The authors add that "the marine and yachting segment has been able to perform this well with only limited government investment and marketing and promotion."[22] While both studies demonstrate the economic importance of yachting, the Grenada study raises questions about how much one specific category, superyachts, actually contribute to the local economy. This study found that for superyachts, the most significant source of economic impact was expenditures related to provisioning, fuel, and berthing. Crews of superyachts also spent on onshore services such as restaurants and entertainment. However, other major categories of spending eluded Grenada: the costs of charters are paid outside Grenada, significant or technical repairs are performed by craftsmen and technicians flown in to Grenada by the owners, and passengers typically "engage in few, if any, on-shore activities."[23] Nevertheless, Grenada and other countries often put in special facilities to attract and accommodate superyachts, similar to what is done for cruise tourism. According to Willard Phillips, an economic affairs officer with the Economic Commission for Latin America and the Caribbean (ECLAC) in Trinidad, "While there is much excitement in the Caribbean about the benefits of superyachts to the regional economy, questions are increasingly being asked about this proposition."[24] Clearly, more detailed studies are needed in other Caribbean destinations to assess the real costs and benefits of superyachts.

Environmental Impacts of Marinas

Like airports, roads, and hotels, marinas can cause significant negative environmental impacts. Inappropriately designed, constructed, and operated marinas cause a range of negative effects, and some of these, such as loss of mangroves, can also reduce resilience to climate change. Properly done, however, marinas can improve degraded land and minimize environmental impacts on pristine coastal and nearshore areas. "Marinas carry a stigma among the general public of *always* causing negative impacts," states marina designer and consultant Esteban Biondi.[25] To the contrary, he explains, "Marinas can be sited, developed, and operated in a sustainable manner." He highlights that degraded waterfronts, for instance, can benefit from the development of recreational and tourism boating infrastructure as part of a renovation and cleanup plan. Biondi concludes that best practices for planning and building marinas (and for coastal construction in general) involve design solutions that are resilient, seek positive (or at least neutral) environmental impacts, maximize social and economic benefits, and add economic value to the project (see Case Study 3.1).

Biondi says that proper engineering design of marinas and other coastal structures is fundamental to mitigating environmental impacts, including erosion, accretion, and severe damage during extreme events such as hurricanes.[26] He believes that many projects cause unacceptable shoreline impacts because their design, construction, and operation have not followed good engineering design guidelines. Biondi believes that best practices in engineering studies, and sound design principles, should be seen as investments in a higher-value project. Positive outcomes are achieved when developers understand that basic studies are an investment to improve the design, as opposed to a cost to get a permit.

In addition to coastal engineering issues, he highlights that ecological features can be integrated into a marina design, adding aesthetic value and/or reducing construction costs—an approach known broadly as *environmental design*.[27] He adds that the concept of *structural resiliency*, which is rather new in marina design, and specifically relates to climate change adaptation, is, at its core, traditional "good engineering design." This involves assessing extreme events properly and designing structures and systems that can respond well when design conditions are exceeded.[28]

Biondi argues that while such practices can be very effective, they are often not followed by developers and regulatory agencies in the Caribbean. Although marina developers and operators in the Caribbean and Latin America are aware that these facilities are exposed to increasingly severe and unpredictable hurricanes and sea level rise, they do not typically include consideration of climate change or the need for adaptation in practice. Unfortunately, marina developers often do not undertake all recommended engineering studies, or follow their recommendations, even if those steps would likely result in reduced costs of construction, maintenance, and repairs after extreme weather events. Biondi makes the case that the integration of environmental design approaches in marina planning and design meets the sustainability criteria of international guidelines such as PIANC's *Working with Nature*[29] in a practical and effective manner.[30]

Social Impacts

Even less attention has typically been paid to the social impacts of marinas, or to how they might be used to help address local economic, social, and cultural needs. In fact, throughout the Caribbean region, marinas have become a flashpoint for conflicts between coastal residents, including fishing communities, and wealthy outsiders such as tourists. Promoters of marinas argue that they provide positive social impacts, including facilities for police and customs officials to check boats and their passengers, monitor illegal activity, and conduct safety inspections. Critics, meanwhile, argue that marinas tend to attract a less desirable international clientele and may serve as a gateway for drugs, prostitution, and other illegal and antisocial activities.[31] These negative social impacts are difficult to verify and may well be based more on fear than reality. Two other social concerns are, however, more credible. One is limited job creation, and the other is displacement of local coastal and fishing communities.

Developers frequently inflate the number of local jobs marinas will bring during the construction and operations phases. The Tyrell Bay Marina on Carriacou in Grenada promised to bring 125 direct and 300 indirect new jobs to the island, for example. They estimated that when fully built, the marina and its range of facilities would generate a total of 150 to 200 direct and indirect jobs. But in early 2017, the owners admitted that during the multiyear construction stage, the project had only generated 20–40 jobs at any one time (see Case Study 3.3). In Costa Rica, Marina Pez Vela in Quepos pledged to provide training programs in conjunction with the National Learning Institute (INA) "so that locals can acquire the relevant skills" to work in the marina.[32] However, the developer committed only a few thousand dollars for job training, and by late 2011, only "about 20 people work[ed] at the marina facility, most in sales and cleaning or security positions." It was also not clear how many of these workers were local. Ever optimistic, however, the marina operators predicted that when the hotels, condos, and shopping center were completed, "an estimated 3,000 direct and indirect jobs would have been created."[33]

As a marina designer and consultant, Esteban Biondi provides an innovative approach to social sustainability applied to marina design.[34] He argues that authentic guest experiences add value to marinas, and that local residents are "the best suited to deliver authentic experiences."[35] From a business standpoint, he says, offering these experiences through interactions with local people can bring both added value and enhanced profitability of a marina project. Biondi argues that direct connections with local businesses and community members can have positive socio-economic impacts, such as reducing economic leakage and providing memorable guest experiences.[36] He believes that developers can proactively implement the principles of sustainable tourism in the marina planning process, and thereby achieve economic success as well as social and environmental sustainability (see Case Study 3.1).

Marinas, Yachting, and Climate Change

According to Ivor Jackson, a Caribbean-based architect specializing in environmental land use and tourism planning, yachting destinations can become vulnerable to climate change if they have poorly designed and engineered infrastructure; poorly manage their boatyard services, including yacht storage on land; and lack well-managed hurricane shelters.[37] Climate change is already heightening the susceptibility of marinas to environmental damage, while inadequate social policies and practices, and poor community relations, can make it more difficult for marinas to respond effectively to climate change impacts. Marinas, boatyards, and related infrastructure are vulnerable to high winds, high energy waves, and storm surges, all of which are increasing in the era of climate change. According to Jackson, the Caribbean's most important yachting destinations and marinas have all suffered recent impacts from winds, waves, and storm surges (Table 3.2). He mentions several marinas and yacht basin bulkheads that

Table 3.2 Climate-related threats to important yachting destinations, from Puerto Rico to Trinidad[38]

Yachting sub-region	Yachting destination	Destination rating		Recent impact		Hazard threat	
		Services	Cruising	Wind	Surge	High	Medium/Low
Northwest region	Puerto Rico	E	G	*	*	*	
	USVI	E	G	*	*	*	
	BVI	E	E	*	*	*	
Leeward islands and Guadeloupe	St. Maarten/St. Martin	E	G	*	*	*	
	St. Barts	G	F	*	*	*	
	Antigua/Barbuda	E	E	*	*	*	
	Guadeloupe	E	F				*
Windward islands and Barbados	Martinique	G	G				*
	St. Lucia	G	G		*		*
	St. Vincent/Grenadines	F	E		*		*
	Barbados	G	F		*?		*
Southern region	Grenada/Grenadines	G	E		*		*
	Trinidad & Tobago	E	F		*		*

(E = Excellent; G = Good; F = Fair)

are especially vulnerable to sea level rise and extreme effects of wave and storm surge, including Nelson's Dockyard, Jolly Harbour, and Catmarina in Antigua, Rodney Bay in St. Lucia, and Chaguaramas in Trinidad.[39]

Sea level rise caused by ocean warming has implications for the planning and environmental management of marinas. According to Jackson, careful planning is needed to "increase the useful life of marina infrastructure against the rise in sea level and to maintain structural integrity against storm waves and surge." It is vital to set adequate heights for bulkheads and berthing piers, and provide adequate structural reinforcement for the foundations of pier piles and bulkhead footing.[40] Sea level rise is also threatening coral reefs, which in some places, including the BVI, Antigua/Barbuda, and St. Vincent and the Grenadines, offer protected yachting anchorages. As Jackson states, "Sea level rise can be expected to have adverse impacts on the protective function of coral reefs, except where reef growth is fast enough to maintain wave energy attenuating functions at existing levels."[41]

At the same time, several factors are increasing the navigational difficulties for sailing and cruising among the Caribbean's fragile coral reefs. Increased storms, numbers of boats, pollution, and runoff are all contributing to reduced visibility around coral reefs. In addition, sediment deposition associated with more frequent and intense storms is reducing channels and anchorages. One solution is to increase the depth of existing channels and ports, especially for large luxury yachts and tall ships (such as windjammer cruisers), which have deeper draughts than bareboat charters or twin hull catamarans. While incidents of yachts running aground on unmarked reefs have increased with the growth of bareboat charters,[42] authorities have been reluctant, sometimes for financial reasons, to implement adequate buoyage (marker) systems.

According to Esteban Biondi, while predictions of sea level rise are available, the impacts of climate change-induced storms are less certain. More intense storms can generate higher offshore waves and increased storm surge height. Higher water levels due to sea level rise may allow storm waves to overtop breakwater structures. This is typically not a major issue for breakwaters in deeper areas, but it may be significant in shallower waters and mild slope shorelines.[43] Biondi notes that traditional engineering design of marinas, done properly, has long incorporated structural resiliency as a goal. Such designs must now consider climate change impacts as well. Coastal structures should not fail abruptly when design conditions are exceeded. Additionally, marina design and construction should facilitate recovery after storms.[44] Best practices such as these almost always come down to following *and exceeding* existing guidelines and regulations.

Certification under Blue Flag for Marinas

One way to ensure that marinas are sustainably designed, built, and operated is to follow voluntary certification programs. In the Americas, there are two leading marina certification programs, Clean Marinas and Blue Flag. Clean Marinas includes a "family" of programs that originated in U.S. Environmental Protection Agency recommendations, but which are run by individual states.[45] One state program, the California Clean Marinas program, has expanded to Mexico.[46] The program uses best management practices designed to protect waters from pollution, and allows marina operators, yacht clubs, and municipal port authorities to gain certification. In addition, Clean Marinas has recently developed guidelines for addressing resilience, which can be used by marinas in the Caribbean as part of a climate change adaptation strategy (see Case Study 3.1).

The second certification program is Blue Flag, which is designed for marinas, beaches, and boats. Blue Flag is probably the oldest and most widely recognized sustainable marine tourism certification program. Founded in France in 1985 by the nonprofit organization Foundation for Environmental Education (FEE), by April 2016, Blue Flag had certified 676 marinas in 32 countries, and 3,494 beaches in 45 countries.[47] By late 2016, there were nine Blue Flag-certified marinas in the Caribbean, including in The Bahamas, Puerto Rico, U.S. Virgin Islands, St. Maarten, and Martinique. Blue Flag is administered by a national jury in each country that evaluates the marinas; these juries are overseen by FEE International. While the Blue Flag certification process does not include a third-party audit, certified marinas are subject to unannounced inspections by FEE. If the marina is not in compliance, Blue Flag certification can be suspended temporarily or withdrawn completely, depending on the severity of the infraction.

Blue Flag's certification for marinas includes 25 criteria divided into four broad categories: 1) environmental education and information; 2) environmental management; 3) safety and services; and 4) water quality. Most criteria are "imperative," meaning a marina must comply with them, while some are listed as "guidelines," meaning they are preferable but not mandatory. Blue Flag's criteria are designed to ensure compliance with national legislation on environmental impacts, including proper control and disposal of hazardous waste; use of recycling containers; bilge water pumping facilities that separate oily bilge water from other residues; and control of fluids from boat repair and washing areas. Marinas situated in or near marine protected areas (MPAs) must consult with MPA management to ensure "compatible ecosystem conservation and biodiversity goals."[48] However, this and some other criteria are broad and nonspecific.

In 2011, the IGY Isle de Sol in St. Maarten became the first marina in the Dutch Caribbean to be Blue Flag-certified. Its environmental good practices include careful separation of waste oil, black and grey water, and hazardous waste, and posting of Blue Flag rules to help ensure that boat owners comply. [49] IGY is a marina owner and operator that presently operates eight marinas in the larger Caribbean basin: one each in Colombia, Panama, Turks & Caicos, and St. Lucia; two each in the Virgin Islands and St. Maarten; and several in the United States. It recently started its Community Outreach Project, known as "Inspire Giving through You," to encourage yachters to get "off the boats and into the communities where we operate to support local charities and nonprofit organizations" (see Image 3.0.2). The program involves IGY marina staff, boat owners, captains, and crew, who become "the driving force behind participation by rolling up their sleeves and pitching in to help contribute at each of the chosen destinations."[50]

Because Blue Flag certifies existing marinas, rather than those in the planning or construction phases, it is limited in terms of addressing climate change through environmental design measures, such as careful siting to protect mangroves and coral reefs. It also does not address construction methods, such as ensuring that pier piles and bulkheads can withstand sea level rise, strong hurricanes, strong waves, and storm surges. Nevertheless, Blue Flag and other certification programs can help ensure that marinas are operated more sustainably, thereby reducing their impacts on the environment, limiting their contribution to future climate change, and

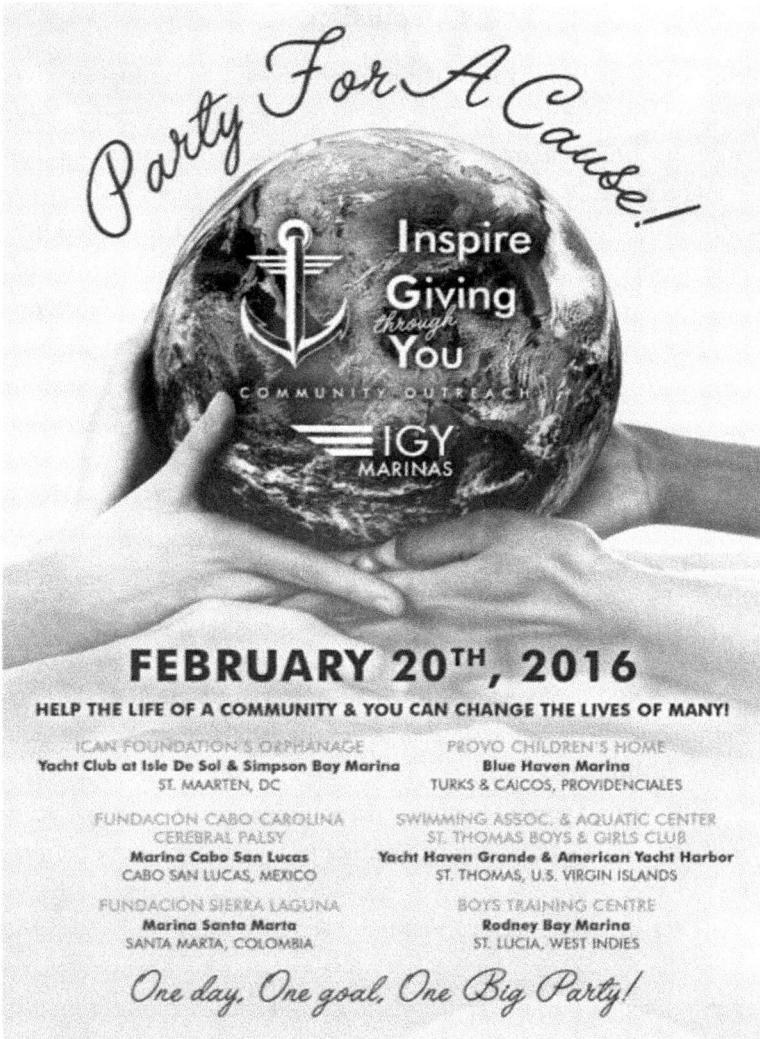

Image 3.0.2 IGY Marinas successfully implemented their first annual "Inspire Giving through You" initiative on Saturday, February 20, 2016. The worldwide service project occurred simultaneously across six countries with over 300 volunteers from eight participating IGY Marina locations[51]

increasing the resilience of local ecosystems and communities. In other words, they can play an important part in helping marinas become part of the solution to climate change threats, rather than part of the problem.

Conclusions

Yachting tourism is on the rise in the Caribbean and offers a range of possible economic contributions. Yet, like other forms of marine (and coastal) tourism, yachting and marinas have the potential to do harm to local and regional ecosystems and communities. Impacts of marinas include inappropriate development that destroys mangroves, coral reefs, and other fragile marine and coastal habitats; poorly run operations that contribute sewage, sediments, oily waste and other pollutants into coastal ecosystems; and generally unsustainable practices at onshore facilities, including intensive use of water and other limited resources. Recreational boats, for their part, can damage coral reefs and other habitats through accidental strikes and poor anchoring techniques; can contribute solid and liquid waste into coastal and offshore waters; and can disturb marine wildlife, among other impacts. Both yachts and marinas produce greenhouse gases (GHGs) that contribute to climate change, and bring additional tourists to already stressed marine and coastal locations. These problems are compounded by the ever-increasing size of many recreational boats, including superyachts and megayachts, which not only exacerbate all of the above impacts, but also require larger and deeper harborages and additional onshore facilities.

While the environmental and social impacts of marinas in the Caribbean and elsewhere can be significant, a growing number of planning and design tools are available to avoid, minimize, mitigate, and compensate for harmful impacts. Voluntary eco-certification programs such as Blue Flag and Clean Marinas, and the incorporation of environmental design principles into integrated planning and construction for marinas, can help reduce negative environmental and social impacts, including those related to climate change. Most promising are holistic programs that address design, siting, construction, and operations of marinas to protect the known and projected impacts of climate change, including increasingly severe and frequent hurricanes, sea level rise, and storm surges. Through the use of such practices, the Caribbean might just be able to sustainably accommodate the growing number and size of recreational boats in the region, as well as the increasing number of tourists who wish to experience the waters and coastlines of the region from deckside. It might also be possible to plan for a future in which the Caribbean remains one of the world's premier yachting destinations, even as climate change and its many impacts bear down upon this part of the world.

Notes

1. Ivor Jackson. (2002). "Potential Impact of Climate Change on Tourism." Issue paper [draft] prepared by Ivor Jackson & Associates for the OAS – Mainstreaming Adaptation to Climate Change (MACC) Project, 13. http://www.oas.org/macc/docs/tourismissues.doc

2. Andre Vincent Henry. (June 2013). "Improving the Business Climate for the Marine and Yachting Sector in Grenada," 12. http://www.thegcic.org/2013/07/economic-impact-of-the-yachting-on-grenada-2013/

3. In contrast, islands in the south Caribbean, close to the South American continent, get very little rainfall and are considered to be outside of the Hurricane Belt. This includes Aruba, Bonaire, Curacao, Providencia Island, San Andrés, and Belize, as well as Barbados, Grenada, and Trinidad and Tobago.

4. Ivor Jackson. (2002). Op cit., 12-13.

5. Eliza Mackintosh and Kara Fox. (2017). "A week after Irma, Caribbean Devastation is Laid Bare." CNN World, September 14, 2017; Chris Morris. (2017). "Puerto Rico's Losses from Hurricane Maria May Top $72 Billion." Fortune, September 26, 2017; Alphea Saunders. (2017). "Maria Could Cost Dominica Billions of Dollars, Says CDEMA." *Jamaica Observer,* September 26, 2017. http://www.cnn.com/2017/09/13/americas/hurricane-irma-caribbean-one-week-on/index.html

6. Anonymous. (2017). "Hurricane Irma's Impact on Caribbean's Tourism Sector." South Florida Caribbean News, September 14, 2017. https://sflcn.com/hurricane-irmas-impact-on-caribbeans-tourism-sector/

7. Since the 1930s, the term *marina*, which is Italian for a small craft harbor, has been used in the Americas to describe a recreational boating facility. Marinas are distinct from marine ports that handle commercial cargo or cruise ports that handle large pleasure vessels owned by handful of corporations. Today, the term marina, or sometimes *leisure harbor*, is widely used to describe a managed facility for privately owned recreational boats and/or boats used commercially for pleasure activities such as sailing, sport fishing, snorkeling, and scuba diving.

8. Nautical tourism is tourism that combines sailing and boating with vacation and holiday activities. It can be travelling from port to port

in a cruise ship, or joining boat-centered events such as regattas or landing a small boat for lunch or other-day recreation at specially prepared dayboat landings. From Wikipedia. https://en.wikipedia.org/wiki/Nautical_tourism

9. Richard Graves & Associates. (2012). "Marinas." Unpublished PowerPoint. Ft. Lauderdale, FL.

10. Cathy Hawker. (September 23, 2013). "Demand Grows for Caribbean Marinas." *Vacation News,* Latin American edition. www.worldpropertychannel.com/latin-america-vacation-news/caribbean-marinas-barbados-port-ferdinand-yachts-camper-and-nicholsons-international-unna-marina-projects-boating-altman-real-estate-7385.php

11. Cathy Hawker. (September 23, 2013). Op cit.

12. Richard Graves & Associates. (2012). Op cit.

13. Richard Graves & Associates. (2012a). "Marina Business Presentation." Unpublished presentation. Ft. Lauderdale, FL.

14. Image Source: Port Ferdinand.

15. Richard Graves & Associates. (2012). Op cit.

16. Warsash Superyacht Academy. (2017). "What is a Superyacht?" http://www.warsashsuperyachtacademy.com/about/superyacht-industry/what-is-a-superyacht.aspx

17. Cathy Hawker. (September 23, 2013). Op cit.

18. Richard Graves & Associates. (2012). Op cit.

19. Ibid.

20. Ibid. Note: Visitor data taken from the Ministry of Tourism and the Environment. Figures for average length of stay and average daily expenditure taken from Eastern Caribbean Central Bank. Calculations of US$ amounts added by author of this essay.

21. Ivor Jackson. (2002). Op cit., 12.

22. Andre Vincent Henry. (June 2013). Op cit., 7.

23. Ibid., 21–23.

24. Willard Phillips. (January 19, 2017). Email correspondence with Martha Honey.

25. Esteban L. Biondi. (February 2017). "A Sustainable Approach to Marina Development." *Caribbean Compass.* http://www.caribbeancompass.com/sustainable_marinas.html

26. Esteban L. Biondi. Forthcoming. "Pautas y medidas de manejo para el diseño, construcción y operación de marinas." In D. Zárate, E. González, H. Alafita, R. Barba, R. Margain, and J. Rojas (Eds.). *La Evaluación de Impacto Ambiental: Guía para Proyectos Turísticos en Zonas Costeras.* Semarnat, Mexico.

27. Esteban L. Biondi. (2015). "Environmental Management - Designing for the Environment," in *Marina World*, May–June 2015.

28. Esteban L. Biondi. (2015). "Beach and Shoreline Protection." Presentation at 4th Symposium for Innovators in Coastal Tourism, co-hosted by the Center for Responsible Travel and the Puntacana Ecological Foundation. Punta Cana, Dominican Republic, July 22, 2015. http://www.innovators2015.com/presentations/Biondi_Coastal_w_text_22Jul15.pdf

29. PIANC. "Working with Nature." http://www.pianc.org/working-withnature.php

30. Esteban L. Biondi. (2017). "Marinas Working with Nature - Sustainable and Resilient Marina Design." Presented at the International Marina and Boatyard Conference. Ft Lauderdale, January 2017.

31. Martha Honey and Erick Vargas. (2007). Personal interviews with residents along Costa Rica's Pacific coast.

32. Maricarmen Esquivel. (2011). *Coastal Development Decision-Making in Costa Rica: The Need for a New Framework to Balance Socio-Economic and Environmental Impacts.* Unpublished thesis, Master in City Planning, Massachusetts Institute of Technology, 136.

33. Kimberly Barron. (November 27, 2011). "New Quepos Costa Rica Marina Pez Vela Still Struggling to Catch a Wave." *Eye on Costa Rica* blog. http://eyeoncostarica.blogspot.com/2011/11/new-quepos-costa-rica-marina-pez-vela.html

34. Esteban L. Biondi. (July 2014). "Sustainable Marinas: The Social Dimension of Sustainability." Presented at the 3rd Symposium for Innovators in Coastal Tourism, co-hosted by CREST. Grenada, West Indies, July 9–11, 2014. http://www.responsibletravel.org/events/Workshop_9.html

35. Esteban L. Biondi and Albina L. Lara. (September 2015). "Sustainable Marinas – Institutional Framework of Sustainability." Presented at PIANC SMART Rivers 2015. Buenos Aires, September 7–11, 2015.

http://www.pianc.org.ar/_stage/pdf/papers_sr2015/68_paper_Biondi_USA_10.pdf

36. Esteban L. Biondi. (June 2014). "Planning Sustainable Marinas – The Social Dimension of Sustainability." Presented at the PIANC World Congress 2014. San Francisco, June 1–5, 2014.
37. Ivor Jackson. (2002). "Potential Impact of Climate Change on Tourism." Issue paper [draft] prepared by Ivor Jackson & Associates for the OAS – Mainstreaming Adaptation to Climate Change (MACC) Project, 13–14. http://www.oas.org/macc/docs/tourismissues.doc
38. Ibid., 13.
39. Ibid., 14.
40. Ibid., p. 17.
41. Ibid., p. 19.
42. A bareboat charter provides a boat only, exclusive of crew, supplies, fuel, and the like.
43. Esteban L. Biondi, Applied Technology & Management. Personal interview with Martha Honey.
44. Ibid.
45. Florida Clean Marina Program. http://www.dep.state.fl.us/cleanmarina/marina/default.htm
46. Clean Marinas (California). (2015). http://www.cleanmarina.org/thecleanabout.html
47. Blue Flag. (2016). "Blue Flag Sites." http://www.blueflag.global/all-bf-sites/
48. Blue Flag. (April 2016). "Blue Flag Marina Criteria and Explanatory Notes." 8. http://www.blaflagg.org/wp-content/uploads/2016/04/Marina-Criteria-and-explanatory-notes.pdf
49. Island Global Yachting. (2015). "Isle de Sol Marina Rules." IGY Isle de Sol. http://igy-isledesol.im.sonce.net/marina/ids-marina-rules; Island Global Yachting. (2015). "Services." IGY Isle de Sol. http://igy-isledesol.im.sonce.net/services; Island Global Yachting. (2015). "St. Maarten Initiative." IGY Marinas. http://www.igymarinas.com/igy-community-service/st.-maarten-initiative
50. IGY Marinas. "Inspire Giving Through You." http://igymarinas.com/igy-community-service/
51. Image Source: IGY Marinas.

Case Study 3.1

Planning Marinas for Uncertain Futures: Environmental Design and Social Sustainability

by Esteban L. Biondi

Introduction

In response to the threats posed by climate change to recreational boating, and with our current understanding of the impacts of marinas and yachting on the environment, one might assume that sustainability would be a key goal in the planning and design of marinas and other types of recreational navigation infrastructure. Despite extensive professional codes of practice, environmental regulations, design guidelines, and voluntary certification programs, however, too many new marina projects still cause avoidable negative impacts. This is unfortunate, because when environmental design principles and sustainability best practices are followed, most negative environmental impacts can be avoided, minimized, or managed. In some cases, such as when marina projects are developed in disturbed or impacted areas, they can actually produce positive environmental impacts. In addition, positive economic and social impacts created by marinas can actually mean a net positive impact of many marina projects. Finally, marinas can be planned and developed in ways that make them less susceptible to extreme weather events and other impacts of climate change, and can also be designed to minimize their contribution to climate change effects. This case study provides examples of how the concept of "environmental design" can be used to plan marinas that are more sustainable, resilient, and prepared for the types of impacts that climate change will bring to places such as the Caribbean.

Environmental Impacts of Marinas

Typical environmental impacts associated with traditional marina projects include:

- Ecosystem impacts, including loss of wetlands and other aquatic resources, such as coral reefs, mangroves, seagrass beds, oyster beds, mudflats, coastal lagoons, salt ponds, and dune ecosystems;

- Shoreline impacts, such as interruption of sediment transport, increased erosion, and disruption of beach dynamic responses due to improperly designed coastal structures;
- Water quality impacts, such as increased concentrations of pollutants, sediment runoff, discharge of contaminants, and reduction of water exchange; and
- Changes in physical dynamics of coastal, lagoon, estuarine, delta, river, or lake systems, such as salinity changes, suspended sediments, or nutrient loading.

While the engineering knowledge to assess, avoid, mitigate, and compensate these impacts has been available for decades, some marina projects are still built without adequate assessment, proper design, or appropriate materials. The examples below illustrate some common problems and how they might be addressed through better marina planning and design.

Beach erosion, often caused by improperly designed coastal structures, can reduce the protection that natural beach and dune systems provide. For example, Cabo Riviera Marina in the Sea of Cortez (Mexico) has caused severe beach impacts. Erosion is most severe on the marina's very valuable beachfront properties, showing how poor design can negatively impact the economic value of marina projects themselves. These impacts are clearly visible in images showing construction in progress (see Image 3.1.1).

Image 3.1.1 Cabo Riviera Marina and Resort, Phase 1, April 2011[1]

Better design and construction practices can offer simple solutions to problems of erosion. While coastal rock structures or rubble mound breakwaters can cause negative impacts to natural sand transport along open beaches, for example, these same structures built in appropriate locations can create valuable marine habitats. For instance, man-made rock structures used for shoreline protection or marina breakwaters can perform as artificial reefs, creating valuable marine life habitat and even serving as tourism attractions (see Image 3.1.2).

Marinas can also offer opportunities for positive environmental impacts when existing sites are polluted or degraded. For example, a lack of environmental management, along with inadequate boating facilities, have caused severe environmental degradation, negative guest experiences, and unsafe operations in the Caribbean island of San Andrés, Colombia. Marine tours in San Andrés operate from a series of dilapidated private facilities along a protected coast of the island, near the main downtown hotels (Image 3.1.3). A lack of investment and haphazard growth over many years have caused severe environmental degradation. A properly designed boating facility for this location could significantly upgrade conditions for operators and tourists, improve water quality, and restore some of the degraded marine habitat. The national tourism authority has identified this problem and is presently considering the development of a marina to clean up boating operations in this area.[2]

Image 3.1.2 Fish abundance in man-made rock structure in Anguilla[3]

Image 3.1.3 Tour operation in San Andres, Colombia[4]

Environmental Design

Environmental design is a tool proposed to expand best practices in marina design. It considers environmental features proactively as part of marina project design, not just as a tool to mitigate negative impacts.[5] Environmental features become design elements that: (a) add value to a marina project, for example, through improved aesthetics or functionality; (b) reduce costs; and/or (c) provide ecological benefits such as habitat creation and protection of threatened vegetation or wildlife. This approach can be considered an advanced level of *integrated marina design* that leads to a more effective way of conducting environmental impact assessment as an instrument of sustainable development.

One of the most important aspects of environmental design is site selection. The analysis of marina development sites from an environmental point of view, especially when considering the future effects of climate change, should use the following criteria:[6]

- Give preference to properties with natural protection from waves, winds, and currents; that are naturally deep enough for the type of vessels targeted by the project; and that have existing navigable access to open waters to avoid or minimize the need for dredging.
- Give preference to development in areas that have already been impacted. For example, redevelopment of brownfield waterfront properties could result in a net positive environmental impact.

- Give preference to locations that have adequate upland areas to avoid the need to create developable land through filling or draining of wetlands.
- Give preference to locations that are farther away from and less connected to valuable ecological resources, and to locations that will induce less boat traffic through sensitive and valuable marine and coastal resource areas, such as coral reefs and seagrasses.
- Avoid coastal areas with high wave energy and/or strong littoral transport, because coastal structures in those conditions tend to cause more shoreline impacts (and can be more expensive).
- Give preference to locations that are less prone to catastrophic failures or major damage due to extreme events such as hurricanes.
- Avoid areas with significant and/or valuable vegetation cover, such as mangroves.
- Avoid, reduce, and mitigate potential conflicts over uses of water and land, including visual or acoustic impacts.
- Give preference to locations that are conducive to a good physical, functional, and economic integration of the marina with its surroundings.

Environmental design does not just mean reducing negative impacts. It can mean creating positive impacts through such things as using native landscaping materials, or incorporating local ecosystems into marina design. For example, a mangrove shoreline (either created or preserved) can have both ecological and aesthetic functions. Native vegetation can complement pedestrian overwater boardwalks and can provide spaces for recreation and environmental education (see Image 3.1.4). Combinations of structural and natural features can offer efficient solutions, such as creating mangrove or oyster habitats as part of shoreline stabilization structures. In other words, it is possible to design marinas that not only minimize disturbances to natural systems, but that actually help to create and support them. This is the best possible way to plan and build for the many uncertainties of climate change and its expected impacts.

A range of marina planning and development guidelines that incorporate environmental design principles are available, including those offered through coastal and marine engineering professionals, and various certification programs that offer environmental and resilience best practices.

Image 3.1.4 Jupiter Yacht Club in Jupiter, Florida, has natural mangrove vegetation adjacent to the marina[7]

Two prominent examples, summarized below, are Working with Nature, and the Clean and Resilient Marina Initiative.

Working with Nature

Working with Nature (WwN) is an initiative promoted by The World Association for Waterborne Transport Infrastructure, which goes more commonly by the acronym PIANC. This international professional organization, founded in 1885, has long-established design principles that encourage early analysis of environmental issues. Working with Nature started with ports and navigation canals and was later expanded to include marinas.[8] WwN guidelines for marinas include identifying fundamental project objectives and considering site conditions from the perspectives of both natural systems and technical design aspects. WwN incorporates environmental analysis in the design stage, so that a project takes steps to reduce its impact before the environmental impact study is carried out. This is an improvement over the traditional sequential approach typically used in large infrastructure projects, which consists of completing a project design and preliminary engineering first, and then conducting a formal environmental impact study. The best marina is one that avoids potential negative impacts caused by poor siting and design, and then further mitigates unavoidable impacts as part of the value of the project itself.

Clean and Resilient Marina Initiative

As noted above, marina developers in the Caribbean and elsewhere have not typically included in their planning adequate consideration of climate change and the need for adaptation. The Clean and Resilient Marina Initiative of the Gulf of Mexico Alliance, however, has published a number of documents that offer practical recommendations to reduce damage and facilitate recovery after a major weather-related event. *The Clean and Resilient Marina Guidebook*, for instance, calls for the promotion and expansion of resilient and environmentally responsible operations and best management practices at marinas.[9] The Initiative builds on the Clean Marina voluntary certification programs in the United States and provides additional recommendations to strengthen local marinas' ability to withstand extreme events. The Initiative is important in raising general awareness; however, its content is not technical and practical enough to provide concrete measures for addressing specific climate change impacts.

Social Sustainability in Marina Design and Operations

Marinas can be built and developed in ways that improve the lives of the local communities where they are developed. However, typically very little attention is paid to social issues relative to marinas. For example, most developers overlook the value to tourists and resort residents of interacting with local fishing or farming communities. While no specific guidelines exist for addressing social sustainability as part of the marina planning and design process, many marina resort projects have included social sustainability practices in their operations.[10] Integrating social sustainability in marina design and operation is important because: (a) the marina business is a hospitality business, (b) "authentic" guest experiences are high value, and (c) local community members are often best-suited to deliver authentic experiences. Authentic engagement with the local community from project design through operations does present challenges, and requires long-term commitment, resources, and some institutional capabilities.

Nonetheless, developers who proactively incorporate principles of socially sustainable tourism in marinas recognize that it is good business.

As one example, Rodney Bay Marina in Saint Lucia has long been recognized as a major facility for sailboats; it has now been redeveloped to also include megayacht facilities. Through an innovative initiative, the marina partnered with the country's Ministry of Agriculture to offer local farmers direct access to marina guests at The Farmer's Market at Rodney Bay (see Image 3.1.5). This program was conceived by the marina's general manager, Adam Foster, and marketing director Portia Mogal, who developed the vision, obtained support from the government and facility ownership, and implemented this innovative program. When the program started, it had about 20 vendors who traveled from some of the poorest parts of the island to sell their produce. The marina management encouraged its clients to purchase directly from the farmers, and encouraged residents around the facility to visit the marina for their weekly fruit and vegetable shopping. Other businesses inside the marina have also benefited from the increased foot traffic through the facility.[11]

Another example is Puerto Los Cabos, a large coastal tourism resort and marina development project in San José del Cabo, Baja California Sur, Mexico. The project, which includes a 500-slip marina, was developed around a small fishing village called La Playita. The marina includes a basin and fishing village (see Image 3.1.6) for use by local fishermen and operated by a local fishing cooperative.[14] The facility represents a significant

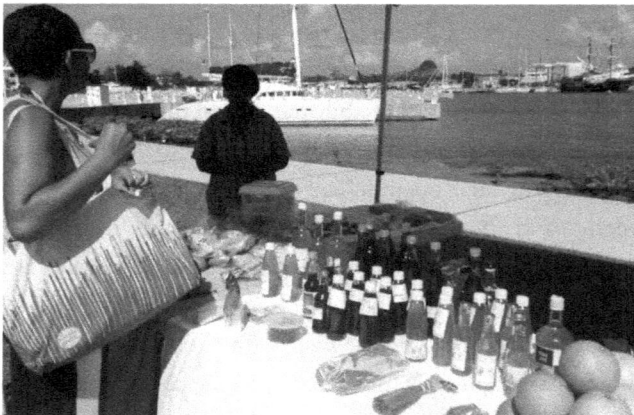

Image 3.1.5 Farmer's market at Rodney Bay[12]

Image 3.1.6 Marina at Puerto Los Cabos, Mexico includes an area dedicated exclusively to local fishermen[13]

investment by the marina and resort in community-oriented infrastructure; it was initially built to very high standards, and was fully repaired by the developer after Hurricane Odile caused considerable damage in late 2014. The fishermen use their small boats, called *pangas*, both for commercial catch and for sport fishing charters operated by the local cooperative. These charters have been very successful, with visiting sport fishermen reporting high levels of satisfaction. While some community activities take place in the fishermen's wharf landing facility and adjacent plaza built by the developer, the Puerto Los Cabos fishermen village has not yet reached its full potential of offering authentic experiences to all resort and marina guests, and thereby benefiting more broadly the local community.

In late 2016, the resort's Hotel El Ganzo, the region's only art hotel, launched an art center and permaculture garden on empty land across from the hotel. The project offers local school children free art classes taught by artists staying at El Ganzo, as well as organic gardening lessons aimed at helping to tackle childhood obesity (see Image 3.1.7). "In Mexico, we have an enormous problem with overweight children," explained Ella Messerli, El Ganzo's general manager. "It is of crucial importance that children recover gardening practices," Messerli added. "This project has the potential of setting an example of what can be achieved when the body, mind, and spirit are nurtured."[16] This is yet another example of how marinas and their associated facilities, such as hotels and resorts, can contribute to the social sustainability and resilience of nearby communities.

Image 3.1.7 Staff and children take part in the opening ceremony of the Art Center and Permaculture Garden[15]

Conclusions

Marina planning has not typically included adequate consideration of their environmental or social impacts, or how they could contribute to protecting and even improving local ecosystems and communities. Additionally, current marina developments in the Caribbean do not typically include consideration of how their activities will contribute to climate change, or how to plan for the more severe and frequent impacts that climate change will likely bring. Best practices for marina development, however, include finding design solutions that are resilient, achieve positive or neutral environmental impacts, maximize social and economic benefits, and add economic value to the project being planned. The concept of environmental design offers one approach to achieving this goal.

While specific solutions proposed following the principles of environmental design might be similar to other processes, they differ radically in their motivation. Solutions are proposed upfront, proactively, as part of the development plan, rather than after the plan is already designed and possibly constructed. They also can add value or reduce costs to a project, as well as reducing environmental impacts. They are often not just technological solutions, and might not conform to usual design and construction practices. Environmental design involves a change in the attitudes and objectives of developers and their technical and design teams, resulting in modification of the design process and outcomes to be more sustainable, resilient, and economically viable.

Social sustainability best practices, meanwhile, incorporate the needs of local communities into design and operation plans. This can include creating new facilities that can be used by local residents to increase income opportunities, such as the Farmer's Market at Rodney Bay and the fishing village at Puerto Los Cabos, both described earlier. In addition to their local economic benefits, such facilities can create opportunities for increased cultural and social interactions between marina users and local residents. Marina facilities can also be used to host activities that benefit local residents in creative ways, such as the art center and permaculture garden created by the Hotel El Ganzo, also described earlier. These examples are but a few of the ways in which marinas can be planned, designed, built, and operated to not only do the least harm, but to actually bring significant benefits to local communities.

Marinas have a perhaps well-deserved reputation of bringing unwanted environmental and social impacts to areas while generating little in the way of local economic development and other benefits. However, with a more proactive approach to planning and design, there is no reason this has to be the case in the future.

Notes

1. Image Source: CREST. (March 2012). "Alternative Development Models and Good Practices for Sustainable Coastal Tourism: A Framework for Decision Makers in Mexico." Washington, DC: Center for Responsible Travel, 83. http://www.responsibletravel.org/resources/documents/reports/Alternative%20Coastal%20Tourism%20in%20Mexico.pdf. Photo use authorized by the Center for Responsible Travel and used with permission in publication cited

2. Minomercio Industria y Turismo. (September 15, 2016). "Inversiones por $23.000 Millones para Nueva Marina de San Andrés." http://www.mincit.gov.co/publicaciones.php?id=37111&dPrint=1

3. Image Source: Bill Fay.

4. Image Source: Esteban L. Biondi. (2014).

5. Esteban L. Biondi. (2015). "Environmental Management - Designing for the Environment." *Marina World*, May–June 2015.

6. Esteban L. Biondi. (Forthcoming) "Pautas y Medidas de Manejo para el Diseño, Construcción y Operación de Marinas." In D. Zárate, E. González, H. Alafita, R. Barba, R. Margain, and J. Rojas, eds. *La Evaluación de Impacto Ambiental: Guía para Proyectos Turísticos en Zonas Costeras*. Mexico: Semarnat.

7. Image Source: Esteban L. Biondi.

8. The author, as a member of PIANC marina group and of the WwN project jury, prepared some guidelines on how to efficiently apply the WwN principles to marinas. Esteban L. Biondi. (September 7, 2015). "Proposal for Marinas Working with Nature." White Paper. Proposal to PIANC Recreational Navigation Commission. Buenos Aires, Argentina.

9. Gulf of Mexico Alliance. (2013). *Clean and Resilient Marina Initiative*. Includes *Guidebook Volumes I and II* plus other documents. http://www .gulfofmexicoalliance.org/2013/05/gomas-clean-resilient-marina-initiative/

10. Esteban L. Biondi. (June 2014). "Planning Sustainable Marinas – The Social Dimension of Sustainability." Presented at the PIANC World Congress 2014. San Francisco, June 1–5, 2014. http://www.pianc .org.ar/_stage/pdf/papers_sr2015/68_paper_Biondi_USA_10.pdf

11. Esteban L. Biondi and Albina L. Lara. (September 2015). "Sustainable Marinas – Institutional Framework of Sustainability." Presented at PIANC SMART Rivers 2015. Buenos Aires, September 7–11, 2015. http://www.pianc.org.ar/_stage/pdf/papers_sr2015/68_paper_ Biondi_USA_10.pdf

12. Image Source: Adam Foster.

13. Image Source: Esteban Biondi. (2013).

14. Esteban Biondi. (June 2014). Op cit.

15. Image Source: Hotel El Ganzo.

16. Ella Messerli, General Manager, Hotel El Ganzo. (December 8, 2016). Personal interview with Martha Honey.

Case Study 3.2

The Future of Grenada's Yachting Sector: Addressing the Climate Change Challenge

by Robin Swaisland

Introduction

Yachting in Grenada began in the 1960s with the advent of the first charter boats and the development of cruising on yachts as a lifestyle. By the late 1960s, Grenada rivalled Antigua and Barbuda in terms of its popularity as a boating destination. Grenada's location at the southern end of the Grenadines, and its own coastal beauty, were important factors in stimulating that growth. During the 1970s and 1980s, there was considerable development of the yachting sector in other Caribbean destinations as well. The British Virgin Islands became a major yacht tourism destination, particularly for charter customers. Antigua and St. Martin became the islands of choice for large luxury charter yachts, and eventually, superyachts, while Trinidad and Tobago became a major service destination for smaller yachts. Unfortunately, Grenada's yachting industry stagnated and actually contracted in the late 1970s and early 1980s, in part due to the country's political upheavals.

In recent decades, hurricanes Lenny in 1999, Ivan in 2004, and Emily in 2005 wrought tremendous damage on Grenada and caused the marine services industry to suffer serious setbacks. Most devastating was Hurricane Ivan, which caused EC$2.4 billion (US$890 million) in damage, or twice the country's GDP at that time. Roughly half of the 800 or so yachts in Grenada were damaged by the storm, including 15 sunk and 50 stranded on land (see Image 3.2.1). Three yachting facilities closed after the hurricane, and others considered moving to safer locations.[1] But over the last decade, yachting has managed to bounce back remarkably well, helped, in part, by investments from internationally recognized brands.

Today, interest in Grenada as a tourism destination has returned, and the country once again benefits from a thriving yachting and marine

Image 3.2.1 2004 Hurricane Ivan's devastation to Spice Island Marines Services' yard, Grenada[2]

services sector. The formation of the Marine and Yachting Association of Grenada (MAYAG) in 1999, and the passing of the *Grenada Yachting Act, 2000,* which recognized the sector's value to the economy and provided some financial incentives, were instrumental in creating an effective public-private partnership that has spurred investment and growth in the yachting industry. This, in turn, has stimulated investment in larger boatyard facilities, marinas, and specialized yacht service businesses. Table 3.3 shows the growth in yacht and visitor numbers in Grenada from 2009 to 2015.

Despite the three exceptionally fierce hurricanes mentioned above, and a few tropical storms since, the insurance industry still classifies

Table 3.3 Numbers of yachts and yachting visitors to Grenada[3]

Yacht and visitor calls							
Year	**2009**	**2010**	**2011**	**2012**	**2013**	**2014**	**2015**
Number of yachts visiting	4,318	4,299	4,940	4,936	4,786	4,996	5,247
Number of yachting visitors	16,187	17,026	19,580	20,060	22,163	24,650	22,118

Grenada as "below the hurricane belt." This means that insurance companies provide year-round coverage to yacht owners based in Grenada. Grenada is exploiting this competitive advantage by offering its boatyards and marinas for storage during hurricane season (Table 3.4). Indeed, during 2014–2016, a major investment in boatyard[4] and marina[5] expansion increased capacity by about 40 percent.

Yachting's contribution to the national economy is hard to calculate precisely, because the Grenada government tracks only two categories, stay-over visitors and cruise passengers. Yachters are included with stay-over visitors. Nevertheless, a 2013 study that interviewed many businesses and reviewed existing government data concluded that the marine and yachting segment "is a major contributor to the economy of Grenada," almost certainly "outstrips the international cruise segment," and "is comparable with the resort tourism segment."[6] Table 3.5 provides a breakdown of the economic impacts of yachting and marine tourism in Grenada. Yachting contributed over US$48 million and 912 direct and indirect jobs (including 750 direct) in 2012, compared with cruise

Table 3.4 Boatyard and marina capacity by numbers of vessels, 2016[7]

Capacity – Number of vessels	
Boatyards	
Grenada Marine	250
Spice Island Marine Services	200
Clarkes Court Bay Boatyard & Marina	200
Carriacou Marine	30
Subtotal	680
Marinas	
Port Louis	159
Le Phare Bleu	60
Whisper Cove	15
Clarkes Court Bay Boatyard & Marina	20
Prickly Bay	24
Carriacou Marine	6
Secret Harbour	53
Subtotal	337
Total	1017

Table 3.5 Summary of economic impact assessment of marine and yachting sector in Grenada, 2012[8] *(Calculated in East Caribbean dollars/EC$. Exchange rate was EC$1.00 = US$0.37 in 2012)*

Segment	Average spending	Number of units	Gross impact in EC$	Gross impact in US$
Charters	11,337	500	5,668,500	2,097,345
Short-term owners	25,256	2,034	51,370,704	19,007,160
Long-term visitors	54,207	857	46,455,399	17,188,498
Superyachts	264,600	50	13,230,000	4,895,100
Gross direct econ impact			116,724,603	43,188,103
Purchases by establishment			16,501,687	6,105,624
Multiplied impact			16,501,687	6,105,624
Total gross impact			149,727,977	55,399,351
Total leakage from imports			(19,345,878)	(7,157,975)
Net impact on GDP			130,382,053	48,241,360
Direct employment impact			750	278
Multiplied (Indirect) employment impact			162	60

tourism, which contributed US$15.2 million and 434 direct and indirect jobs (270 direct) for the 2011–2012 cruise season.[9] In analyzing four different segments of yachting, the study found that in terms of economic impact, the most profitable is long-term stays. In particular, the sub-segment of long-term stays that appears to have the greatest potential is second homes, where boat owners base and store their yachts in Grenada.[10]

In addition, the study looked at the yachting sector's *economic leakage* (or loss from the local economy) in four categories: repairs and maintenance, provisioning, dining and accommodation, and fuel. It found that leakage is relatively low, just over US$7 million, or about 13 percent. In contrast, in the Caribbean as a whole, leakage from the tourism and travel industry ranges from a low of 50 percent to a high of 90 percent.[11] Finally, the study concluded that "Grenada's yacht tourism sector is better placed than any other country in the Caribbean to take advantage of the two major lines of business in the sector—cruising and services." It added that there are opportunities for Grenada to "take advantage of its position at the southern end of the best cruising grounds in the Caribbean" and to "significantly expand its share" of the yacht tourism market. The study concluded that while to date, much of the sector's growth "has been spontaneous," at a strategic level, the government should promote "policies for business retention and business expansion of this sector."[12] In fact, given the yachting sector's economic benefits, the Grenada government is deliberately targeting it for growth. A new National Export Strategy is currently being designed, with "marine services and yachting" as one of the priority areas.[13]

Reducing Yachting's Contribution to Climate Change

While the marine and yachting sector is a significant contributor to Grenada's economy, its climate footprint is relatively small. Compared with air transport, which accounts for about 5 percent of global GHG emissions[14] and 2 percent of global CO_2 emissions,[15] the impact of sailing yachts on climate change is very much less—only 0.0095 percent of global CO_2 emissions are caused by yachts.[16] Even though some yachters do use air transport at the beginning and/or end of their visits, the length of their stay in Grenada, several months in many cases, reduces the ratio of economic impact (money spent in country) to GHG emissions.

While low, however, the carbon footprint from yachts and marinas does need to be addressed. As one report states, "Good seamanship and good economics underline the need to operate a yacht efficiently, and measures that lower fuel consumption can serve to reduce your carbon emissions at source." Much of the emphasis in the yachting community, however, has gone into reducing emissions of noxious and sooty fumes, such as sulfur oxides, rather than reducing CO_2 and other GHG emissions. Superyachts are, of course, big consumers of fossil fuels. Only about 50 superyachts visit Grenada each year, compared with over 4,000 of other types of pleasure crafts. The impact of individual boats is mostly en route, based on the distance traveled to reach Grenada, rather than during their short stays at anchor or in a marina.

For yachts that remain berthed in Grenada for any length of time, their carbon footprint is mainly from electricity use. Grenada's yachts and marinas, like its entire tourism sector, is a heavy consumer of electricity, most of which is generated from fossil fuels by Grenlec, a private utility company owned by a U.S. firm. For the yachting sector, electricity consumption varies throughout the year, with January being the heaviest month. In Grenada's largest marina, Port Louis, monthly consumption peaks at about 230 kWh (kilowatt-hours) in January and drops to 75 kWh in May. Because of Grenlec's monopoly, the installation of renewable energy in Grenada has been slow. Until recently, domestic solar and wind systems accounted for about 1 MW (megawatts) of generation, while Grenlec's solar photovoltaic (PV) projects added a further 1.12 MW in mid-2016. Together, this represents only about 7.5 percent of Grenada's peak demand. Grenlec's goal is to generate 20 percent of demand using renewable sources by 2020.[17] These renewable energy measures are making modest reductions to the carbon footprint of Grenada's tourism industry, including the yachting sector, and this will continue to improve over the coming years.

While a few marinas in Grenada have installed solar PV systems, restrictions from Grenlec on interconnection between such systems and the grid have discouraged wider adoption of onsite renewable energy generation. Where achieved, however, the benefits have been worthwhile. For example, Le Phare Bleu, which is a boutique resort and marina, has installed a system with the capacity to satisfy all its energy requirements during daylight hours (an average of 10,000 kWh per month). This has halved their GHG emissions. Like an increasing number of marine service sites, this property has also fitted LED lights throughout and installed energy efficient air conditioning units and restaurant coolers.[18]

Impact of Climate Change on Grenada's Yachting Sector

As mentioned earlier, unusually fierce hurricanes over the past decade caused considerable damage to marinas and yachts in Grenada. In 2004, for instance, Hurricane Ivan damaged half the yachting fleet and forced some marinas to close. Other impacts related to climate change are also beginning to affect the yachting sector, although their long-term ramifications are less clear. Loss of coral reef through bleaching and ocean acidification has been minimal so far, but physical damage to beaches from Hurricane Lenny in 1999, and to a lesser extent, Hurricane Ivan in 2004, is still evident. This reduces the coastal zones' utility for marine activities and resilience to future storm events. The severity and frequency of storms in the North Atlantic is predicted to increase, producing regular extreme long frequency swells with hurricane force impacts. The Grenada Government and UNESCO produced a useful report, *Wise Practices for Coping with Beach Erosion,* which calls for new developments (including marinas and boatyards) to be set "a 'safe' distance landward of the vegetation line," to stabilize sand by conserving and restoring beach cover, and to stop mining of sand and dunes as construction materials.[19]

According to a study by CARIBSAVE, a one-meter rise in sea level will destroy over 70 percent of Grenada's coastal tourism properties.[20] While there are skeptical views that counter even modest scientific predictions, the impact of climate change may well be not only severe, but will arrive much sooner than some believe. The increasing severity and frequency of storms in the North Atlantic could mean that the sort of impacts Hurricanes Lenny and Ivan produced will become more common. Marine tourism installations and essential national infrastructure could be threatened. For coastal tourism properties, including boatyards and marinas, the impacts of storm surges, as well as sea level rise, will eventually be terminal. Yachting and marine service installations are all vulnerable to sea level rise, sea surges, and major rain events. Each yard and marina needs to conduct its own risk assessment to determine the appropriate mitigation and adaptation steps required for business survival. A development plan that recognizes which steps would be under their control, and which would require the involvement of government and other stakeholders, should then be drawn up. Bearing in mind the degree of uncertainty, a *scenario planning* approach is advisable.

Conclusion: Ensuring that Grenadian Yachting Survives Climate Change

The first step for all marine tourism businesses is to educate themselves about climate change, both its impacts and likely timing. Grenadians have already made strides in this regard, through events such as the GIZ-sponsored Climate Change and Coastal Tourism educational workshops given by CREST in 2015. These workshops trained government officials, tourism business owners, and local residents on the impacts of climate change on the tourism industry, and how the industry can either contribute to the problem or help to solve it. Those trained with the information were then able to share it within their communities.[21] Recognizing the vital contribution that yachting and marine services make to its national economy, Grenada should assist with furthering the educational process and provide strategic leadership.

As traveler awareness increases about climate change, the quality of Grenada's environmental profile will become increasingly important to holiday purchasers. The island's *Pure Grenada*[22] brand will develop increasing commercial value in a highly competitive market. This must be accompanied, however, by concrete climate mitigation steps. Opportunities exist, for instance, to further reduce the carbon footprint of the yachting sector. The *Yacht Carbon Offset* program works with yacht owners to quantify GHG emissions from a vessel's engines, generators, tenders, water-toys, and even helicopters.[23] As the program's website explains, "Carbon Offsetting represents a pro-active response to your yacht's CO_2e (carbon dioxide equivalent) emissions and is both straightforward and pragmatic. The principle is to ensure that for each tonne of CO_2 emitted by your yacht's engines, a tonne of CO_2e emissions have been saved elsewhere, through independently approved renewable power, methane recovery, and other projects."[24] Further opportunity exists for the development of local offsets in terms of forest, coral, and mangrove replanting and restoration, so that yacht owners can contribute to offset programs that provide a direct return to Grenada.

In addition, programs such as Blue Flag (see Essay 3.1) certify marinas and boats (as well as beaches) for environmental sustainability, including reducing GHG emissions through fossil fuel reduction and use of renewable energy. Grenada's marina and yacht owners should join such initiatives, because they not only contribute to GHG reduction, but also reflect well on the country's environmental credentials. As the climate crisis accelerates, the frequency of big disasters will increase. The political and business communities in Grenada need to recognize this and prepare accordingly. In addition, the international support and assistance that has been enjoyed by distressed small island states in the past will not necessarily be available in the future. Indeed, Grenada has already experienced this phenomenon: support commitments made after Hurricane Ivan dwindled away when the international community shifted aid to the victims of the Asian tsunami just three months later. Self-reliance will be essential, with the emphasis on homegrown solutions to Grenada's national problems.

Notes

1. Organisation of Eastern Caribbean States. (September 7, 2004). "Grenada: Macro-Socio-Economic Assessment of the Damages Caused by Hurricane Ivan." http://www.gov.gd/egov/docs/reports/Ivan-Report-07-09-04.pdf
2. Image Source: Nick Bruce.
3. Table Source: Grenada Tourism Authority *Compendium of Annual Statistics*. Used with permission from Robin Swaisland.
4. A boatyard is a landside facility that is used to store and arrange parts that have been taken off boats so they can be worked on. It is for the repair and maintenance of the boats and yachts.
5. A marina is a dock or basin with moorings and supplies for yachts and small boats.
6. Andre Vincent Henry. (June 2013). "Improving the Business Climate for the Marine and Yachting Sector in Grenada." *The Marine and Yachting Sector in Grenada. Economic Impact Assessment – Final Report*, 7. http://grenadaidc.com/LinkClick.aspx?fileticket=RXkaiLkLGAg%3D&tabid=110

7. Table Source: Marine & Yachting Association of Grenada. (June 2016). Used with permission from Robin Swaisland.

8. Table Source: Adapted from: Andre Vincent Henry. (2013).

9. Business Research & Economic Advisors (BREA). (September 2012). *Economic Contribution of Cruise Tourism to the Destination Economies. A Survey Based Analysis of the Impacts of Passenger, Crew and Cruise Line Spending. Volume 1, Aggregate Analysis.* http://www.f-cca.com/downloads/2012-Cruise-Analysis-vol-1.pdf

10. Andre Vincent Henry. (June 2013), 8.

11. Ibid., 53–55.

12. Ibid., 8.

13. Linda Straker. (April 27, 2016). "New Export Strategy Being Developed." *Now Grenada.* http://www.nowgrenada.com/2016/04/new-export-strategy-developed/

14. Davide Ross. (May 6, 2009). *GHG Emissions Resulting from Aircraft Travel.* Carbon Planet. v9.2. http://studylib.net/doc/18714451/ghg-emissions-resulting-from-aircraft-travel

15. Air Transport Action Group. (2016). "Facts & Figures." http://www.atag.org/facts-and-figures.html

16. International Maritime Organization (IMO). (2015). *Third IMO Green House Gas Study 2014. Executive Summary and Final Report.* London, 44. http://www.imo.org/en/OurWork/Environment/PollutionPrevention/ AirPollution/Documents/Third%20Greenhouse%20Gas%20 Study/GHG3%20Executive%20Summary%20and%20Report.pdf

17. Grenlec. (May 20, 2016). "Grenlec's Largest Solar Project." http://www.grenlec.com/Blog/TabId/126/ArtMID/657/ArticleID/105/Grenlecs-Largest-Solar-Project.aspx

18. This is a Grenada Hotel and Tourism Association project funded by the CARICOM Development Fund.

19. National Science and Technology Council Grenada, Ministry of Agriculture, Forestry, Land and Fisheries Grenada, University of Puerto Rico, Caribbean Development Bank and UNESCO. *Wise Practices for Coping with Beach Erosion.* UNESCO, Caribbean Development Bank, and Government of Grenada. http://www.unesco.org/csi/act/cosalc/grenb.pdf

20. M. Simpson, J.F. Clarke, D.J. Scott, M. New, A. Karmalkar, O.J. Day, M. Taylor, S. Gossling, M. Wilson, D. Chadee, H. Stager, R. Waithe, A. Stewart, J. Georges, N. Hutchinson, N. Fields, R. Sim, M. Rutty, L. Matthews, and S. Charles. (2012). *The CARIBSAVE Climate Change Risk Atlas (CCCRA)*. UKaid Department for International Development (DFID), Australian Agency for International Development (AusAID) and CARIBSAVE Partnership. Barbados, West Indies.

21. For more information on this project and fact sheets about climate change and coastal tourism in the Grenada, visit http://responsible-travel.org/whatWeDo/cruiseAndCoastalTourism.php

22. Pure Grenada. http://grenadagrenadines.com/

23. Yacht Carbon Offset. http://www.yachtcarbonoffset.com/index.html

24. Yacht Carbon Offset. "Why Offset?" http://www.yachtcarbonoffset.com/why-offset.html

Case Study 3.3

Tyrell Bay Marina, Carriacou, Grenada

by Martha Honey

Introduction

Carriacou, one of three islands that comprise Grenada, is a tranquil tourism byway in a string of Eastern Caribbean islands known as the Grenadines. But for more than a decade, a debate has simmered here over a new 160-berth marina, with haul-out storage for 200 or more vessels, that is being built in the northeast corner of Tyrell Bay's delicate ecosystem. The controversy over the new Tyrell Bay Marina has pitted environmental protection against job creation and economic development, local public opinion against high-level political connections, and wealthy foreign yachters against local fishing communities. The controversy has also been fueled, in part, by misinformation stoked by a lack of clear, transparent government regulations, company plans, and community outreach. As a result, while the project is pitched as bringing badly needed economic benefits to the island, on the eve of its promised opening in 2017 there was still considerable distrust and suspicion among residents of Carriacou, and opposition from national and international environmental groups.[1] Also unresolved, even in the final stages of construction, is how this new marina will cope with the realities of climate change—most importantly, sea level rise and increasingly strong and unpredictable storms.

The Development of Tyrell Bay

Carriacou, a 13-square-mile island with a population of about 6,500 permanent residents, has no full-scale marina. Tyrell Bay's natural cove, however, has long offered yachters safe haven from high sea swells, Atlantic storms, and hurricanes. Tyrell Bay's calm, protected waters have also accommodated passenger and cargo ships at times of the year when the swells at the main jetty in Hillsborough, the island's principle town, are too large and rough for safe docking. The government is, therefore, planning to relocate its passenger and cargo ports to Tyrell Bay, next to the new marina. This will likely shift the hub of Carriacou's economic life from Hillsborough to Tyrell Bay, which is an issue of concern to Hillsborough's merchants and a number of tourism businesses.

The parent company of the new Tyrell Bay Marina is the Carriacou Development Corporation (CDC), whose two principals are Jerome McQuilkin, a Carriacou businessman with shipping experience, and his partner John (Johnny) Walker, an engineer and businessman from Trinidad. They have promised that the new marina, expected to cost US$25 to $30 million, will generate jobs and tourism investment and turn Carriacou into a year-round yachting destination. Studies in the region have shown that yachters spend far more than cruise passengers while onshore, and bring various economic benefits to Caribbean islands (see Essay 3.1).

Environmental Impacts of the Marina Project, and Government Response

Tyrell Bay has a small-scale boatyard with capacity for 25 yachts, and basic amenities including fuel, mini-marina, a do-it-yourself labor yard, and a haul out area with a washdown catchment, ensuring that no toxic paints go back into the sea. Described in a sailors' guide as "one of the more environmentally friendly" boatyards in the region, the Tyrell Bay Yacht Haul Out is, however, inadequate to meet the increasing number of yachts visiting the island.[2] While it is widely recognized that Carriacou needs a proper marina, the Tyrell Bay project has been wrought with controversy over its environmental impacts. As described in the project's 2002 Environmental Impact Assessment (EIA), the new marina is to include facilities for yacht repair and storage, piers and jetties "constructed on concrete piles driven into the seabed," a customs and immigration office, shops, a restaurant, and its own desalinization plant and sewage treatment plant, ensuring it will "have no impact on local utilities."[3] The EIA gave the marina project a green light, concluding, "A full service marina will bring great economic benefits to the island of Carriacou with the potential to double the tourist receipts, fill existing hotel rooms and justify expansion of hotel capacity." Dredging for the marina began in 2003.

Local and international environmental concern has focused on the project's destruction of mangroves and "mangrove oyster beds" where the shellfish grow on tree roots. The mangroves are ecologically important as breeding grounds and nursery habitat for marine organisms, including economically important species such as snapper, lobster, and conch. They also act as critical buffers against storms, increasing the resilience of the area against the effects of climate change. Environmental and community activists argue that the Tyrell Bay Marina project has already caused a serious decline in the oyster beds found in the mangroves, and that this indicates water quality has also declined. As the original 2002 EIA report explained, while "the oysters are not harvested for any substantial commercial benefit and historically do not represent any essential part of [the] local diet," they "are considered an accurate indication of water quality [and] therefore particular attention must be given to eliminate or minimize any possible negative impacts this project may have on the area."[4] In 2010, a government-appointed expert mission recommended that there should be no further expansion of the marina because of its "negative impact on the Oyster Bed."[5]

Amid growing public concerns about environmental impacts, in 2008, the Grenada government, led by the liberal center-left National Democratic Congress (NDC) party, rejected the CDC's request for an additional seven acres of land, and then halted the project completely. In September 2009, the NDC government created and declared the Sandy Island Oyster Bed Marine Protected Area (SIOBMPA) (see Image 3.3.1).[6]

Image 3.3.1 Sandy Island, Carriacou[7]

The protected area is located on the southwestern tip of Carriacou and encompasses a string of small islands and the Tyrell Bay mangrove system, which includes a significant amount of the area earmarked for the marina project.

New Government and a Project Restart

A new government, headed by the conservative center-right New National Party (NNP), assumed office in early 2013. To the dismay of marina opponents, incoming Prime Minister Keith Mitchell announced that, despite the impact on the oyster beds and the new MPA, the project could move forward and even expand its size. The CDC quickly resumed dredging and land reclamation. In addition to giving the green light to resume construction, the government's Grenada Investment Development Corporation (GIDC) granted the CDC significant duty-free concessions on imported supplies and materials for constructing the marina. The marina's new stores and workshops servicing yachts will also be allowed to sell duty-free goods to yachters. Similar benefits have been given to other marinas in Grenada, according to project developers.[8]

At the June 2013 relaunch ceremony, the marina developers and their government supporters announced that when fully operational, the marina is expected to provide 125 direct jobs and 300 indirect jobs.[9] More recently, CDC owners have tempered these projections, saying that during the construction stage, they have generated between 20 and 40 jobs at a time, with 90 percent going to locals. They also project that when fully built, the marina will support 150 to 200 direct and indirect jobs, most of which will go to locals. Information from local observers and the author's site visits, however, found that as of mid-2014, only four local residents had been employed in construction, three as machine operators and one as a night watchman.[10] By mid-2016, there were 10 workers, eight locals and two from Trinidad, while in early January 2017, there were reportedly 15 workers, including 10 from Carriacou. With unemployment on the island running over 40 percent, many in Carriacou worry that the CDC's projections are too high, and that the best jobs are likely to go to foreigners because they require skills and training not available in Carriacou.

Project Update and Ongoing Concerns

Despite local, national, and international opposition, marina construction has continued in recent years, and has even accelerated. By early 2017, the marina had begun a modest soft opening of its dry dock and boat repair facilities, with, developers said, an official opening of the wet slip facilities planned for March or April of 2017. The auxiliary shops and workshops, a chandlery selling nautical supplies, restaurants, bars, and other buildings are slated, the company says, to be completed in the near future. Despite the evident frenzy of activities, however, locals remain skeptical that the project will really see the light of day. As one Carriacou tour operator commented as he perused the construction site in early January 2017, "This year marks the fifteenth year of this marina project. God knows when it will be finished." Other local residents, however, have come to support the endeavor. As resident Kit Stonewalling wrote in July 2014, "The Tyrell Bay Marina, sisters and brothers, is a home grown project. . . . With oversight, proper management and a firm commitment from Carriacou Development Corporation to international monitoring and mitigation standards, the marina and mangroves can coexist, boosting the sagging [local] economy. . . . [Carriacou] has the unique opportunity to showcase to the region, and indeed to the developing world, that harmony between vibrant economic development and environment[al] sustainability is attainable—let's go forward confidently."[11]

Environmental concerns, including over destruction of the mangroves, have nonetheless continued. A July 2013 petition from the Mangrove Oyster Bed Protection Community (MOB-PC) contended that the "Marina Project has not only affected the Mangroves and Oyster Bed but has contributed to the drastic depletion of fishes, lambi, lobster, etc. within the Tyrell Bay ecosystem."[12] In February 2014, the United Nations Development Programme (UNDP) added its voice to growing international concern about the project. In a letter to the Government of Grenada, the UNDP warned that "the 2013 expansion approval of the Tyrell Bay marina project . . . could destroy acres of mangrove forest and coral reefs within the SIOBMPA." It added, "Safeguarding this area ensures the health of vital marine and coastal ecosystems. Grenada's tourism-based economy is dependent on its vibrant and rare coral reefs and mangroves."[13]

By mid-2014, critics of the project estimated that nearly 10 acres of mangroves had already been cut, half of them within the MPA. More swaths of mangrove were reportedly cut in the following years. The CDC's McQuilkin disputes these figures. He says that 70 percent of the marina's 14 acres has been reclaimed through landfill—dredging the bay to make it deeper to accommodate all sizes of yachts and using the dredged material to build out the land. He concedes that "some mangroves were lost around the fringes of our land, but we're required to replant five mangrove seedlings for every tree we cut." He says the CDC is still waiting for the government to tell them where they should plant the new mangroves. He contends that at present, the remaining Tyrell Bay's mangrove forest "is extremely healthy," based on periodic water samples they have collected and sent to the United States for analysis. "In many areas the water quality has improved. It's deeper and this has helped clear the way for more fish than before."[14]

McQuilkin further states that the marina construction and operations are based on exemplary environmental practices—"the Rolls Royce for marina standards"—as prescribed in an internationally recognized marina certification program. While he could not remember the name of the certification program, he ticked off a list of environmental measures he says the marina is taking. These include installing a wastewater treatment plant to convert sewage to gray water and prevent the marina and yachts it docks and services from dumping directly into the ocean; use of recycled gray water for lawns and gardens; preventing water contaminated with anti-fouling paints from running into the ocean; safe handling of oil waste; and plans to use alternative energy, principally solar, for creating potable water and "wherever possible." In addition, the CDC is planning to build a new elevated dock outside the mangroves, which will allow water to flow freely beneath into the remaining mangroves and oyster beds. For his part, operations manager Graham Diamond said that he is unaware that the marina's construction is based on any environmental certification program, but that, "I'm sure we will be at the end of the day."[15]

Asked if the new marina has taken measures to address the impacts of climate change, owner McQuilkin answers, "That's a difficult question. We don't have a plan in place per se." However, he emphasizes that a number of their environmental measures, such as water recycling and use of renewable energy, will help to reduce the marina's GHG emissions and mitigate impacts of climate change. As McQuilkin has stated elsewhere, "Our design will make it far less weather sensitive than other marinas."[16] But the reality is that Tyrell Bay Marina, and other marinas throughout the Caribbean, are among the most climate change-vulnerable tourism assets, in part because of their need to straddle the shoreline and near ocean. It seems clear that without additional steps to protect vital coastal ecosystems such as mangroves, or to clearly plan for major storms and other predicted impacts, new marina projects such as Tyrell Bay will likely become future victims of climate change, rather than models for adaptation and resilience.

Notes

1. This case study is based on the author's several trips to Carriacou in recent years, including in January 2017, and her email and phone communications with individuals both involved with, and critical of, the marina.

2. Economic Commission for Latin America and the Caribbean (ECLAC). (April 2003). *Grenada, Carriacou, and Petite Martinique: The Yachting Sector.* Prepared as part of the Dutch-funded project NET/00/79 "Development of a Regional Marine-based Tourism Strategy." 6, 23, 38.

3. Lena Downs and Associations with Delta Logistics, Ltd. (March 2002). *Ecology and Natural Resources* and *Marine Engineering and Hydrology.* Environmental Impact Assessment of Tyrell Bay Marina and Haul-Out Facility. Prepared for Jerome McQuilkin and Associates, ii, iii, vi.

4. Lena Downs and Associations with Delta Logistics, Ltd. (March 2002), iii.

5. Letter from Nelson Andrade Colmenares, Coordinator, Caribbean Environment Programme, Regional Co-coordinating Unit, United Nations Environment Programme (UNDP) to the Honorable Members of the Government of Grenada. (February 17, 2014).

6. C-FISH. (2017). Sandy Island Oyster Bed, Carriacou. http://www.c-fish.org/where-we-work/carriacou/

7. Image Source: Samantha Hogenson, Center for Responsible Travel (CREST).

8. Jerome McQuilkin, Co-Owner, Carriacou Development Corporation, and Graham Diamond, Operations Manager. (January 7–10, 2017). Telephone interviews with Martha Honey.

9. Government of Grenada. (June 3, 2013). "Tyrell Bay Marina Project Ready to Move Forward." http://www.gov.gd/egov/news/2013/jun13/03_06_13/item_1/tyrell_bay_marina_project.html

10. Orlon Jules, Chairman, Mangrove Oyster Bed Protection Community, Inc. (MOB-PC). (August 2014). Personal communication with Martha Honey.

11. Kit Stonewalling. (July 2, 2014). "Letter: Tyrell Bay Marina a Plus for Carriacou and Petite Martinique." *Caribbean News Now.* http://www.caribbeannewsnow.com/topstory-Letter%3A-Tyrell-Bay-Marina-a-plus-for-Carriacou-and-Petite-Martinique-21844.html

12. Orlon Jules, Chairman, Mangrove Oyster Bed Protection Community, Inc. (MOB-PC). (July 12, 2013). "Petition to Protect and Conserve Our Threatened Tyrell Bay Ecosystem."

13. Letter from Nelson Andrade Colmenares, UNEP. (February 17, 2014). Op cit.

14. Jerome McQuilkin, Co-Owner, Carriacou Development Corporation. (January 10, 2017). Telephone interview with Martha Honey.

15. Graham Diamond, Operations Manager, Carriacou Development Corporation. (January 6 and 7, 2017). Telephone interview with Martha Honey.

16. Grenada Embassy USA. (June 24, 2014). "Tyrell Bay Marina Ready to Sail." Press release. http://www.grenadaembassyusa.org/wp-content/uploads/2014/06/TYRELL-BAY-MARINA-READY-TO-SAIL.pdf

CHAPTER 4

Cruise Tourism

Overview—Cruise Ship Holidays and Climate Change: The Lure of Playgrounds at Sea

Martha Honey

Today, the Caribbean is "the dominant cruise destination, accounting for more than a third (35.5 percent) of global deployment capacity market share,"[1] according to the Florida-Caribbean Cruise Association (FCCA). Cruises represent a key pillar of the Caribbean tourism industry, competing toe-to-toe for travelers with sun-and-sand resorts. Indeed, cruise ship vacations are the fastest growing sector of the leisure travel industry,[2] with ship size and numbers, passengers, ports, and profits all on the rise. The number of cruise passengers globally jumped nearly 50-fold in the past five decades—from 500,000 in 1970 to 1.5 million in 1980, 4 million in 1990, and 24 million in 2016.[3]

As with other sectors of the tourism industry, cruise ships and their activities (both at sea and on land) contribute to climate change, and have become increasingly vulnerable to its impacts. In terms of the industry's contribution to climate change, a study by the Swedish Environmental Research Institute found "that shipping [both cargo and cruise] is one of the fastest growing sectors in terms of greenhouse gas (GHG) emissions" and that "GHG emissions from ships in the port are projected to increase by 40 percent to 2030 in a business as usual (BAU) scenario."[4] At the same time, the cruise industry is also being forced to cope with damage and disruptions linked to climate change. According to an analysis by researchers at the Caribbean Maritime Institute in Jamaica, "Over the last 35 years, the intensity of hurricanes in the Caribbean has been increasing. In the last 15 years, extreme events resulting from climate change have produced widespread damage to infrastructure, housing, and hotel and recreational facilities, including the shoreline for accommodating cruise activities."[5] Increasingly, cruise ships are also forced to delay or cancel departures or divert course and alter itineraries to avoid extreme weather events. Despite the cruise sector's enormous investment in ships and supporting infrastructure, it is somewhat surprising that, at least until recently, efforts by the cruise lines to either reduce their own carbon footprint or to find ways to mitigate and adapt to the impacts of climate change have been relatively modest and piecemeal. Large cruise lines have "lagged behind hotels and airlines when it comes to sustainable travel," Randy Durband, CEO of the Global Sustainable Tourism Council, told *The New York Times* in January 2017.[6]

History and Growth of Caribbean Cruise Tourism

In the mind of most Americans, international cruise tourism most probably dates from the *Titanic*'s star-crossed 1912 transatlantic voyage. However, the creation story of the modern cruise industry, writes Elizabeth Becker in *Overbooked: The Exploding Business of Travel and Tourism,* really dates from 1966. That is the year that Ted Arison, the son of a multimillionaire shipping magnate, emigrated from Israel to Miami and founded what became Carnival Cruise Lines. Southern Florida was, as Becker details in her popular examination of the tourism industry, "the petri dish for developing mass tourism,"[7] and Miami's retirees and snowbirds from the north flocked on board the first cruise ships heading for sun-and-fun Caribbean holidays. Today, in addition to the Caribbean (including Central America and Mexico), the other leading cruise destinations are the Mediterranean, Alaska, Western and Northern Europe, and the Pacific/Asia.

The cruise industry continues to grow in the number and size of cruise ships. By 2016, there were 448 cruise ships operating globally, with another 26 ocean, river, and specialty ships scheduled to be launched in 2017.[8] According to *Cruise Critic*, when it comes to cruise ships, "This is the year for superlatives—the biggest, the most luxurious, the most technologically advanced."[9] Indeed, ship size increased from an average of 500–800 passengers in the 1970s to today's newest ships, dubbed "floating cities," which accommodate from 3,000 to 6,780 guests, with crews of 2,000 or more.[10] In addition to ships, the cruise industry owns, leases, or uses an array of onshore infrastructure, including cruise terminals and port facilities; cruise villages or shopping complexes; sightseeing buses, and occasionally, boats and trains; and a growing number of small private islands and enclaves across the Caribbean, including ones in The Bahamas, Haiti, Belize, and the Dominican Republic.

Cruise tourism is dominated by three mega-lines—Carnival Corporation, Royal Caribbean Cruises Limited, and Star Cruises (often referred to as Norwegian Cruise Line)—making it the most consolidated sector of the tourism industry. Together, these three corporate conglomerates control 90 percent of the U.S. market.[11] The largest is Carnival, with more than 100 ships, nine distinct cruise lines, and revenues in 2011 of $15.8 billion;[12] it accounts for over 50 percent of the North American market. Next is Royal Caribbean (RCL), with five distinct lines plus TUI Cruises (a joint venture with the large German tour operator, TUI), making up 25 percent of the North American market. The third, Star Cruises, includes Norwegian Cruise Lines (NCL), which it acquired in 2000, and several subsidiary lines, with eight distinct classes of ships and accounting for some 14 percent of the North American market. Beyond the "Big Three," the rest of the market is made up of independent cruise lines, niche operators, *pocket cruise ships* (usually under 200 passengers), and river cruises. The cruise sector overall is segmented into four main classes—luxury, premium, contemporary, and budget—with the mass-market premium and contemporary categories accounting for 70 percent of passenger capacity between 2006 and 2010.[13]

The growth of the Caribbean cruise tourism industry has both mirrored worldwide trends and been subject to its own economic, geographic, and political forces. Following the 9/11 terrorist attacks, cruise lines pulled some ships out of the Mediterranean and redeployed them in the Caribbean, capitalizing on the region's image as a safe, terror-free travel destination. Responding to the public's post-9/11 fear of flying, cruise lines opened new ports along U.S. coastlines, including Baltimore,

New York, Houston, Galveston, New Orleans, Bar Harbor (Maine), San Francisco, and Charleston (South Carolina). As one cruise executive who worked on establishing these new home ports explained in an interview, "After 9/11 we realized there [was] an opportunity. We [could] move our ships to home ports located near large population centers. This is an advantage of having a moveable asset (a ship). So, the industry moved ships to some 30 new North American home ports. This meant that passengers no longer had to fly to South Florida, the hub of the industry. They could instead drive to a home port closer to home."[14] In addition to establishing new home ports, cruise lines offered discounts to attract a wider clientele, and expanded the ports of call in Mexico and the Caribbean.

To protect its economic position and public image, the cruise sector has become increasingly consolidated in its public relations and advocacy (lobbying) associations. The Cruise Lines International Association (CLIA) was founded in Washington, D.C. in 1975 by the major cruise lines to serve as "a unified voice and leading authority of the global cruise community."[15] For decades, CLIA worked closely with its 15,000 travel agents to promote cruises as less expensive and more glamorous alternatives to land-based Caribbean hotels. A major regional trade organization, the Florida-Caribbean Cruise Association (FCCA), was founded in 1972 and is composed of lines operating in the waters surrounding Florida, the Caribbean, and Latin America. According to its website, "The FCCA works with governments, ports and all private/public sector representatives to maximize cruise passenger, cruise line, and cruise line employee spending, as well as enhance the destination experience and the amount of cruise passengers returning as stay-over visitors."[16] Its widely-cited research and publications are designed, the association says, "to create a better understanding of cruise passengers; improve the landside product delivery; and maximize cruise tourism's benefits."[17]

The Cruise Industry's Economic Model

Cruise tourism is the most profitable sector of the tourism industry, generating US$40 billion in revenue annually.[18] Carnival Cruise Lines and other mega-lines sell vacation packages using a highly competitive business strategy that depends on the U.S. market, but avoids many U.S. laws and regulations through legal loopholes in maritime law. To appeal to the mass market, the cruise sector "developed a business model reflecting the mobility of its assets: the cruise industry sells itineraries, not destinations, implying a greater flexibility in the selection of ports of call and adaptability to changing market conditions."[19] In addition, it adjusts its prices to keep occupancy close to full. In 2013, after a string of accidents at sea sent consumer confidence tumbling, Carnival's chief executive officer explained how the cruise line could afford to drastically slash fares: "It's not what the passengers pay to book their cruise that counts," CEO Arnold Donald told CBS News, "It's what they spend once they're on board that moves the bottom line."[20]

The sector's economic success is made possible, in part, by a legal loophole—the *flag of convenience*, which has become a centerpiece of its business model. Although cruise ships are floating hotels, they have successfully exploited this maritime practice, originally intended for commercial cargo ships.[21] Carnival, Royal Caribbean, and Norwegian Cruise Lines, while headquartered in Florida and carrying mainly American passengers, have registered their ships in Liberia, Panama, Bermuda, and increasingly, The Bahamas. According to Caitlin Burke, "Cruise lines have been circumventing U.S. statutes and regulations since as early as the 1920s."[22] In practice this means, writes Elizabeth Becker, that the major cruise lines "essentially have no minimum wages, labor standards, corporate taxes or environmental regulations and [the countries registering the ships have] only a flimsy authority over the ships flying their flags. All these countries require is that ship lines pay a handsome registration fee."[23]

As a longtime cruise industry executive put it, "There are very few U.S.-flagged cruise ships for several reasons, mostly related to finances."[24] To be classified as a U.S.-flagged ship, according to this executive, there are several criteria: the ship must be built in a U.S. shipyard, owned by a U.S. company, registered in the United States, and staffed by a U.S. crew paid according to U.S. minimum wage laws. Only one major cruise ship, NCL's *Pride of America,* was built in the United States (in 2005) and is registered there; it is currently being used in Hawaii.[25]

A 2012 Lynchburg (Virginia) College Business School case study looked at the advantages that Carnival Cruise and RCL get from both foreign flags and U.S. maritime laws. The report stated:

> Both trade on the New York Stock Exchange and pay millions in stock incentives to American executives and they reported combined profits of more than $2 billion in their most recent annual reports to the U.S. Securities and Exchange Commission. However, Carnival and Royal Caribbean take advantage of maritime laws to avoid paying U.S. taxes, gain immunity from American labor laws, avoid U.S. courts in workplace disputes, and fend off new environmental regulations. . . . This gives tiny tropical countries regulatory power over one of Florida's major industries. At stake are hundreds of millions of dollars in cruise ship revenues. Both companies caution investors that their tax privileges are key to future profit growth.[26]

The flag of convenience loophole has allowed the cruise industry to circumvent U.S. labor laws and policies. Because cruise lines are not subject to local hiring laws, ships can hire from wherever they choose, and therefore have one of the most globalized labor markets in the world. Even though over one-third of cruise ships operate in the Caribbean, "only a smattering of staff is from around the Caribbean basin," explained one cruise industry official.[27] Enduring confined quarters and constant exposure to passengers, crew members are required to work an average of 80 hours a week and are expected to provide a higher level of service than is typical within most land-based hotels.[28] While cruise ship officers, entertainers, and retail workers may receive wages comparable to those paid for equivalent jobs in the United States, the bulk of the staff earn far below average U.S. salaries. Cleaning staff and engine room crew earn as little as US$400 a month, while waiters typically receive US$50 a month in salary and are expected to earn the bulk of their income from tips, which can be up to US$1,500 a month.[29]

The International Transport Workers Federation (ITF) works on behalf of seafarers to set global standards for employment conditions, recruitment, and training and safety at sea; they also track cruise labor policies and practices. According to the ITF, some 200,000 people work on cruise ships around the world. "Many are drawn to the industry, as it is a way to visit distant places, meet new people, and earn money at the same time. But the job isn't always as glamorous as it sounds," writes ITF Seafarers.[30] "Below decks on virtually all cruise ships," states the ITF, "there is a hidden world of long hours, low pay, insecurity, and exploitation. Those who work continuously below deck, like in the galleys (ship kitchens), rarely see the light of day, let alone the shimmering sea of the Caribbean."[31]

Cruise line profits have also been facilitated by a growing emphasis on onboard entertainment, shopping, and spending. While the image is that cruise vacations are both reasonably priced and paid for in advance, the reality is that onboard passenger spending is enormous.[32] According to the FCCL's 2010 study, cruisers spend an average of US$1,770 per person per week for their cruise, including on-ship and onshore expenditures, while non-cruise vacationers spend an average of US$1,220 per week.[33] The United Nations' World Tourism Organization (UNWTO) finds, "On-board spending is an increasingly important part of cruise line income, ranging between 25 percent and 35 percent of total income," with gambling and beverages accounting for half the total.[34]

Costs and Benefits of Cruise Tourism for Caribbean Destinations

The UNWTO finds that cruises operating in the Caribbean "are often considered as destinations in themselves," with ports of call being "merely added attractions." This creates, according to the UNWTO, "a significant rivalry between cruise ships and their shore side destinations."[35] This is compounded as coastal cities and island states compete with one another to attract cruise tourism, and cruise line negotiators have become adept at playing off one destination against another. While the terms vary from port to port, in most cases in the United States and Caribbean, port authorities finance infrastructure and facilities, including dredging harbors and building the docks and terminals needed to attract and maintain cruise lines.[36] In recent years, cruise corporations have also gotten into the business of port facility construction and ownership, sometimes with local governments or other partners. Examples include Carnival's terminals at Turks and Caicos,[37] Amber Cove in the Dominican Republic,[38] and plans for a $70 million facility on Tortuga Island, Haiti.[39] According to Canadian cruise expert Ross Klein, "The positive is that cruise ships and their passengers have modern facilities, however, the negative is that the economic impact on the local economy is further reduced as income from these terminals go[es] to offshore, foreign-registered corporations."[40]

Operating cruise ports can potentially gain from cruise tourism in five different ways: 1) cruise passenger and crew spending; 2) cruise line employment for onshore offices, marketing, and tour operations; 3) purchases of goods and services; 4) port services, taxes, and fees; and 5) cruise ship maintenance.[41] Lured by the combination of direct, indirect, and induced economic benefits, many coastal and island governments and communities seek to attract cruise tourism as a way of quickly increasing visitor numbers and stimulating economic development. As a report by the World Monuments Fund explains, "Viewed in isolation, cruise ship tourism [has] had demonstrable economic benefits that make plain why policy makers turn to cruise ship tourism as a source of economic development."[42]

In addition, home ports where cruise ships start and end voyages are considered to provide more economic gains for the destination. Compared with ports of call, home ports have the potential to generate additional revenue because ships may purchase provisions locally and passengers may spend extra days in this port. According to a Canadian study, "Economic output impacts per cruise ship visit are about eight times larger at home ports, like Vancouver or Seattle, than at ports of call, like Victoria, because ship provisioning, refueling, and hotel stays occur at home ports but not at ports of call."[43] Home or *drive to* ports, which expanded dramatically in the United States after 9/11, are relatively rare in the Caribbean. The Bahamas, the Dominican Republic, and Puerto Rico are among the few Caribbean destinations with home ports as well as ports of call. In late 2015, Havana, Cuba, the Caribbean's newest cruise destination, became a home port for MSC Cruises, a family-owned Italian company with a fleet of 15 mid-sized ships with capacities of 2,000 to 4,000 passengers (see Image 4.0.1).[44]

In the rivalry between cruise ships and shoreside destinations, cruise companies strive to maximize the flow of onshore spending back to the

Image 4.0.1 The MSC Opera at home port in Havana, Cuba, June 2017[45]

ship. Within a typical cruise port, a sizable portion of businesses and real estate are owned or leased by the cruise lines, thereby helping them to capture a greater percentage of the tourist dollar. "Cruise corporations benefit from economies of scale and offer goods at competitive prices, making it difficult for local business owners to compete," explains an analysis of cruise tourism in Alaska. "They also have established contractual relations with local firms to provide tours to cruise guests, who book these tours online before the cruise or on board the ship, with the cruise lines taking a commission. The onboard advertising of these partner companies gives the firms a significant comparative advantage over other tour operators selling their services on shore."[46] To promote onshore tours and shopping, cruise lines employ outside firms such as Onboard Media[47] to run their marketing and sales program and ensure standardized delivery systems. The goal, according to another study, is to ensure that "[t]he majority of these expenses are captured within the cruise ship."[48]

Both independent and industry-commissioned studies find that most onshore tours are purchased onboard the ship and include a hefty commission. A 2015 study of 35 destinations by Business Research and Economic Advisors (BREA), commissioned by the FCCA, found that the cruise lines' commissions are usually 100 percent of the base cost (Table 4.1). This means that for a $120 tour that a passenger buys

Table 4.1 Passenger onshore visits and expenditures by destination, 2014/2015[49]

Destinations	Average price of tour purchased from			Local effective price of a tour
	Cruise Line	Onshore	Other[a]	
Antigua & Barbuda	$ 67.29	$ 29.26	$ 58.51	$ 43.52
Aruba	$ 61.88	$ 26.90	$ 53.81	$ 38.43
Bahamas	$ 91.25	$ 39.67	$ 79.35	$ 50.29
Barbados[b]	$ 75.32	$ 32.75	$ 65.49	$ 45.35
Belize	$ 67.98	$ 29.55	$ 59.11	$ 48.90
Bonaire	$ 54.51	$ 23.70	$ 47.40	$ 30.62
British Virgin Islands	$ 72.90	$ 31.70	$ 63.39	$ 42.77
Cabo San Lucas	$ 73.61	$ 32.00	$ 64.01	$ 53.19
Cayman Islands	$ 56.99	$ 25.77	$ 49.56	$ 32.69
Colombia[b]	$ 56.26	$24.46	$ 48.92	$ 42.38
Costa Maya	$ 85.21	$ 37.05	$ 74.09	$ 34.80
Costa Rica	$ 139.34	$ 60.58	$ 121.17	$ 57.81
Cozumel	$ 76.11	$ 33.09	$ 66.19	$ 41.53
Curacao	$ 59.53	$ 26.92	$ 51.77	$ 40.24
Dominicia	$ 61.77	$ 27.93	$ 53.72	$ 42.81
Dominician Republic[b]	$ 87.75	$ 39.68	$ 76.30	$ 48.02
Ensenada	$ 53.64	$ 24.26	$ 46.65	$ 32.72
Grenada	$ 52.76	$ 23.85	$ 45.87	$ 30.19
Guadeloupe[b]	$ 125.52	$ 56.75	$ 109.14	$ 80.08
Guatemala	$ 85.42	$ 38.63	$ 74.28	$ 46.02
Honduras	$ 62.41	$ 28.22	$ 54.27	$ 38.81
Jamaica	$ 75.18	$ 34.00	$ 65.38	$ 45.42
Martinique[b]	$ 75.33	$ 34.06	$ 65.50	$ 50.54
Mazatián	$ 55.85	$ 25.25	$ 48.57	$ 34.67
Nicaragua	$ 80.51	$ 36.41	$ 70.01	$ 51.46
Progreso	$ 58.65	$ 26.52	$ 51.00	$ 31.65
Puerto Rico (San Juan)[b]	$ 75.94	$ 34.34	$ 66.03	$ 41.26
Puerto Vallarta	$ 73.63	$ 33.29	$ 64.03	$ 40.08
St. Kitts & Nevis	$ 73.40	$ 33.19	$ 63.83	$ 53.25
St. Lucia	$ 76.18	$ 34.45	$ 66.24	$ 44.19
St. Maarten	$ 66.60	$ 30.11	$ 57.91	$ 41.06
Tobago	$ 76.40	$ 34.55	$ 66.43	$ 56.32

Table 4.1 Passenger onshore visits and expenditures by destination,
2014/2015[49] *(Continued)*

Destinations	Average price of tour purchased from			Local effective price of a tour
	Cruise Line	Onshore	Other[a]	
Trinidad	$ 68.31	$ 30.89	$ 59.40	$ 40.57
Turks and Caicos	$ 64.03	$ 28.95	$ 55.67	$ 37.66
U. S. Virgin Islands	$ 71.41	$ 32.29	$ 62.10	$ 36.33
All Destinations[a]	$ 66.36	$ 28.85	$ 57.71	$ 43.65

[a]Includes purchases made through travel agents and purchases made through an unspecified channel.
[b]Only includes passengers onboard cruise ships making transit calls.

onboard, only about $60 goes to the onshore tour operator; the cruise line and its agent retain the other $60. Tours purchased from tour operators via the Internet sell for about the same amount, while tours bought onshore from independent operators sell for about half the price, or approximately the base price without the commission.

Similarly, onshore shops promoted by the cruise lines also pay a commission, which again is typically up to 100 percent. The BREA study calculated that "Average per passenger expenditures ranged from a low of US$42.58 in Trinidad to a high of US$191.26 in St. Maarten and averaged US$103.83 per passenger visit across the 35 destinations." While shore excursions were the most popular expenditure, in terms of total spending, passengers spent more for "watches and jewelry" than any other category. Nearly 20 percent of passengers purchase watches and jewelry from duty-free shops, spending on average US$187.64 per person.[50] Very little of expenditures from duty-free shops are retained by the destinations, however, since most are owned by international chains.

Cruise Passenger Head Tax, and Other Taxes and Fees

There is often a tug-of-war between cruise lines and destinations over the passenger or "head tax," a fee paid by cruise lines to the port authority or government for each passenger on board. Cruise lines incorporate head taxes for all ports on an itinerary into what passengers pay for the cruise, even if they do not go ashore.[51] The amount and terms of head taxes vary widely, as they are negotiated individually between cruise lines and each port. In 2016, Caribbean head taxes ranged from US$1.50 in Guadeloupe and St. Kitts & Nevis to US$15.00 in Jamaica, US$18.00 in The Bahamas, and a high of US$60.00 in Bermuda,[52] with the average being $8.92. Generally, home ports do not receive head taxes from cruise lines, since it is argued that these destinations receive other significant economic advantages.

Over the years, cruise lines have bargained hard to keep down head taxes, successfully forcing, for instance, Alaska to reduce its head tax from US$46 to US$34.50 in 2010.[53] In late 2001, following the 9/11 terrorist attacks, *The Royal Gazette* newspaper in Bermuda reported, "The Florida Caribbean Cruise Association and individual companies have been pressing governments throughout the Caribbean to reduce passenger [head] taxes to help an industry that has been crippled since September 11." In fact, as a UNWTO report explained, the 9/11 attacks caused a repositioning of ships to the Caribbean and an opening of dozens of new ports along U.S. coastlines, which brought "a boon for destinations close to the United States."[54] Under pressure, several destinations, including Puerto Rico and Costa Rica, did agree to reduce their already modest head tax, and Bermuda agreed to drop plans to raise its head tax from US$60 to US$80.[55]

The head tax is typically used to directly build or upgrade onshore cruise infrastructure and to help destinations and cruise lines recoup their onshore investments. For instance, the US$7 head tax in Belize is split, with US$3 going to the Belize Tourism Board and US$4 going to the Tourism Village, a duty-free shopping complex co-owned by Royal Caribbean and Diamonds International.[56] According to press reports, cruise lines do not always pay head taxes to ports, even though they are embedded within what passengers pay for the cruise. In 2011, an expose in the *Jamaica Gleaner* revealed that although the head tax had already been collected from passengers, "the cruise lines mostly honour this obligation in the breach. They owe Jamaica more than US$12 million."[57]

Caribbean governments have long discussed the possibility of creating a common cruise policy in an effort to increase economic benefits to ports of call. A 2003 report proposed that Caribbean states should develop a regional policy toward cruise ship tourism with several key objectives: "to increase the collective bargaining power of destinations in the negotiations with cruise ships and maximise [sic] on-shore expenditures by cruise ship passengers, establish environmental standards for cruise operations, and [create] mechanisms to increase the benefits of cruise activities to national economies."[58] That year, the CTO also proposed that all the countries in the region involved in cruise tourism impose a common $20 per passenger head tax, with revenues to be placed in a fund that would be spent on marketing, security, and environmental protection.[59] However, even this modest proposal "caused an uproar" from cruise lines, forcing the CTO Chairman to announce in 2004 that the proposal was being withdrawn due to unspecified "problems regarding legality and compliance."[60]

Revenue from Cruises versus Overnight Tourism

In assessing the economic value of the cruise industry in the Caribbean, it is instructive to compare the contributions of cruise tourism and stay-over tourism. Studies have consistently found that overnight visitors spend more per day, more in taxes, and more overall, because they stay far longer in the destination. A 2005 Bermuda government report stated, for instance, that while cruise tourism made "a significant contribution to the Bermuda economy," air passengers outspent cruise ship passengers by a ratio of 7 to 1.[61] The Caribbean Tourism Organization (CTO) estimated in 2003 that 19 Caribbean countries generated US$7.3 billion from overnight tourism, and only US$1.1 billion from cruise tourism, even though the total number of arrivals in each sector was about the same (just over 18 million). Total in-country expenditures averaged $994 per overnight visitor and only $77 per cruise passenger, or 13 times more for overnight visitors.[62] In terms of taxes, stay-over visitors typically pay considerably more as well. The Caribbean Tourism Organization (CTO) estimated that government income from taxes for each cruise passenger per visit in the early 2000s was US$17 ($9 in head tax plus about $8 in sales tax), while governments collected on average US$133 in taxes from each overnight tourist per visit—meaning eight times more revenue from each overnight visitor.[63]

One example from a Caribbean nation helps to shed light on the relative benefits of cruise versus stay-over tourism. In the 2014–2015 cruise season, Antigua & Barbuda received 527,000 cruise visitors, but "continue[d] to have one of the lowest spends by cruise passengers in the region," just US$67 per passenger or about US$40 less than the regional average.[64] That season, according to the BREA study described earlier, Antigua & Barbuda's total earnings from cruise tourism were US$34.2 million.[65] In contrast, in 2014, the country received 249,300 stay-over visitors (less than half the number of cruise visitors), who generated about US$283 million, or over eight times more than cruise tourists.[66] This is on par with the Caribbean as a whole, where, as noted earlier, the Caribbean Tourism Organization calculated that stay-over tourism generated almost seven times more than cruise tourism for roughly the same number of visitors, and 13 times more per stay-over tourist when compared with cruise passengers.[67]

Environmental Footprint of the Cruise Industry

While cruise tourism brings relatively modest economic benefits to destinations, the industry has created a range of environmental problems at sea and in port. These include air pollution (see Image 4.0.2), sewage, gray water, hazardous waste, and solid waste at large scales (Case Study 4.1). According to the Environmental Protection Agency (EPA), a ship carrying upwards of 3,000 passengers and crew produces about 210,000 gallons of raw sewage a day, or enough to fill ten backyard swimming pools.[68] Every year, the North American cruise industry generates

Image 4.0.2 A cruise ship emits pollution while coming into port[69]

an estimated 50,000 tons of food waste and 100,000 tons each of glass, tin, and burnable waste.[70] And, as Teri Shore of the Bluewater Network writes, "Inadequate and poorly enforced U.S. federal laws allow cruise ships to legally dump treated sewage and dirty water from laundries into ports, harbors, and coastal waters. Raw sewage, food wastes, and garbage can be dumped offshore at three miles or more, depending on the size and type of waste. . . . Only plastics and oil are clearly forbidden from overboard disposal."[71]

For several decades, NGO, media, and government attention focused most squarely on the environmental impacts of cruise ships discharging their waste at sea. An international treaty called MARPOL, or the International Convention for the Prevention of Pollution from Ships, was first enacted in 1973 and has been revised over the years. MARPOL was designed to regulate the dumping of waste, including oils, lubricants, fecal sewage, solid waste, and gas emissions, by both cruise and cargo ships in international waters and waters under national jurisdiction. In international waters, cruise ships are subject to the regulations of the International Maritime Organization (IMO), which includes both MARPOL and SOLAS, the International Convention for the Safety of Life at Sea. Initial enforcement of these agreements was weak, however, and by the 1980s, alarm bells sounded when garbage dumped by cruise ships started washing up on Florida's beaches and the Gulf of Mexico's coastlines. A 2003 report by the Organization for Economic Cooperation and Development (OECD) stated that "the shipping industry [both cruise and cargo] had strong financial incentives to circumvent MARPOL regulations" because it was cheaper to pay fines than stop dumping.[72] As one cruise official recalls, "The maritime world in the '80s and '90s thought of the ocean as bottomless, and they could dump their trash into it."

Monitoring of cruise industry practices is notoriously difficult because of the nature of ocean travel, leading to companies and employees trying to skirt environmental rules. In 1993, Princess Cruises was fined $500,000 after a couple on a cruise videotaped several crew members dumping 20 plastic bags of garbage off the Florida Keys. This led to more surveillance—by passengers, the U.S. Coast Guard, the U.S. Environmental Protection Agency (EPA), and others—and to more fines. Between 2003 and 2013, four cruise ships received fines ranging from

US$200,000 to US$2 million for illegal dumping of oil, fuel, sewage, untreated wastewater, and ballast water.[73] In the Caribbean, the number of prosecutions has been less than in the United States, which probably reflects the latter's greater enforcement capacity.[74]

Despite the fines, the cat-and-mouse sea chase between cruise lines and enforcement agencies has continued, with increasingly innovative methods to avoid detection. In December 2016, Princess Cruise Lines agreed to pay US$40 million, the largest penalty of its kind to date, after discovery of a "magic pipe" that had been used since 2005 to illegally dump raw bilge waste from the ship's engines and fuel systems directly into the ocean. Under federal law, ships are supposed to properly dispose of oily wastewater and sludge by passing it through an oil-water separator on board, burning it in an incinerator, or offloading it when a ship is in port to be taken to a waste facility. Court documents showed illegal practices by four other Princess ships, with ships' officers and crews, motivated by cost savings, conspiring to cover up what was going on. As part of the settlement, the U.S. federal court in Miami also required parent company Carnival to submit 78 cruise ships across its eight brands to a five-year environmental compliance program.[75] The court also ordered the cruise line to pay the engineer who exposed the "magic pipe" a $1 million reward. "Without the courageous act of a junior crewmember to alert authorities to these criminal behaviors of deliberately dumping oil at sea, the global environmental damage caused by the Princess fleet could have been much worse," U.S. Coast Guard official Scott Buschman said in a statement.[76]

In addition to illegal dumping of waste, *legal* dumping can also cause problems. Current U.S. federal law requires that cruise ships dump only treated wastewater if they are within three nautical miles of shore,[77] while international wastewater regulations allow cruise ships and other commercial vessels to discharge untreated sewage into the ocean when they are beyond 12 nautical miles from shore and moving at designated speeds.[78] These rules, which were designed mainly to reduce the amount of nuisance pollution affecting ship passengers and coastal communities, assume that the ocean has nearly unlimited capacity to absorb and treat chemical and biological waste. They do not reflect current scientific knowledge about the lasting impacts of pollutants on marine and coastal environments, including fragile ecosystems such as coral reefs. An estimated 70 percent of cruises take place in biodiversity hotspots, including environmentally sensitive areas in the Caribbean and Alaska. Existing rules also do not pay much attention to the climate change impacts of ocean dumping, which have little to do with ship speed or distance from coastlines. And they certainly do not consider the number and size of vessels within the cruise industry, both of which have grown enormously in the past few decades.

Increasing attention is also being paid to the environmental impacts of cruise tourism on land, including ports of call, home ports, and the coastlines and islands where cruise ships dock and discharge passengers. Concerns include the degradation and destruction of coral reefs by anchoring cruise ships, large numbers of snorkelers and divers, and sunscreen pollution; cutting of shoreline mangroves and seagrasses to build cruise docks and other coastal infrastructure; costly dredging of harbors to accommodate increasingly large cruise vessels; air and noise pollution from cruise engines kept running when ships are in port; improper disposal of black water, gray water, and hazardous waste; and oily waste from accidental collisions, groundings, fueling spills, and bilge pumping (Case Study 4.1). In general, environmental impacts are greatest in ports located in sensitive or fragile areas, while vessels berthing at already established urban ports cause less harm. There is, however, growing recognition that historic cities such as Venice and Barcelona in Europe; Charleston, South Carolina, in the United States; and Havana, Cuba, in the Caribbean; can also suffer damage from large numbers of cruise visitors.[79]

The FOE Report Card and Environmental Monitoring

According to Friends of the Earth (FOE), which issues periodic Cruise Ship Report Cards, the environmental record of all large cruise lines is uneven. Its 2016 *Report Card* compared the environmental impacts of 17 major cruise lines and 171 cruise ships.[80] It ranked major cruise lines according to three environmental criteria—sewage treatment, air pollution reduction, and water quality compliance—plus overall transparency. FOE then averaged the grades for each of the criteria to calculate the final grade for each cruise line.

To determine a cruise line's Sewage Treatment grade, FOE highlights the gaps between cruise ships that have adopted the most advanced sewage treatment systems and those that still use decades-old technology. In addition to calling for an upgrade to the almost 40 percent of cruise ships that use old technology, FOE continues to push the U.S. Environmental Protection Agency to update the ship sewage treatment standards under the U.S. Clean Water Act to bring these polluting ships into the twenty-first century. Under the current American administration, this appears highly unlikely to happen. To determine the Air Pollution Reduction grade, FOE looked at whether ships have installed shoreside power hookups for use when docking at a port, if they have smokestack *scrubbers* designed to remove the sulfur from ships' emissions to comply with North American standards (see more discussion below), and if they use cleaner fuel than required by U.S. and international law. In determining the Water Quality Compliance grade, FOE examined each ship's level of compliance with Alaska's water quality regulations to protect the state's coastal waters.

In 2016, both Norwegian Cruise Lines (with 14 ships) and Disney Cruises (with 4 ships) received the highest grade of "A" in both the Sewage Treatment and Water Quality Compliance categories. For Air Pollution Reduction, Princess Cruises (with 17 ships) received B+, the highest grade awarded to any cruise line. The Transparency grade was based upon how well the cruise lines responded to FOE's request for information. Disney was the only cruise line in 2016 to earn an "A" for transparency by responding fully to information requests.[81] Every other cruise line, as in previous years, refused to confirm its current environmental technologies, resulting in failing grades for transparency.

The FOE Report Card aims to both educate the traveling public and encourage more reforms within the cruise industry. According to *The Guardian*, "FOE's report card offers a clear, apples-to-apples comparison that makes it easy for consumers to find the most responsible vacation bet."[82] Increasingly, however, FOE's survey has been criticized by the cruise industry for not presenting a full picture of performance and environmental initiatives. In 2014, and again in 2016, the Cruise Lines International Association (CLIA), mentioned previously, announced it would not work with FOE because the survey's methodology was "misleading and inaccurate,"[83] and the report card "does not advance the public's understanding in a meaningful or objective manner."[84] The cruise lines followed suit, refusing to provide information to FOE, even though they had voluntarily done so for earlier surveys. Many cruise lines do publish annual sustainability reports, which not coincidentally contain most of the information that FOE used for its analysis.[85]

The cruise industry's criticism of the FOE survey is not isolated; cruise associations and corporations have repeatedly challenged independently produced data, and at times, have threatened legal action. In May 2016, for instance, Royal Caribbean International made a legal complaint against *The Guardian* for an article describing the "supersized pollution problem" posed to the port of Southampton by RCL's newly launched *Harmony of the Seas*, the world's largest cruise ship.[86] And in a debate at the 2017 ITB Berlin Convention, the world's largest travel industry meeting, a CLIA official vigorously disputed data produced by academic and scientific institutions and NGOs.[87] Both CLIA and FCCA produce a steady stream of reports on the economic contribution and environmental stewardship of cruise lines, which are, in turn, often viewed skeptically by academic and NGO researchers.[88] As a World Monuments Fund report on cruise tourism notes, "[A]cademic and professional literature on cruise ship tourism and its impacts is surprisingly limited."[89]

Cruise Industry Responses

Dogged by bad press, government fines, and NGO campaigns, cruise lines have recently taken a series of steps to try to clean up some of their practices. As Cruise Critic, an industry watchdog group, writes, "[C]ruise lines continue to make important strides to improve their environmental policies—some lines more extensively than others. . . . Green technologies are being incorporated into newly built ships and are sometimes retrofitted onto older ones," including solar panels, exhaust scrubber systems to reduce emissions, and advances in hull design so ships cut through water more efficiently. "Some cruise lines also collaborate with nonprofit organizations and government agencies to collect data about the ocean's health and climate changes (Case Study 4.3)."[90] The cruise industry has also developed a voluntary code of conduct, placed environmental officials on

many of their ships, and instituted a range of other sustainability practices.[91] Royal Caribbean, for instance, has been working with international NGOs, including Conservation International and World Wildlife
Fund, to develop a range of environmental programs (Case Study 4.2).

In addition to significant GHGs (as described later in this essay), fuel
emissions from cruise ship smokestacks also contain sulfur and other
harmful pollutants. Cruise ships typically burn bottom-of-the-barrel
bunker fuel, which is what remains of crude oil after gasoline and distil-
late fuel oils are extracted. These dirty fuels release high levels of a number of noxious gases when burned, including many known carcinogens.[92]
While new scrubber technology (described below) brings cruise ships into
compliance with North American emission rules, the cruise industry lags
well behind the land transportation sector in terms of basic diesel fuel
standards. For instance, international shipping rules allow use of fuel with
up to 35,000 parts per million of sulfur (3.5 percent), and Emission Control Area rules limit sulfur to 1,000 parts per million (0.1 percent); in
contrast, on-road diesel truck fuel has been limited to 15 parts per million
(0.0015 percent) of sulfur.[93]

According to Daniel Rieger, a transport officer at the German environment group Nature and Biodiversity Conservation Union (NABU),
"Cruise companies create a picture of being a bright, clean and environmentally friendly tourism sector. But the opposite is true. One cruise ship
emits as many air pollutants as five million cars going the same distance
because these ships use heavy fuel that on land would have been disposed of as hazardous waste."[94] A study by the environmental organization Oceana found, "These emissions add to the smog in the air, create
dead zones and algae blooms in the ocean, and contribute to acid rain,
global climate change and respiratory diseases like asthma. Yet, cruise ship
air emissions are almost entirely unregulated."[95] The EPA calculates that
"each day an average cruise ship is at sea it emits more sulfur dioxide
than 13 million cars and more soot than 1 million cars."[96] While sulfur
is not a direct greenhouse gas, it has impacts on human health and the
marine environment. Take, for instance, the scathing 2016 article in *The
Guardian* on the maiden commercial voyage by the world's largest cruise
liner. According to the article, "As [Royal Caribbean's] *Harmony of the
Seas* sets sail from Southampton docks on Sunday she will leave behind a

trail of pollution—a toxic problem that is growing as the cruise industry and its ships get even bigger."[97] While in port and close to U.S. and some European coasts, the *Harmony* and other cruise liners must burn low-sulphur fuel or use abatement technologies, Southampton residents contend that fumes from cruise liners and cargo ships are contributing to the port city's highly polluted air.

The solution promoted by a growing number of U.S. and Canadian ports is electric plug-ins, which allow ships to hook up to city power grids and turn off their engines in port. According to the Port of Vancouver's EcoAction brochure, the electrical hookup program for cruise ships is eliminating 3,000 tons of GHGs annually, the equivalent of "taking 770 cars off the road for a year."[98] Princess, Holland America, Disney, Norwegian, and Celebrity have retrofitted some or all their ships to use onshore hookups.[99] But there has been industry pushback to this seemingly elegant solution. Cost has been the biggest stumbling block—CLIA estimates that retrofitting costs $1 million per cruise ship, while shoreside facilities cost many times more, and often accommodate only one or two vessels at a time.[100] In addition, for Caribbean island states dependent on fossil fuel-based electricity, shore hookup is not a practical or eco-friendly solution.

The major cruise lines, as well as industry associations, all report that cruise corporations are investing a lot in new technologies and practices to ensure the sector's sustainability. As Helge Grammerstorf, National Director for CLIA in Germany, said at the 2017 ITB Berlin trade show, "Our industry is investing a lot to make it more environmentally friendly."[101] That same month, CLIA released a study detailing the cruise industry's "leadership in environmental performance" in air emissions and wastewater treatment practices. The study, written by two independent U.S. academics and commissioned by CLIA, "found that although cruise ships represent less than 1 percent of the global commercial maritime fleet, the industry's actions have substantially contributed to the maritime community's initiatives in environmental stewardship."[102] Many cruise experts, however, argue that the sector can, and must, do more in terms of air emissions, wastewater treatment, and many other areas in order to play a leadership role in *greening* the entire industry. Cruising's continued prosperity depends on a healthy, resilient, and sustainable environment.

Indeed, as another panelist at ITB Berlin, Dietmar Oeliger from NABU, told the audience, "We believe that the cruise industry must be and should be the innovation driver going forward."[103]

Impacts of Climate Change on the Cruise Industry

Like other sectors of the tourism industry, cruise tourism is both impacted by and contributes to climate change. Cruise tourism's onshore facilities are particularly vulnerable because they are concentrated along low-lying coastlines and in coastal waters. Assets include beaches, coral reefs, and other natural ecosystems; constructed assets such as port facilities and marinas, restaurants, bars, and shops; and onshore cultural and historic sites. In addition, climate change has indirect and secondary impacts on the flow of tourists, as well as goods and services (Figure 4.1).

As Ivor Jackson writes in an early study of climate change impacts in the Caribbean, "Cruise tourism like yachting is water dependent and so its infrastructure is largely coastal. Cruise ship piers (or cargo piers used for cruise ships) are designed to accommodate large vessels and structurally should be less vulnerable than hotel or yachting infrastructure to hurricane waves and storm surge." However, Jackson notes, "Damage by Hurricane Georges [in 1998] to the cruise ship pier at Port Zante, St. Kitts indicates that impact can be extensive where design flaws exist. Loss of docking revenue and passenger revenue resulting from damage to the

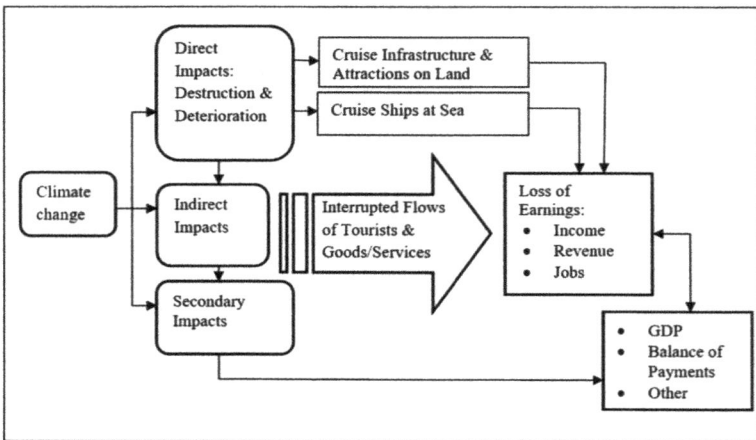

Figure 4.1 Impacts of climate change on cruise tourism[104]

pier was significant."[105] The pier was rebuilt in 1999, but again destroyed that same year by Hurricane Lenny. When rebuilt again, the cruise pier was redesigned with "massive revetments" (barricades) at both ends to protect cruise ship bulkheads.[106] In a similar case, Hurricane Wilma (2005) caused extensive damage to two of Cozumel, Mexico's three piers and forced cruise ships to divert to alternative destinations (Case Study 4.3). From 2000 to 2009, the Caribbean experienced more category 5 hurricanes than during any other 10-year period, with 27 named tropical storms in 2005 alone. Apparently as a result of climate change, hurricanes are now developing at lower latitudes and becoming more intense in shorter times with increased maximum wind intensity.[107]

Jackson contends that a major impact from increasingly frequent and fierce hurricanes is disruption to the flow of cruise sector goods and services, and the forced rescheduling of cruise ship itineraries.[108] In recent years, a growing number of cruise ships have been diverted or otherwise affected in the face of unpredicted or underestimated storms. During the 2014–2015 cruise season, for instance, Royal Caribbean was forced to divert a half dozen or more vessels due to hurricanes: *Liberty of the Seas* was rerouted from Bermuda to Saint John, Canada, due to Joaquin;[109] a number of vessels had to change their itinerary routes in the Eastern Caribbean to avoid Danny;[110] *Adventure of the Seas* had to alter its itinerary two weeks in a row because of first Danny, and then, Erika;[111] and *Explorer of the Seas* switched course as Gonzalo bore down on Bermuda.[112] That same year, Carnival Cruises also diverted ships due to Hurricanes Joaquin and Erika.[113] While Port Saint John reported an economic boon from the unexpected arrival of 11 diverted cruise ships,[114] the altered itineraries upset passengers and cost the cruise lines and scheduled ports financially. With climate change-induced storms, heavy rainfall, and higher-than-normal temperatures all predicted to intensify, researchers are warning that travelers may well begin to move away from the Caribbean, to the detriment of the islands and their cruise and other tourism sectors.[115]

Impacts of the Cruise Industry on Climate Change

In terms of impacts on climate change, the cruise industry's contributions are primarily of two types—GHG emissions into the atmosphere and waste effluents into the ocean. According to the International Maritime Organization, shipping globally (both cruise and cargo) contributes about 2.4 percent of manmade GHGs.[116] The U.S. Environmental Protection Agency (EPA) reports that this includes nearly one billion tons of carbon dioxide (CO_2)[117] and 870,000 tons of nitrogen oxide each year.[118] According to British science writer Fred Pearce, "Ships are as big a contributor to global warming as aircraft—but have had much less attention from environmentalists."[119] George Monbiot of the British-based Climate Outreach Information Network calculated that every passenger traveling round-trip from Southampton, UK, to New York, NY on the Cunard Line's *Queen Elizabeth II* is responsible for 9.1 tons of GHG emissions, which amounts to "almost 7.6 times as much carbon as making the same journey by plane."[120] Both international shipping and aviation are exempt from Kyoto Protocol rules on carbon emissions.[121] But while "green pressure," plus efforts to cut fuel costs, have led airlines to pledge to cut emissions by 50 percent by 2050, "shipping companies are keeping their heads down," according to Pearce. Amazingly, he notes, they also plead poverty, arguing before the International Maritime Organization (IMO) that because the cruise lines are registered in poor developing countries, they should not have to cut carbon emissions.[122]

Recently, the cruise industry has made modest progress toward reducing GHG and other emissions. In 2015, the United States and Canada implemented cleaner fuel standards for large ships, both cruise and cargo. But rather than using cleaner fuel, many cruise ships have installed technology that "scrubs" the sulfur from ship smokestacks, sometimes using seawater pumped through the stacks to do so. (By 2017, for instance, 60 Carnival ships had been retrofitted with such scrubber systems.[123]) This process, known as exhaust gas cleaning systems (EGCS) technology, removes sulfur and other contaminants from a ship's airborne emissions, but often dumps the water back overboard, where it contributes to the release of GHGs. A study by Swedish and British researchers determined that "when sulfuric acid is added to seawater by scrubbers, carbon dioxide is freed from the ocean surface. Each molecule of sulfuric acid results in release of two molecules of carbon dioxide as the ocean attempts to retain its alkaline balance."[124] In other words, seawater scrubber technology robs

Peter to pay Paul, reducing the amount of noxious emissions, but adding to climate change impacts of the cruise industry.

Other technologies are being employed on an experimental basis to both improve efficiency and reduce GHG emissions. Beginning in the late 1990s, for example, Royal Caribbean became the first cruise line to use gas turbine engines on a number of its ships. This marked a considerable improvement over conventional diesel-guzzling cruise ship engines in terms of reducing sulfur and nitrogen oxide emissions. It is an expensive alternative, however, and also produces higher volumes of CO_2.[125] In any case, by 2014, gas turbine engines were on the cusp of being, according to one German study, "quickly superseded by more viable solutions."[126] According to the cruise industry, experiments are underway to test liquid natural gas (LNG) as a new cleaner type of engine fuel. At the ITB Berlin travel show in March 2017, CLIA's Helge Grammerstorf expressed on a panel on cruise tourism and climate change, "There have been several ships ordered that will use liquefied gas engines," and they are expected to be ready no later than 2020. He stated that LNG supplies are sufficient to last the lifetime of ships, which can be up to 40 years. "It's an investment in the future and we're ahead of this," the executive added. Others on the panel, while welcoming this initiative as "laudable" because it will reduce CO_2 emissions, argued that "LNG is just a transition" and that the long-term solution must be found in renewable energy sources.[127]

Conclusion: Building a Sustainable Caribbean Cruise Industry

For countries in the Caribbean, cruise tourism has long raised a host of environmental, social, and economic concerns. Over the years, a handful of politicians, academics, NGOs, and tourism associations have questioned the region's deep dependence on cruise tourism, especially given its relatively modest economic contributions when compared with stay-over tourism. As Ivor Jackson has noted, "Some may argue that the level of investment in deep water basins, berths and shopping complexes for cruise tourism is not justified when compared to the level of return in visitor expenditure and revenue to governments." He cites, for example, the US$22 million-plus investment by the government of Antigua &

Barbuda to deepen and extend the St. Johns Deep Water Harbour basin, and to build additional piers to accommodate larger cruise ships.[128] The statistics tend to bear out Jackson's concerns about the level of government investment in cruise infrastructure, as described earlier in the section on economic benefits.

In the mid-2000s, the Center for Responsible Travel (CREST) and INCAE, a Costa Rican-based business school, conducted cruise tourism studies in Belize, Costa Rica, and Honduras. The studies included a set of recommendations for how governments in Central America could better manage cruise ship tourism to mitigate "adverse social and environmental effects" while "increasing the economic benefits for a wide sector of the local population."[129] The proposed reforms recommended that governments negotiate collectively with cruise lines to:

1. Coordinate policies on such issues as the passenger or head tax, port use fees, duty-free sales, selection of local vendors, and payment of commissions, to "eliminate the descending spiral of competition" that pits ports against one another;
2. Ensure that cruise ship tourism "complies with international, regional, and national norms related to health, safety, and protection of the environment";
3. Establish regional zoning policies to prevent port and wharf construction for cruise ships in fragile and pristine areas such as near coral reefs and wetlands, restrict tourism numbers in pristine natural or culturally sensitive areas, and separate cruise passengers and stay-over tourists;
4. Ensure that public funds collected via the head tax or other cruise surcharges are not invested "in infrastructure that directly favors the cruise lines" such as tourist "villages" and other port concessions; and
5. Provide training and establish policies to help local vendors more effectively market their crafts, cuisine, and cultural attractions to cruise passengers.[130]

The CREST/INCAE studies also stressed that countries should focus on strengthening the facilities, attractions, infrastructure, and quality of the tourism experience for higher-value onshore stay-over tourism, because this puts far more revenue into the local economy than does cruise tourism.[131]

In December 2009, tourism ministers from the Association of Caribbean States (which includes Central America) met and formed an *Ad-Hoc Working Group for the Creation of the Association of Caribbean Cruise Ship Destinations* to "contribute to the exercise of greater leverage in discussions with the [cruise] industry." The tourism ministers defined their goals as moving toward "regional unification" of the Caribbean cruise ship destinations, and establishing "a united front to develop policies and strategies to increase the benefits of Cruise Ship Tourism in their destinations."[132] This initiative represented the first successful effort to create a Caribbean and Central American-wide association of cruise states to work collectively to increase the benefits of cruise tourism. While it was an important step, however, so far it has had no concrete achievements in terms of collective action. As of 2017, the larger goal, as summarized in a 2003 report, "to increase the collective bargaining power of destinations in the negotiations with cruise ships and to . . . establish environmental standards for cruise operations [while increasing] the economic benefits of cruise activities to national economies" remains unmet.[133]

Given the vulnerability of cruise ships and their coastal port facilities to the impacts of climate change, destinations need to work together to craft mitigation and adaptation strategies and sustainability standards. As maritime experts Fritz Pinnock and Ibrahim Ajagunna put it, "The survival of cruise tourism in the Caribbean requires regional governments to find a more creative way for adaptation of the industry to the effect[s] of climate change."[134] Pinnock and Ajagunna are among a small but growing number of analysts examining what Caribbean destinations must do to reduce the climate-related impacts of cruise tourism. Their recommendations include the following:

1. Adopt and enforce coastal land-use planning strategies that include cruise and yachting sectors. The St. Kitts & Nevis Tourism Master Plan was one of the earliest and most comprehensive such plans in the Caribbean.

2. Improve protection of existing installations, redesign at-risk facilities, and where feasible, build flexibility into design so that adjustments can be made as more reliable data and resources are available. Ports should reduce waste of water and electricity in all aspects of operations. For instance, some ports are already using desalination and solar photovoltaic panels to reduce fossil fuel consumption.[135]

3. Ensure coastal structures incorporate design and construction techniques to withstand increasingly frequent and fierce storm winds and sea surges. Planning regulations and building codes should include coastal engineering design standards such as minimum ground-floor elevations for buildings and warehouses, and incentives for use of renewable energy.

4. Establish effective early warning and evacuation systems for people, and emergency planning with designated safe shelters from storms for cruise ships and yachts. Trinidad has become a regional hurricane shelter, and while both Trinidad and Grenada are considered outside the hurricane belt, both need to develop comprehensive hurricane emergency plans.

5. Protect coral reefs, mangroves, and seagrasses from damage caused by construction of new cruise terminals, dredging of harbors for larger ships, and illegal cruise ship mooring. Cruise lines need to pay for damage, as well as replanting lost corals and seagrasses. Given that replanting often fails, however, ports must be vigilant in preventing damage and protecting these fragile ecosystems as important economic assets and as GHG sinks and storm buffers.

6. Beware of the effects of construction, maintenance, and upgrading of cruise ports on other economic activities, particularly fishing. For instance, bottom dredging to accommodate larger cruise ships in the Key West Harbor Channel destroyed coral and sponges, including within the protected Florida Keys National Marine Sanctuary. This reduced habitat for bait fish for tarpon, a key attraction for the local sport fishing industry, and led to an economic downturn in Key West's sport fishing tourism.[136]

7. Regulate and reduce GHG and other harmful air emissions in port and near shore. Cruise ships have typically kept their engines running in port, causing both air and noise pollution. At a minimum,

North American emissions rules should be extended to cover the Caribbean as well.

The bottom line is that Caribbean states would benefit from a coordinated region-wide policy that takes steps to increase cruise tourism's economic benefits and reduce its environmental impacts, including air emissions, waste dumping, and dredging in coastal waters that contribute to climate change while lessening coastal resilience. Caribbean states may find that by limiting and regulating cruise tourism, while also increasing and strengthening higher-value stay-over tourism, they will retain more tourism revenue, decrease climate impacts, and protect and maintain healthy coastal and marine ecosystems.

Notes

1. Florida-Caribbean Cruise Industry Association. (2015). "Cruise Industry Overview – 2015." Pembroke Pines, Florida. http://www.f-cca.com/downloads/2015-Cruise-Industry-Overview-and-Statistics.pdf
2. Florida-Caribbean Cruise Industry Association. (2015). Op cit.
3. Cruise Lines International Association, Inc. (December 2016). *2017: Cruise Industry Outlook.* p. 7. https://www.cruising.org/docs/default-source/research/clia-2017-state-of-the-industry.pdf?sfvrsn=0
4. Hulda Winnes, Linda Styhre, and Erik. Fridell. (2015). "Reducing GHG Emissions from Ships in Port Areas." *Research in Transportation Business & Management,* 17. Gothenburg, Sweden: Swedish Environmental Research Institute, 73–82. http://ac.els-cdn.com/S2210539515000590/1-s2.0-S2210539515000590-main.pdf?_tid=40b5838e-2459-11e7-96ee-00000aab0f01&acdnat=1492535321_b6584bb2bc9d737ed7811f4a052c6c26
5. Ibrahim Ajagunna and Fritz Pinnock. (2016). "The Impact of Climate Change on Cruise Tourism: A Case Study from the Caribbean." Unpublished paper prepared for the Center for Responsible Travel.
6. Shivani Vora. (January 8, 2017). "Going Green Picks Up Steam." *The New York Times.* Travel Section. p. 9.
7. Elizabeth Becker (2013). *Overbooked: The Exploding Business of Travel and Tourism.* New York: Simon & Schuster, 141.

8. Cruise Lines International Association, Inc. (December 2016). Op cit., 15.

9. Colleen McDaniel. "New Cruise Ships in 2016." *CruiseCritic*. http:// www.cruisecritic.com/articles.cfm?ID=2089

10. Cruise Critic. "The Biggest Cruise Ships in the World." http://www. cruisecritic.com/articles.cfm?ID=1431

11. Ross Klein. (September 2003). "Charting a Course: The Cruise Industry, the Government of Canada and Purposeful Development." Canadian Centre for Policy Alternatives. http://www.policy.ca/policy-directory/Detailed/558.html

12. Caroline Cheong. (2012). "Cruise Ship Tourism: Impacts and Trends. A Literature Review." Draft paper, World Monuments Fund, New York City, 4.

13. United Nations World Tourism Organization (UNWTO). (2010). *Cruise Tourism–Current Situation and Trends*. Madrid, Spain: United Nations World Tourism Organization, 61–66.

14. Off the record telephone interviews with author, 2013 and 2017.

15. PRNewsire. (March 15, 2016). "FCCA and CLIA Announce Strategic Partnership: The Cruise Industry's Leading Associations to Produce Quarterly Magazine." http://www.prnewswire.com/news-releases/fcca -and-clia-announce-strategic-partnership-300233923.html

16. Florida-Caribbean Cruise Association. http://www.f-cca.com/about. html

17. PRNewsire. (March 15, 2016).

18. Statista. "Revenue of the cruise industry worldwide from 2008 to 2015 (in billion U.S. dollars)." https://www.statista.com/topics/1004 /cruise-industry/

19. Jean-Paul Rodriguez and Theo Notteboom. (2012). "The Cruise Industry: Itineraries, Not Destinations," *Port Technology International*, 54, 13–16. http://people.hofstra.edu/jean-paul_rodrigue/downloads /PT54-17_3.pdf

20. CBS News. "After Recent Cruise Disasters, Carnival Tries to Right the Ship." September 6, 2013. http://www.cbsnews.com/8301-505263 _162-57601051/after-recent-cruise-disasters-carnival-tries-to-right-the-ship/

21. Ninety percent of commercial vessels calling on U.S. ports fly foreign flags. Bill McGee. "Why are Cruise Ships Registered in Foreign Countries?" *USA Today*, January 8, 2013. http://www.usatoday.com/story/travel/cruises/2012/12/11/why-are-cruise-ships-registered-in-foreign-countries/1760759/

22. Caitlin E. Burke. "A Qualitative Study of Victimization and Legal Issues Relevant to Cruise Ships. Senior Honors Thesis. Recreation, Parks and Sport Management." University of Florida. http://www.cruiseresearch.org/Legal%20Issues%20Relevant%20to%20Cruise%20Ships.html

23. Elizabeth Becker. (2013). Op cit., 139.

24. Off the record interviews with author, 2013 and 2017.

25. Bestcruisebuy.com. "Norwegian Pride of America." http://www.bestcruisebuy.com/ship/76/Pride_of_America.html

26. Atul Gupta and Aaron Cox. (May/June 2012). "Royal Caribbean Cruises Ltd.: Innovation at a Cost?" *Journal of Business Case Studies*. 8(3), 274–76. https://www.cluteinstitute.com/ojs/index.php/JBCS/article/view/6987/7062

27. Off the record interviews with author, 2013 and 2017.

28. Caroline Cheong. (2012). Op cit., 6.

29. Elizabeth Becker. (2013). Op cit., 127–28.

30. ITF Seafarers. "Inside the Issue: Cruise." http://www.itfseafarers.org/ITI-cruise.cfm

31. Ross Klein. (December 2001/January 2002). "High Seas, Low Pay: Working on Cruise Ships." *Our Times: Canada's Independent Labour Magazine*. http://www.cruisejunkie.com/ot.html

32. Elizabeth Becker. (2013). Op cit., 146–47.

33. Florida-Caribbean Cruise Association. (2011). "Cruise Industry Overview - 2011. State of the Cruise Industry." Pembroke Pines, Florida. http://www.f-cca.com/downloads/2011-overview-book_Cruise%20Industry%20Overview%20and%20Statistics.pdf

34. United Nations World Tourism Organization (UNWTO). (2010). Op Cit., 16.

35. Ibid., 33.

36. Off the record interviews with author, 2013 and 2017.

37. Pamela Weiler. (2015). "Perspectives of Cruise Tourism by Stakeholders: A Case Study of Grand Turk, Turks and Caicos." Masters dissertation. Oxford, UK: Oxford Brookes University.
38. D.G. Molyneaux. (September 17, 2015). "New Cruise Port to Open in Dominican Republic." *Miami Herald*. http://www.miamiherald.com/living/travel/cruises/article3562694.html
39. *Travel Weekly*. (August 4, 2014). "Carnival to build port on Haiti's Tortuga Island." http://www.travelweekly.com/Cruise-Travel/Carnival-to-build-port-in-Haiti
40. Christina Kamp. "Crusade Against the *Environment." Tourism Watch*. https://www.tourism-watch.de/en/content/crusade-against-environment
41. Juan Gabriel Brinda and Sandra Zapata-Aguirre. (2008). "The Impacts of the Cruise Industry on Tourism Destinations." Monza, Italy.
42. *Harbouring Tourism: Cruise Ships in Historic Port Communities.* Report of an International Symposium held in Charleston, South Carolina. February 6–8, 2013. New York: World Monuments Fund. http://www.jbna.org/IS%20-%20Charleston-Report.pdf
43. Brian L. Scarfe. (2015). "Cruise Ships in Historic Ports: Victoria as a Port of Call." *Harbouring Tourism: Cruise Ships in Historic Port Communities.* Report of an International Symposium held in Charleston, South Carolina. February 6–8, 2013. New York: World Monuments Fund, 57. http://www.jbna.org/IS%20-%20Charleston-Report.pdf
44. Deborah Stone. (July 6, 2015). "MSC Cruises to Homeport in Cuba's Capital Havana." *The Express*. http://www.express.co.uk/travel/cruise/589232/MSC-Cruises-homeport-Havana-Cuba
45. Image Source: Samantha Hogenson, Center for Responsible Travel.
46. Lee K. Cerveny. (July 2005). "Section 3: Southeast Alaska and the Emergence of Tourism." *Tourism and Its Effects on Southeast Alaska Communities and Resources: Case Studies from Haines, Craig, and Hoonah, Alaska.* The Forest Service, USDA Research Paper PNW-RP-566, 26.
47. Onboard Media. http://www.onboard.com/
48. Jean-Paul Rodriguez and Theo Notteboom. (2012). Op cit., 13–16.
49. Table Source: BREA. (October 2015). *Economic Contribution of Cruise Tourism to the Destination Economies, Volume 1*, 41.
50. Business Research and Economic Advisors (BREA). (October 2015). *Economic Contribution of Cruise Tourism to the Destination Economies:*

A Survey-based Analysis of the Impacts of Passenger, Crew and Cruise Line Spending. Vol. 1: Aggregate Analysis Prepared for Florida-Caribbean Cruise Association and Participating Destinations, 8–12.

51. Center for Responsible Travel (formerly Center on Ecotourism and Sustainable Development). (2006). *Cruise Tourism in Belize: Perceptions of Economic, Social & Environmental Impact.* CREST: Washington, DC, 11.

52. National Tourism Offices. (May 2016). "Tourism Related Taxes." Obtained from Caribbean Tourism Organization; Government of Bermuda. (2017). "Passenger Taxes." https://www.gov.bm/print/12856; Keith Archibald Forbes. (2017). "Bermuda's Cruise Ship Calls in 2017." Bermuda-Online. http://www.bermuda-online.org/cruises.htm. This document mistakenly lists Bermuda's head tax as $48, but in email correspondence, the Bermuda government stated that it is $60.

53. *Cruise Critic.* (June 24, 2010). "Alaska Cruise Head Tax Reduction Signed into Law." http://www.cruisecritic.com/news/news.cfm?ID=395

54. United Nations World Tourism Organization (UNWTO). (2010). Op cit., 21.

55. Stephen Breen. (January 25, 2002). "Cruise Lines Warn Tax Hike May Deter Tourists." *The Royal Gazette.* http://www.royalgazette.com/article/20020125/NEWS/301259971

56. Center for Responsible Travel (formerly Center on Ecotourism and Sustainable Development). (September 2006). Op cit., 11.

57. Jim Walker. (May 22, 2011). "Cruise Lines Owe Jamaica More Than $12,000,000 In Unpaid Taxes?" *Cruise Law News.* http://www.cruiselawnews.com/tags/head-tax/

58. Adam Dunlop. (December 21, 2005). "Issues and Challenges in Caribbean Cruise Ship Tourism." Economic Commission for Latin America and the Caribbean (ECLAC), limited LC/CAR.L.75, 20. http://www.eclac.org/publicaciones/xml/5/39735/L.075.pdf

59. IPS Correspondents. (September 26, 2003). "ECONOMY-CARIBBEAN: Cruise Ship 'Head Tax' Makes Waves." Inter Press Service News Agency.

60. Gay Nagle Myers. (June 26, 2004). "CTO Drops Cruise Head Tax Plan." *Travel Weekly.* http://www.travelweekly.com/Destinations2001-2007/CTO-drops-cruise-head-tax-plan/

61. Ministry of the Environment, Government of Bermuda. (2005). *State of the Environment Report*, 161. https://wedocs.unep.org/rest /bitstreams/16276/retrieve

62. Caribbean Tourism Organization Statistical Compendium. (2004). Table 5.1. Cited in CREST-INCAE. (January 2007). *Cruise Tourism Impacts in Costa Rica & Honduras: Policy Recommendations for Decision Makers*. Commissioned by the Inter-American Development Bank, Washington, DC, 10. http://www.responsibletravel.org/projects /documents/cruise_tourism_impacts_in_costa_rica_honduras.pdf

63. Caribbean Tourism Organization Statistical Compendium. (2004). Table 5.1. Cited in CREST-INCAE, (January 2007). Op Cit., 10.

64. *Antigua Observer*. (October 9, 2015). Cruise Visitor Spend in Antigua Among the Lowest." http://antiguaobserver.com/cruise-visitor-spend-in-antigua-among-the-lowest/

65. Business Research and Economic Advisors (BREA). (October 2015). *Economic Contribution of Cruise Tourism to the Destination Economies: A Survey-based Analysis of the Impacts of Passenger, Crew and Cruise Line Spending. Vol. 2: Destinations Report*, 3–4. http://www. f-cca.com/downloads/2015-cruise-analysis-volume-2.pdf

66. Eastern Caribbean Central Bank. *Working Paper Series. Volume 1.* Special Edition of the 2015 Interns. December 2015, 4. http://www. eccb-centralbank.org/PDF/working/WP_Special_Editition_2015_ Interns.PDF

67. Caribbean Tourism Organization Statistical Compendium. (2004). Table 5.1. Cited in CREST-INCAE, (January 2007). Op cit., 10.

68. Jeff Spross. "Here's What Happens to Sewage On Cruise Lines." *ThinkProgress*. December 4, 2014. https://thinkprogress.org/heres-what-happens-to-sewage-on-cruise-lines-333d026c8481

69. Govan001. [CC BY 3.0 (https://creativecommons.org/licenses/by-sa/3.0/deed.en)].

70. Ross Klein. (2002). *Cruise Ship Blues: The Underside of the Cruise Ship Industry.* Gabriola Island, BC, Canada: New Society Publishers,7, 84–85.

71. Teri Shore. (2004). "Cruise Ships—Polluting for Fun & Profit." Cited in Martha Honey. (2008). *Ecotourism and Sustainable Development: Who Owns Paradise?* Washington, DC: Island Press, 50–51.

72. OECD. (2002). "Cost Saving Stemming from Non-Compliance with International Environmental Regulations in the Maritime

Sector." STTI/DOT.MTC, 8/Final. OECD, Paris. Quoted in Economic Commission for Latin America and the Caribbean (ECLAC). (December 21, 2005). "Issues and Challenges in Caribbean Cruise Ship Tourism." Limited LC/CAR/L.75, 16–17

73. Ross Klein. "Large Environmental Fines ($100,000 or More)," and "Pollution and Environmental Violations and Fines, 1992 – 2012." Cruiseshipjunkie.com.

74. Economic Commission for Latin America and the Caribbean (ECLAC). (December 21, 2005), 17.

75. Associated Press. (December 2, 2016). "The $40m 'Magic Pipe': Princess Cruises Given Record Fine for Dumping Oil at Sea." *The Guardian*. London. https://www.theguardian.com/environment/2016/dec/02/the-40m-magic-pipe-princess-cruises-given-record-fine-for-dumping-oil-at-sea

76. "Princess Cruise Lines fined $40M for intentionally polluting ocean." UPI, Apr. 20, 2017. https://www.choice102.com/princess-cruise-lines-fined-40m-for-intentionally-polluting-ocean/

77. Jeff Spross. (December 4, 2014). Op cit.

78. CLIA. (March 30, 2017). "New Study Shows Cruise Industry's Leadership in Environmental Performance." https://www.cruising.org/about-the-industry/press-room/press-releases/pr/new-study-shows-cruise-industrys-leadership-in-environmental-performance

79. *Harbouring Tourism: Cruise Ships in Historic Port Communities.* Op cit.

80. Friends of the Earth. (2016). "2016 Cruise Ship Report Card." http://www.foe.org/crucise-report-card. FOE has issued Report Cards in 2009, 2010, 2012, 2013, 2014, and 2016

81. Friends of the Earth. (June 9, 2016) "Disney Cruise Line Regains A Grade for Pollution Transparency." http://www.foe.org/news/news-releases/2016-06-disney-cruise-line-regains-a-grade-for-pollution-transparency

82. Brian Watson. (January 5, 2015). "Murky Waters: The Hidden Environmental Impacts of Your Cruise." *The Guardian.* https://www.theguardian.com/sustainable-business/2015/jan/05/cruise-ship-holidays-environmental-impact

83. The Maritime Executive. (June 9, 2016). Cruise Industry Says Report Card "Regrettable." http://www.maritime-executive.com/article/cruise-industry-says-report-card-regrettable

84. Brian Watson. (January 5, 2015). Op cit.

85. Ibid.

86. John Vidal. (May 21, 2016). "The World's Largest CruiseShip and Its Supersized Pollution Problem." *The Guardian.* https://www .theguardian.com/environment/2016/may/21/the-worlds-largest-cruise-ship-and-its-supersized-pollution-problem

87. Helge Grammerstorf. (March 14, 2017). "The Hot Seat: Climate Fanaticism vs. Losing Touch with Reality!? – The Cruise Industry." CLIA Germany. ITB-Berlin conference presentation. https://www.youtube .com/watch?v=rDg_ECvAl0s. Eugene Kim, a researcher with CREST, attended ITB and provided written notes from this panel discussion

88. Among the most widely cited are *Economic Contributions of Cruise Tourism to the Destination Economies* studies by BREA, which are commissioned by the Florida-Caribbean Cruise Association (FCCA). These studies, conducted every few years, show that cruise tourism in the Americas contributes impressively to national economies and employment. An analysis of BREA's 2015 edition by the Center for Responsible Travel found that BREA's methodology is, in crucial areas, questionable and obscure. In addition, BREA fails to compare, country by country or for the region, the economic impacts of cruise vs. stay-over tourism for 35 Caribbean destinations it covers. Unpublished analysis by Santiago Herrera-Triana, Ph.D. candidate in Economics, Colorado State University, February 2017. Research reviewed by professors Lawrence Pratt, INCAE, Costa Rica and Andrew Seidl, Colorado State University and commissioned by the Center for Responsible Travel. It will appear in a forthcoming (July 2017) CREST publication.

89. Caroline Cheong. (2012). Op cit., 1.

90. Melissa Paloti and Elissa Poma. "Green Cruising." *Cruise Critic.* http://www.cruisecritic.com/articles.cfm?ID=528

91. Ibid.

92. Paul Evans. (April 23, 2009). "Big Polluters: One Massive Container Ship Equals 50 Million Cars." *New Atlas.* http://newatlas.com/shipping-pollution/11526/

93. Friends of the Earth. (2016). Op cit.

94. John Vidal. (May 21, 2016). Op cit.

95. Oceana. (2003). "Needless Cruise Pollution: Passengers Want Sewage Dumping Stopped." Oceana: Washington, D.C., 4.

96. Friends of the Earth. (2016). Op cit.

97. John Vidal. (May 21, 2016). Op cit.

98. Larry Pynn. (August 19, 2014). "Most Cruise Ships Not Tapping into Vancouver Shore Power." *Vancouver Sun.* http://www.vancouversun .com/travel/Most+cruise+ships+tapping+into+Vancouver+shore+p ower/10129179/story.html

99. Erica Silverstein. "The Earth Thanks You: More Cruise Ports Are Going Green." *Cruise Critic.* http://www.cruisecritic.com/articles .cfm?ID=1214

100. Larry Pynn. (August 19, 2014). Op cit.

101. Helge Grammerstorf. (March 14, 2017). Op cit.

102. CLIA. (March 30, 2017). Op cit.

103. Dietmar Oeliger. (March 14, 2017). "The Hot Seat: Climate Fanaticism vs. Losing Touch with Reality!? – The Cruise Industry." NABU. ITB-Berlin conference presentation. https://www.youtube .com/watch?v=rDg_ECvAl0s. Eugene Kim, a researcher with CREST, attended ITB and provided written notes from this panel discussion

104. Kennedy Obombo Magio and Elisa Guillén Arguelles. (2016). Adapted from Ivor Jackson. (2002). "Potential Impact of Climate Change on Tourism." Draft. Prepared for the OAS (Organization of American States). Mainstreaming Adaptation to Climate Change (MACC) Project.

105. Ivor Jackson. (2002). Op cit., 14.

106. Leonard Nurse. (April 15–18, 2012). "Climate Change Impacts and Risks: The Challenge for Caribbean Ports." PowerPoint presentation. STC-13. Georgetown, Guyana.

107. Ibid.

108. Ivor Jackson. (2002). Op cit. 15.

109. Gene Sloan. (October 2, 2015). "Carnival, Royal Caribbean Drop Bermuda Cruises as Joaquin Turns Northward." *USA Today.* https://www.usatoday.com/story/travel/cruises/2015/10/02/ hurricane-joaquin-cruise-ships/73243174/

110. CBS Channel 10 News. (August 22, 2015). "Tropical Storm Danny Changes Royal Caribbean Itinerary." Tampa Bay and Sarasota. http://www.wtsp.com/news/tropical-storm-danny-changes-royal-caribbean-itinerary/235290033

111. Royal Caribbean Blog. (Aug. 26, 2015). "Tropical Storm Erika's Path Forces Royal Caribbean to Change Itinerary of *Adventure of the Seas*." http://www.royalcaribbeanblog.com/2015/08/26/tropical-storm-erika-changes-itinerary-royal-caribbeans-adventure-of-the-seas

112. *Cruise Critic*. (October 17, 2014). "Update: Hurricane Gonzalo Bears Down on Bermuda, Impacts Cruise Itineraries." http://www.cruisecritic.com/news/news.cfm?ID=6031

113. Gene Sloan. (October 2, 2015). Op cit.; Atom Bash. (October 2, 2015). "Hurricane Joaquin Update: Bahamas Battered, Cruises and Flights Greatly Affected." http://atombash.com/hurricane-joaquin-update-bahamas-battered-cruises-and-flights-greatly-effected/

114. CVC News. (October 15, 2015). "Saint John Prepares for Influx of Cruise Ship Activity." New Brunswick, Canada.

115. Ibrahim Ajagunna and Fritz Pinnock. (2016) "The Impact of Climate Change on Cruise Tourism: A Case Study from the Caribbean." Unpublished paper prepared for the Center for Responsible Travel.

116. Hulda Winnes, Linda Styhre, and Erik Fridell. (2015). Op cit., 73.

117. Fred Pearce. (November 21, 2009). "How 16 Ships Create as Much Pollution as All the Cars in the World." *The Daily Mail*. London. http://www.dailymail.co.uk/sciencetech/article-1229857/How-16-ships-create-pollution-cars-world.html

118. United States Environmental Protection Agency. (December 2007). "Control of Emissions from New Marine Compression-Ignition Engines at or Above 30 Liters per Cylinder." http://www.epa.gov/EPA-AIR/2007/December/Day-07/a23556.htm

119. Fred Pearce. (November 21, 2009). Op cit.

120. "Is Cruising Any Greener than Flying?" (December 20, 2006). *The Guardian*. https://www.theguardian.com/travel/2006/dec/20/cruises.green

121. Gard News. (January 16, 2013). "Shipping Emissions Regulations." Insight 209. http://www.gard.no/web/updates/content/20734079/shipping-emissions-regulations

122. Fred Pearce. (November 21, 2009). Op cit.

123. Melissa Paloti and Elissa Poma. "Green Cruising." Op cit.

124. Christina Montgomery. (October 7, 2007). "Cruise-ship Pollution Initiative Actually Contributes to Problem." *The Province*. www.canada

.com/theprovince/news/story.html?id=438279ef-ec5e-42b0-a582-3cce6a54df75. Cited in Ross A. Klein. (December 1, 2009). *Getting a Grip on Cruise Ship Pollution.* Washington, DC: Friends of the Earth, 47.

125.   Justin Schamotta. (2016). "How Are Cruise Ships Powered?" *USA Today.* http://traveltips.usatoday.com/cruise-ships-powered-30089.html; Chavdar Chanev. (November 26, 2015). "Cruise Ship Engine Power, Propulsion, Fuel." CruiseMapper. http://www.cruisemapper.com/wiki/752-cruise-ship-engine-propulsion-fuel

126.   Tony Peisley and A.R. Peisley. (December 29, 2014). "Shore Power Not the Real Solution to Cruise Ship Emissions." Rostock Port. http://www.rostock-port.de/fileadmin/user_upload/pdf/Presse/englisch/2014/PM_2014_12_29_Landstrom-Engl-E-Mail-2014.pdf

127.   Helge Grammerstorf. (March 14, 2017).

128.   Ivor Jackson. (2002). p. 14; Official Website of the Antigua and Barbuda Port Authority. "Deep Water Harbour." http://www.port.gov.ag/content_page.php

129.   CREST (formerly Center on Ecotourism and Sustainable Development) and INCAE. (January 2007). Op Cit., 30–40.

130.   Ibid.

131.   Ibid.

132.   Association of Caribbean States, "Cruise Ship Tourism under the ACS Framework." 19th Meeting of Special Committee on Transport. Paramaribo, Suriname. Apr. 23, 2010.

133.   Adan Dunlop. (August 2003). *Tourism Services Negotiation Issues: Implications for Cariforum Countries.* Caribbean Council, for the Caribbean Regional Negotiating Machinery (CRNM), 46. http://cms2.caricom.org/documents/10185-tourism_and_services_study.pdf

134.   Ibrahim Ajagunna and Fritz Pinnock. (2016). Op cit.

135.   Leonard Nurse. (April 15–18, 2012). Op cit.

136.   Isadmin. (August 20, 2013). "Dredging the Key West Channel for Larger Cruise Ships: Referendum on the Horizon." Last Stand. https://keyslaststand.org/2013/08/dredging-key-west-channel-larger-cruise-ships-referendum-horizon/; Cammy Clark. (September 27, 2013). "Key West Draws a Line in the Water Over a Wider Cruise-Ship Harbor." *The Miami Herald.* http://www.miamiherald.com/latest-news/article1955604.html

Case Study 4.1

Environmental Impacts of Cruise Tourism

by Julia Lewis

Cruise tourism, the dominant type of marine-based tourism in the Caribbean, poses a range of negative impacts on oceans. This case study describes nine different environmental impacts caused by cruise ships, ranging from oil pollution to reef damage. Each of these carries a unique threat to the health of oceans and contributes, directly or indirectly, to climate change. There are, fortunately, real-world solutions and management approaches to help mitigate the damage caused by these dangers and protect marine environments (see also Case Study 4.2). There are also a growing number of laws and regulations, mostly covering U.S. territorial waters, designed to address these environmental issues.[1]

The major environmental impacts of cruise tourism (Figure 4.2) described in this case study include: the release of liquid effluents, including sewage, gray water, bilge and ballast water, and sunscreen; hazardous wastes, including fluids, vapors, and solids; solid waste, including garbage, as well as macerated food waste; air pollution; and physical damage to reefs. Each of these impacts has its own sources and pathways, and each requires different strategies and tools to reduce or eliminate. Some of these will be explored in this case study. The above impacts are also summarized in the illustration below.

Sewage

Sewage, also referred to as *black water*, includes waste from ship toilets and medical facilities. It is estimated that a cruise ship with 3,000 passengers can produce about 15,000 to 30,000 gallons of sewage per day, or 5 to 10 gallons per person. In 2013, cruise ships discharged more than 1 billion gallons of sewage into the oceans, harming fish, shellfish, and the marine environment.[2] Sewage discharge from ships is less diluted, and therefore, can be much more potent, than sewage

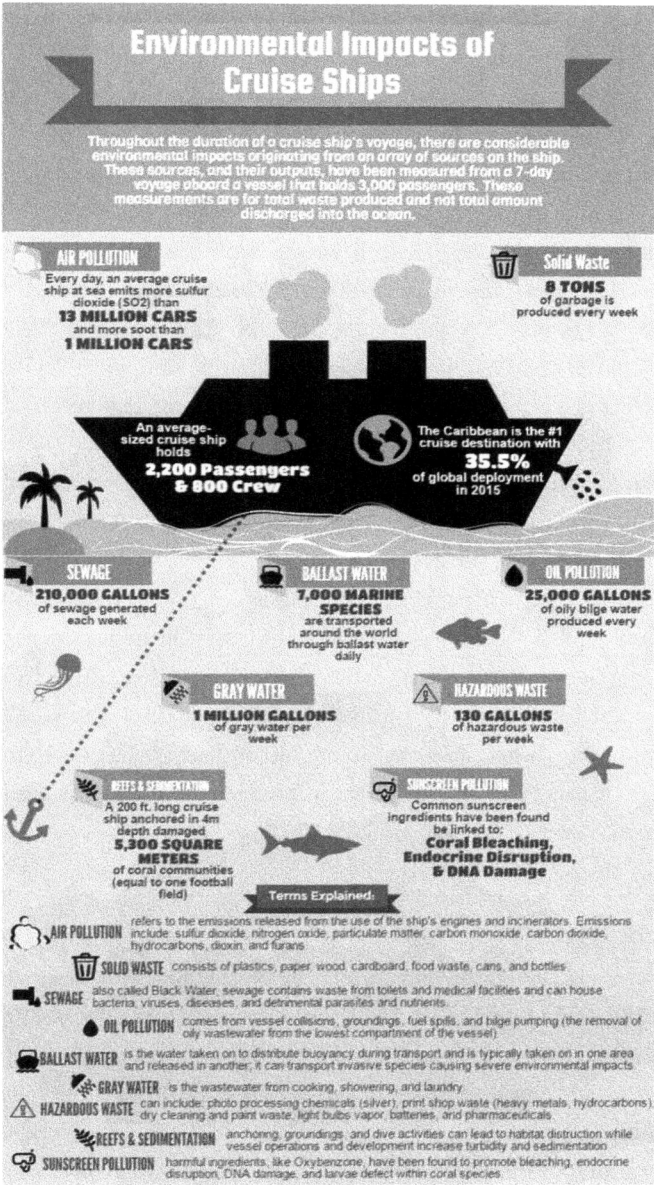

Figure 4.2 Infographic of the environmental impacts of cruise ships[3]

runoff from land.[4] Untreated or improperly treated sewage can lead to viral or bacterial outbreaks that can contaminate shellfish and other food supplies, and pose a serious risk to human health. While New England, California, and Alaska have prohibited sewage discharge close to shore, most U.S. shorelines remain unprotected from this form of pollution.

There are two general technologies for treating sewage aboard vessels: *Advanced Wastewater Treatment Systems* (AWTS) and *Marine Sanitation Devices* (MSDs). While the U.S. Environmental Protection Agency has not updated its regulations on marine sanitation devices since 1976, Alaska has enacted its own sewage treatment regulations that require vessels to utilize high-class AWTS technology. However, even with AWTS technology, treated waste can still discharge increased levels of nitrogen, phosphorous, copper, zinc, fecal coliform, and ammonia in the surrounding waters.[5] In 2009, 72 percent of the ships granted permission to discharge treated waste within Alaskan waters were found to be in violation of the state's legal discharge limits.[6] The environmental organization Friends of the Earth, which has petitioned the EPA to require more suitable regulations for cruise ships' sewage discharge within U.S. waters,[7] has identified numerous technological advancements that would improve treatment of fecal coliform, suspended solids, particulate metals, and volatile/semi-volatile organics.[8]

Gray Water

Gray water is the wastewater runoff from operations such as cooking, showering, and laundry. It is the largest category of liquid waste and may contain fecal coliform, food waste, oil and grease, detergents, shampoos, cleaners, pesticides, heavy metals, and dental waste. On a 3,000-passenger cruise ship, gray water output ranges from 30 to 85 gallons per person per day, or a total of 90,000 to 255,000 gallons per day.[9] Because gray water is not currently regulated under either U.S. law or MARPOL (the International Convention for the Prevention of Pollution from Ships), some states, including Alaska, have developed their own regulations requiring that gray water is treated prior to any discharge.

Bilge Water and Oil Pollution

Petroleum hydrocarbons have negative effects on both egg and larval forms of marine species, as well as on birds and fur-bearing marine species. A ship's oily waste stream can originate from vessel collisions, groundings, fueling spills, and routine bilge pumping, which removes oily wastewater, including runoff from machinery operations, from the bottom compartment (bilge) of the ship. An estimated one-third of the roughly 300 million gallons of petroleum products that reach the world's oceans each year are directly related to routine marine waste removal.[10] Individual cruise ships have the ability to generate 1,300–37,000 gallons of this oily bilge water every day, based on the size of the vessel.[11]

In the United States, bilge water is regulated by the Clean Water Act. These regulations forbid the release of harmful quantities of oil or hazardous substances within 200 miles of the coast. Additionally, the U.S. Coast Guard requires that any discharge within 12 nautical miles of shore be passed through a 15 parts per million (ppm) oily water separator. Beyond 12 nautical miles, vessels en route can discharge oily substances with an undiluted oil content less than 100 ppm. Oily bilge waste is typically pumped through a filter and directly into the water. However, it is hard for enforcement agencies to monitor the proper use of these filters. Oily substances can also be disposed of by using an oil separator device, then incinerating the oil or removing it from the vessel in port.

Regardless of the disposal method, all vessels are required to track their oil disposal in an *Oil Record Book*. Without continuous monitoring, however, it is extremely difficult to locate and track any missteps that may occur within the oil record book. In April 2002, Carnival Corporation pled guilty to six felony charges for polluting the ocean with oily waste as a direct violation of the Clean Water Act. In addition to the plea, Carnival also agreed to pay $18 million in fines and penalties.[12] In order to keep these illegal releases hidden, the company was found guilty of altering the ship's oil record book and rigging the ship's oil content meters, which then allowed the discharge to occur.

Ballast Water

Ballast water is the water taken on by cruise ships and other ocean vessels in order to properly distribute buoyancy during transport.[13] Ballast water has been found to contain marine plants, animals, viruses, bacteria, and invasive species.[14] It is estimated that ballast water transports at least 7,000 marine species each day around the world, and is the leading source of invasive species in marine waters.[15] Ballast water not only poses a threat to biodiversity, but to human health as well. The transported water can carry strains of cholera and introduce toxic algal blooms to the surrounding waters upon discharge.[16]

Globally, there are no regulations applicable to the quality standards of ballast water. Within the United States, ballast water is unregulated beyond 3 miles from the shoreline.[17] California recently adopted measures to regulate the use and quality of ballast water within 3 nautical miles from shore, including requiring ships to be responsible for treating their ballast water[18] and to have a level of "zero detectable living organisms for all organism size classes by 2030."[19] In addition, the U.S. Coast Guard is required to sample ballast water, biofouling, and sediment from a minimum of 25 percent of vessels to ensure they meet the state's requirements.[20]

Hazardous Waste

Hazardous waste usually accounts for the smallest quantity of waste aboard cruise ships, but it can cause significant damage. A cruise ship's hazardous waste can include photo processing chemicals (silver), print shop waste (hydrocarbons, chlorinated hydrocarbons, and heavy metals), dry cleaning waste, paint waste, light bulbs (mercury and fluorescent vapor), batteries, and pharmaceuticals. A 3,000-passenger ship can generate an estimated 15 gallons of photo processing chemicals, 1.5 gallons of tetrachloroethene (PERC), and 1.5 gallons of paint waste every day. In addition, tributyltin (TBT), an anti-fouling agent in marine paint used on boat hulls, has been proven deadly to marine species in high concentrations, and has caused unnatural physiological changes within crustaceans in concentrations as low as 2 parts per trillion.[21] Additionally, TBT can accumulate in sediments and has the ability to bioaccumulate in fish and marine species, eventually reaching the humans who consume them. TBT has been linked to damage within the endocrine system, reproductive system, central nervous system, bone structure, and gastrointestinal tract.

The cruise industry has responded to these concerns by developing a *Cruise Industry Waste Management Practices and Procedures* plan that recommends hazardous waste be incinerated or disposed of onshore, which requires that additional infrastructure be built at the destination country.[22] However, because these recommendations are voluntary, some states, including Alaska, have adopted additional measures to protect their waters from hazardous chemicals, including a prohibition on the sale and use of any TBT-based marine antifouling paint.[23]

Solid Waste

Solid waste on cruise ships consists of plastics, paper, wood, cardboard, food waste, cans, and bottles, plus any additional waste generated by passengers.[24] It is estimated that each passenger produces about 3.5 kilograms of solid waste per day.[25] Within the United States, the *Marine Protection, Research, and Sanctuaries Act* prohibits transporting garbage from the United States for the purpose of dumping into the ocean without a permit.[26] In addition, the *Act to Prevent Pollution from Ships* (APPS) bans the discharge of any garbage within 3 nautical miles of U.S. shores, and specific forms of garbage within 12 nautical miles. Under APPS, the dumping of plastics is not permitted anywhere within U.S. waters.[27]

There is a lack of clarity when it comes to incinerating or macerating solid waste and disposing of it within gray water or other waste or discharge streams. Although MARPOL "generally prohibits the discharge of all garbage into the sea,"[28] monitoring and enforcement are needed by individual countries to adequately protect the marine environment. While regions such as the Antarctic, Baltic Sea, and North Sea have already adopted bans on dumping solid or macerated waste, in-port infrastructure is needed for such bans to be a success.[29] Most cruise ships have the capacity to collect and sort solid waste, but they often report a lack of adequate waste treatment centers once in port. In the Caribbean, the lack of in-port waste treatment facilities has delayed the adoption of a ban for the dumping of garbage into the ocean.[30]

Air Pollution

On cruise ships, air pollution originates from the burning of high-sulfur fuel, as well as the use of on-board incinerators, both of which release into the atmosphere a range of harmful gases including sulfur oxides (SOx), nitrogen oxides (NOx), particulate matter, carbon monoxide, CO_2, and hydrocarbons.[31] Carbon dioxide is a direct greenhouse gas (GHG)[32] while nitrogen oxide[33] is classified as an indirect GHG; both contribute to climate change. The nitrogen released in these processes contributes to nutrient overloading, dead zones, and algal blooms. Both smog and particulate matter also have adverse effects on human health, causing respiratory problems, asthma, and even death. Incinerators also discharge other toxins, such as dioxin and furans. Studies in California found that air emissions from onboard incinerators can travel as far as 100 miles back to shore and can negatively impact surrounding air quality.[34] California has, therefore, banned the use of onboard incinerators within state waters, that is, within three miles of the coast.

In general, there are three approaches to combating air pollution from cruise ships and other vessels: using low-sulfur fuel, drawing on shore power while in port, and employing onboard emissions capture technology (e.g., "scrubbers"). In terms of fuel quality, national and international air pollution regulations can limit the amount of sulfur ships are permitted to use in their fuel within a specified region. In 2010, for example, the International Maritime Organization (IMO) created the North American Emission Control Area (ECA), which includes the waters off North American and Canadian coasts. The North American ECA includes a 200-nautical-mile low-emission zone where stricter international emissions standards apply to ships.[35] Beginning in 2015, ships were required to shift from 1 percent sulfur fuel to 0.1 percent sulfur fuel inside of the ECA region. Although cruise lines were made aware of these changes in 2009, many complained of the high cost of achieving cleaner fuel standards.[36]

Smokestack scrubbers,[37] which are designed to trap escaping pollutants and keep them from entering the atmosphere, are perhaps the most common form of onboard capture technology. Both Royal Caribbean and Carnival applied for exemptions from ECA fuel standards, stating that they planned to pursue scrubber technology that would allow them to continue to burn old fuel types while treating emissions on board.[38] Carnival was also granted an exemption that stated that its scrubber technology would only need to be used while its ships were within the designated ECA zone.[39] One major challenge to the use of scrubbers and other emission control systems is the cost of installing and maintaining the technology. In addition, while reducing levels of sulfur oxides and other noxious gases, the use of seawater in some types of scrubbers actually contributes to the release of additional GHGs (Chapter 4 Overview).

Increasingly, ports are reducing pollution by providing shore power (high-voltage electrical hookups), which permits cruise ships to turn off their engines and generators while docked. While this can significantly reduce the amount of air pollution within a port, the impact on regional GHG and other emissions depends to a large extent on where the power comes from. Most small island states in the Caribbean get the bulk of their electricity from generators using imported oil, so the net impact of shore power on air pollution and GHG emissions may be negligible.[40] In places where renewable energy from solar, wind, and other sources is available, the use of shore power can have a positive impact not only on air pollution, but on the net carbon footprint of the cruise industry.

Reefs and Sedimentation

According to the United Nations Environment Programme (UNEP), an estimated 58 percent of the world's reefs are potentially threatened by human activity.[41] Cruise industry impacts on reefs include increased sedimentation and breaking of corals, caused primarily by snorkeling, diving, boating, and anchoring.[42] Volume I of this series contains more information on coral reef threats and the impacts of dive tourism, including guidelines for industry.[43] Anchoring and boat groundings have been found to leave severe impacts on coral reefs, with slow recovery for the damaged coral. Anchor damage is directly related to the size of the vessel and length of the anchor's chain, which means that large cruise ships can be much more destructive (see Image 4.1.1).[44] In December 2015, divers videotaped an anchor chain from the *Pullmanter Zenith*, owned by Royal Caribbean Cruises, as it destroyed part of a coral reef in the port of George

Image 4.1.1 A ship's anchor after damaging coral reef in the NOAA Florida Keys National Marine Sanctuary in 1997[45]

Town, Cayman Islands.[46] According to local officials, the ship was in a legal anchorage, and therefore, could not be fined. This was just the latest in a long list of anchor-related coral reef destruction involving the cruise industry; most incidents, however, are not witnessed or videotaped. Accidental groundings can be equally destructive. In March 2017, for example, the 90-meter *Caledonian Sky*, operated by Noble Caledonia, grounded at low tide on a popular reef within a national park at Raja Ampat in Indonesia.[47] An area of some 1,600 square meters was destroyed, which experts say will cost between US$1 and $2 million to eventually restore.

Damage from anchors can be significantly reduced with the implementation of permanent moorings, designated anchorages, and proper education regarding anchoring and mooring in the specified area.[48] Critical or biologically significant habitats should be protected from cruise ship anchoring and travel routes.[49] In 2009, Florida approved a new law called The Florida Coral Reef Protection Act (CRPA),[50] which promotes the ecological and economic importance of the Florida Reef Tract, an area of 330 nautical square miles. The law authorizes the Florida Department of Environmental Protection (FDEP) to "protect coral reefs through timely and efficient assessment and recovery of damages, including civil penalties, resulting from vessel impacts to coral reefs."[51] The law applies to all vessels (commercial and recreational) and requires that any impacts be reported to the FDEP within 24 hours, that grounded or anchored vessels be removed by the responsible operator within 72 hours in a fashion that prevents additional damage, and that parties involved must cooperate with FDEP in completing a damage assessment.[52] CRPA also outlines a fee structure for damaged reefs as well as best practices for removing anchors and/or vessels that have impacted coral reefs.

Increased sediment loading caused by the construction of ports, resorts, marinas, and shipping has also damaged coral reefs and other marine and coastal ecosystems, as described earlier in this volume. Sedimentation results in increased turbidity, which reduces the photosynthetic ability of coral colonies, seagrass beds, and mangroves.[53] The Chapter 3 Overview describes these and other negative impacts of marinas and ports, while Case Study 3.1 offers recommendation for sustainable marina design and construction practices.

Sunscreen Pollution

While not specifically related to the cruise industry, the effect of sunscreens on marine environments has recently become more widely understood. In many tourist destinations, including cruise ship ports of call, locals have noticed a lingering oily sheen around popular diving areas, as well as declining coral reef health in frequently visited areas.[54] Oxybenzone, a UV-blocking ingredient commonly used in sunscreen lotions, can reach the ocean through direct contact as it washes off swimmers and divers. It is also found in sewage sludge and discharge from treatment plants, from where it can enter coastal waters.[55] Oxybenzone may cause coral bleaching, has the ability to damage coral DNA, leads to fatal deformities within coral species, and is an endocrine disruptor, causing defects in coral larvae. Oxybenzone has also been found to affect the embryonic development of algae, sea urchins, fish, and mammals. Other sunscreen ingredients found to be adverse to coral health include noncoated zinc oxide, noncoated titanium dioxide, neem oil, eucalyptus oil, lavender oil, beeswax, oil alternatives (silicone polymers and cyclic siloxanes), parabens, and preservatives.[56]

In terms of preventing sunscreen pollution to protect reefs and other marine life, there are a variety of approaches. One is through pro-reef tourism policies for divers in densely populated recreation areas. In Xcaret and Xel-Ha, Mexico, for example, visitors are asked to wear either bio-degradable sunscreen or no sunscreen while swimming.[57] In 2011, the parks associated with Xcaret ran an educational campaign that distributed over 150,000 samples of biodegradable sunscreen.[58] The United States National Park Service (NPS) launched a campaign, "Protect Yourself, Protect the Reef,"[59] to educate visitors in South Florida, Hawaii, the U.S. Virgin Islands, and American Samoa about sunscreen pollution.[60] NPS suggests that swimmers look for sunscreen products that use natural, mineral-based ingredients such as titanium oxide and zinc oxide, or use sun clothing such as hats and rash guards as an alternative to sunscreen.[61] It is estimated that a behavioral shift in favor of more sun clothing protection could decrease sunscreen pollution in the ocean by as much as 90 percent.[62]

Conclusion

While each of these impacts influence the environment in different ways, they all have a connection to climate change. Some contribute directly, while others duplicate or strengthen negative effects from other factors. Air pollution is perhaps the impact most directly correlated with climate change. As noted earlier, cruise vessels release an array of emissions, but their CO_2 emissions are direct contributors to climate change. In addition to being a GHG, atmospheric CO_2 also contributes to *ocean acidification,* whereby the pH of seawater is decreased by the ocean's absorption of atmospheric CO_2.[63] While burning fuel actively pumps CO_2 into the atmosphere, sewage, hazardous waste, reef damage, and sunscreen pollution all amplify the impacts of ocean acidification. For example, ocean acidification has been shown to negatively impact calcifying species by restricting their ability to produce or replenish their calcium carbonate shells and skeletons.[64] When this impact is combined with sewage contamination, shellfish stocks could be severely threatened as both an ecological component and a local food source. As another example, sunscreens and hazardous waste both contribute to the destruction of coral, and possibly, to coral bleaching.[65] Lastly, physical damage from anchors and groundings poses a clear threat to coral as both an ecosystem and a tourist attraction, including in currently pristine locations such as Cuba.

Moving forward, it is critical for cruise tourism destinations and cruise lines to consider both their direct and indirect impacts on climate change. Caribbean nations need to properly value, monitor, and protect these resources as they strive to combat the effects of global climate change, in part to protect their valuable tourism industry.

Notes

1. This case study is drawn from a 2016 research paper, *Cruising to Cuba: Environmental Impacts of Cruise Ships,* prepared for the Environmental Defense Fund (EDF), which highlights key environmental issues that Cuba, as the Caribbean's newest international cruise destination, might consider as it moves to develop its tourism industry. The paper was written and researched by Julia Lewis and supervised by Dan Whittle (Senior Attorney and Senior Director, EDF Cuba Program) and Valerie Miller (Manager, EDF Cuba Program).

2. Friends of the Earth. (October 2013). "Cruise Ships Flushed More Than 1 Billion Gallons of Sewage into the Oceans Last Year." http://www.foe.org/news/news-releases/2013-10-cruise-ships-flushed-more-than-1-billion-gallons-of-sewage-last-year

3. Image Source: Julia Lewis. (July 2016). Infographic of the Environmental Impact of Cruise Ships. Created with Piktochart Software.

4. Michael Herz and Joseph Davis. (May 2002). *Cruise Control: A Report on How Cruise Ships Affect the Marine Environment.* Washington, DC: The Ocean Conservancy. http://www.cruiseresearch.org/Cruise%20Control.pdf

5. Ross Klein. (2009). "Getting a Grip on Cruise Ship Pollution." Published by Friends of the Earth.

6. Ibid.

7. Earthjustice. (2013). "Cleaning Up Sewage Flows from Cruise Ships." http://earthjustice.org/cases/2014/cleaning-up-sewage-flows-from-cruise-ships#

8. Earthjustice. *FOE vs. US EPA: Complaint for Declaratory and Injunctive Relief.* 2014. http://earthjustice.org/sites/default/files/files/MSDComplaint04302014.pdf

9. Michael Herz and Joseph Davis. (May 2002). Op cit.

10. Ibid.

11. Ibid.

12. Martha Brannigan. (April 22, 2002). "Carnival Admits Guilt, Will Pay Pollution Penalties of $18 Million." *The Wall Street Journal.* http://www.wsj.com/articles/SB1019428261294696440

13. Ross Klein. (2009). Op cit.

14. Ibid

15. Michael Herz and Joseph Davis. (May 2002). Op cit.

16. Ibid.

17. Ross Klein. (2009). Op cit.

18. U.S. Department of Agriculture. (2016). "Invasive Species State Laws and Regulations." https://www.invasivespeciesinfo.gov/laws/ca.shtml

19. California State Government. (2015). *Assembly Bill No. 1312 Chapter 644.* http://ct3k1.capitoltrack.com/Bills/15Bills/asm/ab_1301-1350/ab_1312_bill_20151008_chaptered.pdf

20. Ibid.

21. Alaska Report. (2016). "Unregulated Pollution Threatening Resurrection Bay." http://alaskareport.com/science2.htm

22. Cruise Lines International Association (CLIA). (2016). "Waste Management." http://www.cruising.org/about-the-industry/regulatory/industry-policies/environmental-protection/waste-management

23. Stephanie Showalter and Jason Savarese. (October 2004). Restrictions on the Use of Marine Antifouling Paints Containing Tributyltin and Copper. White Paper commissioned by the California Sea Grant Extension Program. http://nsglc.olemiss.edu/Advisory/Antifouling.pdf

24. Ross Klein. (2009). Op cit.

25. Michael Herz and Joseph Davis. (May 2002). Op cit.

26. Ross Klein. (2009). Op cit.

27. Ibid.

28. International Maritime Organization. (2016). "Prevention of Pollution by Garbage from Ships." http://www.imo.org/en/OurWork/Environment/PollutionPrevention/Garbage/Pages/Default.aspx

29. Mike Melia. (2009). "Caribbean Cruise Ships Dump Garbage at Sea." *SFGATE.* http://www.sfgate.com/news/article/Caribbean-cruise-ships-dump-garbage-at-sea-3169729.php

30. Ibid.

31. Michael Herz and Joseph Davis. (May 2002). Op cit.
32. Organisation for Economic Co-operation and Development. (2017). "Air and GHG Emissions." https://data.oecd.org/air/air-and-ghg-emissions.htm
33. GreenHouse Gas Online. "Other Indirect Greenhouse Gases – Nox." http://www.ghgonline.org/othernox.htm
34. Ross Klein. (2009). Op cit.
35. U.S. Environmental Protection Agency. (2016). "Ocean Vessels and Large Ships." https://www3.epa.gov/otaq/oceanvessels.htm
36. *Cruise Critic*. (2016). "ECA and the Cruise Industry: What Cruisers Need to Know." http://www.cruisecritic.com/articles.cfm?ID=1700
37. Stop Cruise Ship Pollution. (2016). "Cruise Ships Emissions in Sydney Harbour Must Be Brought in Line with International Best Practice." http://www.stopcruiseshippollution.org/solutions.html
38. U.S. Environmental Protection Agency. (2013). Letters Between U.S. Government and Carnival Corporation. https://www3.epa.gov/otaq/documents/oceanvessels/carnival-letter-epa-uscg-response-8-8-13.pdf
39. Ibid.
40. U.S. Department of Energy, Office of Energy Efficiency and Renewable Energy. (2017). "Island Energy Snapshots." https://energy.gov/eere/island-energy-snapshots
41. United Nations Environment Programme. (2016). "Tourism's Impact on Reefs: An Ecosystem Under Threat." http://www.unep.org/resourceefficiency/Business/SectoralActivities/Tourism/Activities/WorkThematicAreas/EcosystemManagement/CoralReefs/TourismsImpactonReefs/tabid/78799/Default.aspx
42. Ibid.
43. Kreg Ettenger, ed., with Samantha Hogenson. (2017). *Marine Tourism, Climate Change, and Resilience in the Caribbean, Volume I: Ocean Health, Fisheries, and Marine Protected Areas.* New York and Washington, D.C.: Business Expert Press and the Center for Responsible Travel.
44. United Nations Environment Programme. (2016). Op cit.
45. Image Source: NOAA, Creative Commons.
46. Caribbean360. "Investigation Launched as Video Shows Cruise Ship Damaging Cayman Islands Reef." 2015. http://www.caribbean360.

com/news/investigation-launched-as-video-shows-cruise-ship-dam-aging-cayman-islands-reef#ixzz4iVBJrulD

47. Basten Gokkon. (March 10, 2017). "British-Owned Cruise Ship Wrecks One of Indonesia's Best Coral Reefs." *The Guardian*, U.S. Edition. https://www.theguardian.com/environment/2017/mar/10/british-owned-cruise-ship-wrecks-one-of-indonesias-best-coral-reefs

48. United Nations Environment Programme. (2016). Op cit.

49. Michael Herz and Joseph Davis. (May 2002). Op cit.

50. Brett Godfrey. Florida Department of Environmental Protection Coral Reef Conservation Program. (June 2010). *Management Options to Prevent Anchoring, Grounding, and Accidental Impacts to Coral Reef and Hardbottom Resources in Southeast Florida – Phase 1.* Completed for Southeast Florida Coral Reef Initiative (SEFCRI) Maritime Industry and Coastal Construction Impacts (MICCI) Focus Team and Florida Department of Environmental Protection. http://www.reefresilience.org/pdf/Godfrey_2009.pdf

51. Ibid.

52. Ibid.

53. Michael Herz and Joseph Davis. (May 2002). Op cit.

54. Craig Downs, E. Kramarsky-Winter, R. Segal, J. Fauth, S. Knutson, O. Bronstein, F.R. Ciner, R. Jeger, Y. Lichtenfeld, C.M. Woodley, P. Pennington, K. Cadenas, A. Kushmaro, Y. Loya. (October 20, 2015). "Toxicopathological Effects of the Sunscreen UV Filter,Oxybenzone (Benzophenone-3), on Coral Planulae and Cultured Primary Cells and Its Environmental Contamination in Hawaii and the U.S. Virgin Islands." *Arch Environ Contam Toxicol.* doi: 10.1007/s00244-015-0227-7

55. Zifeng Zhang, Nanqi Ren, Yi-Fan Li, Tatsuya Kunisue, Dawen Gao, and Kurunthachalam Kannan. (2011). "Determination of Ben-zotriazole and Benzophenone UV Filters in Sediment and Sewage Sludge." *Environmental Science and Technology* 45, 3909–16. dx.doi.org/10.1021/es2004057

56. Craig Downs. (2016). "Sunscreen Pollution." Alert Diver Online. http://www.alertdiver.com/Sunscreen-Pollution

57. Frommer's. (2016). "Sustainable Travel and Ecotourism." http://www.frommers.com/destinations/mexico/713380

58. Lori Robertson. (2012). "Travelers' Impact on Coral Reefs." BBC. http://www.bbc.com/travel/story/20120802-travellers-impact-on-coral-reefs

59. National Park Service. "Protect Yourself, Protect the Reef!" https://cdhc.noaa.gov/_docs/Site%20Bulletin_Sunscreen_final.pdf

60. Ibid.

61. Ibid.

62. Craig Downs. (2016). Op cit.

63. NOAA. (June 2016). "What is Ocean Acidification?" http://ocean-service.noaa.gov/facts/acidification.html

64. NOAA. PMEL Carbon Program. "What is Ocean Acidification?" http://www.pmel.noaa.gov/co2/story/What+is+Ocean+Acidification%3F

65. Craig Downs. (2016). Op cit.

Case Study 4.2

How are Cruise Lines Addressing Sustainability and Climate Change? A Look at Royal Caribbean Cruises Ltd.[1]

by Samantha Hogenson

Introduction

There is no shortage of bad press about cruise lines when it comes to sustainability. For a cruise line, however, environmental stewardship both at sea and in port is not only critical in the global fight against climate change, but also for a much more practical reason—to protect the products on which the business is built, including pristine marine environments and healthy port destinations. In this case study, we look at positive actions taken by one of the "big three" Caribbean cruise companies, Royal Caribbean Cruises, for a snapshot of where cruise line sustainability is today. It is important to note that most of the material for this case study comes from Royal Caribbean itself, especially its annual *Sustainability Reports*, rather than from independent reports or investigations. In addition, the significant negative environmental impacts of cruise tourism, as discussed in Essay 4.0 and Case Study 4.1, are not considered in this case study, which focuses instead on positive efforts of one cruise company.

Royal Caribbean Sustainability Programs

Royal Caribbean Cruises Ltd. (RCL) is one of the three largest cruise companies in the world, with a 2015 market share of 23.1 percent.[2] The company currently operates six brands with a combined 47 ships,[3] including the three largest cruise ships in service: *Harmony of the Seas* (see Image 4.2.1), *Allure of the Seas*, and *Oasis of the Seas*, each with a capacity of over 6,000 passengers.[4]

Royal Caribbean was one of the first major cruise lines to have a sustainability department, with an onboard recycling initiative begun in

Image 4.2.1 Royal Caribbean's Harmony of the Seas, which sails in both the eastern and western Caribbean, is the world's largest cruise ship[5]

1992 that eventually became its "Save the Waves" program.[6] Major topics on RCL's radar have included GHG emissions reduction, wastewater and solid waste management, and destination and ocean stewardship.[7] According to RCL's website, "For nearly 40 years, our company has carried out a strong commitment to environmental stewardship by following strict company policies, practices, regulations and special initiatives that we call Above and Beyond Compliance."[8] In 1997, RCL met the voluntary standards of ISO 9001:2000 for quality and became the first cruise line to meet ISO 14001:2004 for the environment.[9] Beginning in 2013, it became one of the first organizations in the United States to file its annual *Sustainability Report* using the internationally recognized GRI G4 (Global Reporting Initiative, 4th generation) reporting guidelines, which Royal Caribbean uses to cover a wide range of social, economic, and environmental issues.[10]

Save the Waves

RCL launched environmental efforts through a program called Save the Waves in 1992.[11] Initially created in partnership with Conservation International to simply reduce, reuse, and recycle waste, Save the Waves initiatives have expanded through the years. RCL states, "As our knowledge of the oceans grew, so did our program, which evolved into a broader sustainability platform aimed at preserving the oceans and protecting coastal communities. In 2015, we took a step back and formalized that program into an official platform that spans all operations from our new building to our charitable giving."[12] Save the Waves involves collaboration with educational institutions, conservation-focused NGOs, and agencies that help develop and strengthen policy for environmental stewardship. To help monitor and enforce Save the Waves guidelines, an environmental officer has been present on each RCL ship since 1996.[13] Environmental officers are "responsible for training crewmembers in the company's policies and procedures, and the ways in which Save the Waves affects each employee."[14]

Supplier Guiding Principles

Recognizing the supply chain's large role in cruise operations, RCL created Supplier Guiding Principles in 2014 to help suppliers adhere to standards in a number of areas, including environmental performance. The principles apply to transport, appliances and consumer goods, and food-sourcing components of the cruise line's supply chain.[15] According to RCL's *2014 Sustainability Report,* "We also set forth the following environmental expectations of our suppliers: use energy and natural resources efficiently; support activities that reuse and recycle materials; and continually look for ways to minimize their environmental impact and improve environmental performance."[16]

Philanthropic Efforts

RCL strives to support marine conservation through The Ocean Fund, which was established in 1996. The Ocean Fund's primary objectives are to "support efforts to restore and maintain a healthy marine environment, minimize the impact of human activity on the marine environment, and promote awareness of ocean and coastal issues and respect for marine life."[17] Between 1996 and 2015, the Ocean Fund "contributed $13.7 million to 81 non-profit organizations and institutions around the world for projects that relate to ocean science and marine conservation, climate change, key marine species, education, and innovative technologies."[18]

Examples of projects with implications for the Caribbean, as listed in the *2014 Sustainability Report*,[19] include:

- CARIBSAVE program in Jamaica to establish climate change-resistant coral in nurseries and transplant them into protected areas to foster growth;
- Central Caribbean Maritime Institute program that uses environmental monitoring data and climate simulation experiments to understand the resilience of corals in the Cayman Islands impacted by climate change;
- North American Marine Environment Protection Association (NAMEPA) program that educates K-12 students in the Caribbean Basin about the harmful effects of marine debris and how to mitigate the impacts;
- University of Miami's OceanScope program, which measures atmospheric and oceanographic data from cruising RCL ships.[20]

GHG Emissions

According to Royal Caribbean Sustainability and Corporate Responsibility Manager Miguel Peña, minimizing carbon emissions is one of the cruise line's main challenges.[21] Cruise ships consume most of their energy in propulsion, and improving the efficiency of how ships move has been a focus for RCL. As a result, RCL claims to have developed some of the lowest emission-producing ships in the industry.[22] Its new ships are incorporating designs that allow for *air lubrication*[23] and reconfigured hulls that reduce drag. RCL reports its newest ships generate 20 percent less CO_2 than ships only 5–10 years old, while existing ships have been upgraded to improve propulsion efficiency by up to 10 percent.[24] For over two dozen of RCL's older ships, "hydrodynamic improvements and speed management measures," as well as HVAC and mechanical upgrades, have removed an estimated 50,000 metric tons in annual emissions.[25]

RCL continues to commit millions of dollars every year toward testing and implementing new technologies and initiatives to help meet emission reduction goals. According to 2014 and 2015 *Sustainability Reports*, accomplishments have included:

- Nearly 25 percent reduction in GHG emissions per available cruise passenger day since 2005.[26]
- 52 percent reduction in refrigerants consumption since 2008.[27]
- Advanced Emission Purification systems installed on 19 existing and five new ships,[28] with four full ship installations and fully certified *emissions abatement*[29] systems.[30]
- Over 30 ships covered by advanced wastewater purification systems,[31] and 90 percent better performance than International Maritime Organization standard for discharged bilge water.[32,33]
- 100 percent of operational waste repurposed on 17 ships,[34] and nearly 32 million pounds of recycled waste in 2015. According to RCL, "The benefits from avoided landfill greenhouse gas emissions are estimated to be similar to that of saving nearly 23 million trees."[35]

Destination Stewardship

Royal Caribbean has established partnerships with a number of international organizations to strengthen destination sustainability and stewardship programs. Contribution to the well-being of port destinations is often an area where the cruise industry is criticized for lack of action, although Royal Caribbean has attempted to make strides, with varied levels of success. In 2010, RCL launched the Sustainable Shore Excursion Program in partnership with Sustainable Travel International. The goal is to help operators align with globally recognized best practices and obtain certification from a Global Sustainable Tourism Council (GSTC) accredited program. By the end of 2015, nearly 70 tour operators had participated in the program.[36] Among its 2020 Sustainability Goals, RCL has pledged to increase the number of sustainable tours offered to guests by certifying 1,000 RCL tours to GSTC standards.[37] A source close to the project, however, shares that this admirable goal is ambitious, given that only 70 operators had participated in the program in the first five years.[38]

In 2014, Royal Caribbean became a founding member of a public-private partnership called the Sustainable Destinations Alliance for the Americas, along with the Caribbean Tourism Organization, the Organization of American States (OAS), and Sustainable Travel International. According to the 2014 report, the Alliance "seeks to improve the way tourism is managed and to enhance the global competitiveness of the [Caribbean] by embedding sustainability into the day-to-day management and marketing of destinations."[39] Following successful pilots in St. Kitts, Cozumel, and Roatán, 7 destinations in the Caribbean were selected for the first implementation phase, and the Alliance plans to expand to over 30 destinations.[40] Again, while this goal is admirable, no major update was provided by Royal Caribbean in their *2015 Sustainability Report,* nor in other literature. A source with knowledge of the Alliance notes that the U.S. State Department did not provide funding to the OAS to continue the project.[41]

Most recently, in 2016, RCL and the World Wildlife Fund (WWF) announced a promising five-year global partnership. According to WWF, "Through the partnership, Royal Caribbean will aim to achieve ambitious and measurable sustainability targets that reduce the company's environmental footprint, raise awareness on the importance of ocean conservation among Royal Caribbean's more than 5 million passengers worldwide, and support WWF's ocean conservation work."[42] Their detailed targets, among others, include addressing supply chain sustainability, emissions reductions, and implementation of destination stewardship initiatives through 2020.[43] Destination Stewardship goals established through the partnership are described in Table 4.2. Jim Sano, WWF's Vice President for Travel, Tourism and Conservation, says, "The travel industry can either be a threat or an opportunity to protect and restore our planet. Royal Caribbean Cruises Ltd. is the first major cruise line to endorse the Global Sustainable Tourism Tour Operator and Destination certification program, and identify an actionable plan to implement it through its supply chain. By mobilizing all the stakeholders, including industry, government and travelers, across the tourism industry, we have the opportunity to achieve conservation at scale."

Table 4.2 WWF/RCL partnership destination stewardship 2020 targets[44]

Beginning in 2016, RCL will support up to three WWF ocean tourism and coastal conservation projects per year to advance ongoing conservation efforts and continue to drive sustainability within the tourism industry.
By the end of 2017, working with partners such as WWF & GSTC, RCL will support the implementation of GSTC's destination assessment in two destinations, as well as RCL private destinations, to identify sustainability and environmental threats and develop corrective action plans in concert with destination managers and local stakeholders.
By 2018, RCL will set a target for RCL private destinations to become GSTC-certified to the applicable GSTC standard.
WWF and RCL will continue to pursue alignment with WWF ocean conservation priorities and WWF's Marine and Coastal Tourism Strategy.

Conclusions

Royal Caribbean Cruises Ltd. is working to help destinations plan for a sustainable future, fund marine science projects, and lessen their own contribution to climate change. The *2015 Sustainability Report* states that stewardship goals for 2015–2020[45] include:

- 35 percent reduction in carbon emissions from 2005 levels.
- 85 percent decrease in waste to landfills from 2007 levels.
- Discharged processed bilge water will be purified to an effluent quality three times more stringent than international standards.
- 125 percent reduction of waste recycled from ships from 2007 baseline.
- Responsibly source 90 percent of its global wild-caught seafood by volume.
- 100 percent sourcing of cage-free eggs and gestation crate-free pork by 2022.[46]
- 80 percent of guests and 100 percent of crew and key people in RCL destinations will be familiar with the Save the Waves program and The Ocean Fund."[47]

But is this enough? Climate change, pollution, lack of sustainable energy options, and other problems are already impacting the tourism i ndustry in the Caribbean. More intense and erratic storms are threatening destinations and the travelers who visit them, including cruise ship passengers. RCL experienced this firsthand in September 2016, when the *Anthem of the Seas*, en route to Bermuda, was caught in the middle of tropical storm Hermine, featuring 90 mph winds and huge storm swells.[48] There is still a tremendous amount of work to be done by cruise lines in terms of climate change and contributing to a sustainable future. There does seem to be an understanding within RCL, however, that the very essence of their business depends on the health and vibrancy of the oceans and the overall environment. A glimmer of hope is found in Royal Caribbean Cruises' recognition that business as usual is no longer an option for cruise lines, and in their efforts to move their operations toward a more climate-friendly and resilient future.

Notes

1. This case study was largely drawn from Royal Caribbean Cruises Ltd.'s *2014 Sustainability Report, 2015 Sustainability Report,* and the Environment section of the corporate website, all accessed via http://www.rclcorporate.com/environment/. Facts and figures that are not cited as other sources can be found in these sources
2. Cruise Market Watch. (2016). "2015 World Wide Market Share." http://www.cruisemarketwatch.com/market-share/
3. Royal Caribbean Cruises Ltd. (2016). *2015 Sustainability Report,* 33. Downloadable at http://www.rclcorporate.com/environment/
4. *Cruise Critic.* (2016). "The Biggest Cruise Ships in the World." http://www.cruisecritic.com/articles.cfm?ID=1431
5. Image Source: FaceMePLS from The Hague, The Netherlands (Harmony of The Seas) [CC BY 2.0 (http://creativecommons.org/licenses/by/2.0)], via Wikimedia Commons.
6. Royal Caribbean Cruises Ltd. (2017). Royal Caribbean and the Environment. http://www.rclcorporate.com/environment/
7. Royal Caribbean Cruises Ltd. "Environment." http://www.rclcorporate.com/environment/
8. Ibid.

9. Royal Caribbean International. "Outreach and Achievements." http://
www.royalcaribbean.com/ourCompany/environment/envOutreach.
do; For specifics on ISO 9001:2000 quality management systems,
visit http://www.iso.org/iso/catalogue_detail?csnumber=21823. For
specifics on ISO 14001:2004 environmental management systems,
visit http://www.iso.org/iso/catalogue_detail?csnumber=31807

10. Royal Caribbean International. (2014). "Royal Caribbean and the Environment." http://www.royalcaribbean.com/ourCompany/environment
/rcAndEnvironment.do. To learn more about the Global Reporting
Initiative G4 guidelines, visit https://www.globalreporting.org/resource
library/GRI-An-introduction-to-G4.pdf

11. Royal Caribbean Blog. (August 29, 2011). "Royal Caribbean Brings
to Spain Its Environmental Policies." http://www.royalcaribbean-
blog.com/category/category/save-waves

12. Royal Caribbean Cruises Ltd. "Environment: Save the Waves."
http://www.rclcorporate.com/environment/

13. Royal Caribbean Cruises Ltd. (2015). *2014 Sustainability Report,*
66. http://www.rclcorporate.com/content/uploads/2014-RCL-Sus-
tainability-Report.pdf

14. Royal Caribbean Cruises Ltd. (2015), 66. Learn more about the Environmental Officer's role at https://www.royalcaribbeanpresscenter.
com/video/634/an-advocate-for-the-environment-the-role-of-royal-
caribbeans-environmental-officers/

15. Ibid., 81.

16. Ibid.

17. Royal Caribbean International. "The Ocean Fund." http://www.roy-
alcaribbean.com/ourCompany/environment/oceanFund.do

18. Royal Caribbean Cruises Ltd. (2015). Op cit., 48.

19. Ibid.

20. Royal Caribbean Cruises Ltd. (2016). Op cit., 31.

21. Author's interview with Miguel Peña, Royal Caribbean Cruises Ltd.
Responsibility Manager, July 1, 2016.

22. Royal Caribbean Cruises Ltd. (2015). Op cit., 59.

23. Air lubrication is when air bubbles are created at the front of the ship's
hull, which reduce resistance or drag as it moves across the ocean.

24. Royal Caribbean Cruises Ltd. (2015). Op cit., 59.
25. Ibid.
26. Royal Caribbean Cruises Ltd. (2016). Op cit., 4.
27. Royal Caribbean Cruises Ltd. (2015). Op cit., 55.
28. Royal Caribbean Cruises Ltd. (2016). *2015 Sustainability Report*, 13. http://www.rclcorporate.com/environment/
29. *Abatement* refers to technologies applied or measures taken to reduce pollution and/or environmental impacts.
30. Royal Caribbean Cruises Ltd. (2015). Op cit., 55.
31. Royal Caribbean Cruises Ltd. (2016) Op cit., 4.
32. *Bilge water* is oil-contaminated water collected from engine spaces.
33. Royal Caribbean Cruises Ltd. (2015). Op cit., 55.
34. Royal Caribbean Cruises Ltd. (2016). Op cit., 15.
35. Ibid., 6.
36. Ibid., 28.
37. Ibid., 5.
38. Anonymous interview with author, 2017.
39. Royal Caribbean Cruises Ltd. (2015). Op cit., 53.
40. Ibid., 53.
41. Anonymous interview with author, 2017.
42. World Wildlife Fund. (March 29, 2017). "WWF and Royal Caribbean Partnership: 2016 Annual Report." https://c402277.ssl.cf1.rackcdn.com/publications/1003/files/original/Royal_Caibbean_WWF_Annual_Report.pdf?1490799218
43. World Wildlife Fund. (2016). "Partnerships: Royal Caribbean Cruises Ltd." http://www.worldwildlife.org/partnerships/royal-caribbean-cruises-ltd
44. World Wildlife Fund. (June 30, 2016). "WWF and Royal Caribbean Cruises Ltd. (RCL) Increase Commitments to Long-Term Ocean Health." http://www.worldwildlife.org/blogs/on-balance/posts/wwf-and-royal-caribbean-cruises-ltd-rcl-increase-commitments-to-long-term-ocean-health
45. Royal Caribbean Cruises Ltd. (2016). Op cit., 5.
46. Royal Caribbean Blog. (December 3, 2015). "Royal Caribbean Commits to Using Cage-Free Eggs and Gestation-Crate Free Pork."

http://www.royalcaribbeanblog.com/2015/12/03/royal-caribbean-commits-using-cage-free-eggs-and-gestation-crate-free-pork

47. Royal Caribbean Cruises Ltd. (November 24, 2015). "More Bubbles Mean Better Mileage: 7th Annual Report Shows How Innovation Drives Environmental Gains." http://www.rclcorporate.com/more-bubbles-mean-better-mileage-7th-annual-report-shows-how-inno-vation-drives-environmental-gains/

48. Daily Mail. (September 5, 2016). "Not Exactly Smooth Sailing! The Moment Cruise Ship is Battered by Hermine's 90mph Winds and Huge Waves as the Tropical Storm Veers Away from the US." http://www.dailymail.co.uk/news/article-3773620/Tropical-storm-Her-mine-drifts-slightly-sea-continues-path-east-coast.html

Case Study 4.3

Climate Change and Cruise Tourism in Cozumel, México

by Kennedy Obombo Magio and Elisa Guillén Arguelles

Introduction

Since at least 2012, the Mexican Caribbean island of Cozumel has vied with The Bahamas as the Caribbean's leading international cruise tourism destination. Cruise tourism is, in fact, the main source of income for Cozumel's local government.[1] Yet, Cozumel is experiencing major challenges to this industry, including security concerns, socio-economic and environmental problems, and climate change impacts, including stronger storms, higher temperatures during summer, and rising sea level. Understanding the relationship between climate change and cruise tourism is important so that key stakeholders, including policymakers, the cruise industry, scientists, and academics, can formulate appropriate strategies to address potential impacts and protect Cozumel's leading position as a cruise destination.

Cozumel is a 30-mile-long island located off the eastern coast of Mexico's Yucatán Peninsula, opposite the coastal town of Playa del Carmen and close to the Yucatán Channel. It has a population of about 80,000 permanent residents. Cozumel is home to a mix of tourists, including cruise ship *day trippers* who spend from five to nine hours onshore; all-inclusive, stay-over hotel guests, mainly from the United States, who typically stay three to four days; low-budget backpackers from Europe and other parts of Mexico; and long-stay expatriates and retirees with homes in Cozumel.[2] The main attractions include more than 30 nearby Mayan archeological sites, as well as unique biodiversity, including coral reefs, mangroves, wetlands, salt marshes, and wildlife including manatees, stingrays and other marine life (see Image 4.3.1).

In 2016, Cozumel set a new record with 4.3 million visitors, a 7.5 percent increase over 2015 according to SECTUR, Mexico's Ministry

Image 4.3.1 Sites seen while snorkeling in Cozumel, Mexico[3]

of Tourism.[4] This included 3.7 million cruise passengers and 843,221 stay-over visitors, most of whom arrived by plane through Cancun's international airport; a smaller number of day visitors arrive via ferry from Riviera Maya.[5] Tourism and related commerce accounts for 78 percent of the island's economic activities, with the remaining 22 percent comprised mainly of fishing, agriculture, ranching, manufacturing, and construction.[6] There are 45 hotels on Cozumel with 4,098 rooms and an average occupancy rate of 46.6 percent.[7] According to the port authority, investments in new hotels and megaresorts on the island's east coast are currently underway to accommodate growing visitor numbers and expand the island's tourism-dependent economy.[8]

Economic Importance of Cruise Tourism in Cozumel

Cozumel's cruise infrastructure includes three piers, which receive about 1,600 ships a year (see Image 4.3.2).[9] Virtually all (96 percent) of Cozumel's cruise passengers come from the United States, the United Kingdom, and Canada.[10] In 2012, cruise passengers spent on average US$89, while stay-over visitors spent an average of US$538 for their total visit,[11] generating a combined total tourist spending of US$44.89 million.[12] According to a 2016 SECTUR study, cruise

Image 4.3.2 Multiple ships at Puerta Maya Port in Cozumel, Mexico[13]

passenger spending had increased to an average of about \$120,[14] while overnight tourists spent \$538 for an average stay of three days.[15] In other Mexican ports, cruise passengers spent on average only \$75. Cozumel is higher, SECTUR concludes, because of its "natural attractions and the growing number of providers of tourist services."[16] The findings of a 2014–2015 cruise season study by Business Research & Economic Advisors (BREA) are similar. This study, commissioned by the FCCA, determined that from May 2014 to April 2015, 2.97 million cruise passengers arrived in Cozumel, and 2.54 million (85 percent) disembarked. On average, those who disembarked spent \$120,[17] or virtually the same as SECTUR's 2016 findings.

The BREA study also determined that Cozumel generated US\$366 million in direct cruise sector expenditures from passenger, crew, and cruise line purchases, making it the third highest among the 35 destinations covered in this study.[18] The study identified three principal sources for the economic benefits Cozumel derives from cruise tourism: onshore expenditures by passengers, including shore excursions and retail purchases of clothing and jewelry; onshore spending by crew, which mainly comprises purchases of food and beverages, local transportation, and clothing and electronics; and expenditures by the cruise lines for supplies, such as food and beverages, port services (navigation and utility services), and port fees and taxes, such as wharfage and dockage fees.[19] The BREA study also found that cruise tourism in Cozumel generated direct employment for 6,114 residents, paying US$37.9 million in annual wages, or just over US$6,000 per employee. These were the highest employment numbers among the 35 destinations BREA studied.[20]

Climate Change Impacts on Cruise Tourism in Cozumel

Given Cozumel's economic dependence on cruise tourism, address-ing climate change is crucially important. Climate change will directly impact core tourism resources (hotels, ports and marinas, airports, and other infrastructure), cultural sites, and natural assets, and indirectly, the flow of tourists, goods, and services (see the Chapter 4 Overview and Case Study 4.1 for more information on such impacts). The Geography Institute at the National Autonomous University of Mexico (UNAM) has identified Cozumel as one of five areas most vulnerable to sea level rise in the Mexican Caribbean.[21] Much of the island's tourism infrastructure and attractions are located along the shoreline and nearshore, including three cruise ship piers, more than ten boat yards and marinas, roads, restau-rants, hotels and resorts, as well as beaches and coral reefs. In 2005 alone, three hurricanes—Emily, Stan, and Wilma—caused losses in Cozumel of more than four billion pesos (about US$400 million) and generated 7,400 insurance claims.[22,23]

Wilma, a category 5 hurricane, was declared the most intense tropical storm ever recorded in the Atlantic.[24] The hurricane made landfall in Cozu-mel, moving over the island from south to north, with the eye passing di-rectly over the northern tip. The strength of the storm, coupled with its slow movement, created catastrophic winds, wave action, and rain, which caused tremendous damage to both beachfront and inland areas. (There were, for example, as many fallen electricity poles on Avenue 65, which is 12 blocks inland, as there were on Melgar Street, which runs along the beachfront.[25]) In the aftermath of Wilma, César Patricio Reyes Roel, the general coordina-tor of Mexico's ports and marinas, urged cruise ships scheduled for Cozumel to use alternative destinations such as Progreso in the Yucatán Peninsula.[26]

Overall, the hurricane caused an exodus of about 9,000 tourists from Cozumel and damaged 98 percent of the island's hotels; 15 required complete reconstruction, including eight in the downtown area that were

Image 4.3.3 The pier in Cozumel destroyed by Hurricane Wilma[27]

swept away during the storm.[28] In addition, one of the island's three main cruise piers was completely destroyed (see Image 4.3.3), and another was extensively damaged and shut down for several months to allow for repairs. With temporary repairs, this pier was able to resume operations, but eventually a new one had to be built.[29] Although Cozumel's cruise ship piers, and cargo piers used for cruise ships, should be able to withstand large hurricane waves, their destruction may be explained by inadequacies in the original design and construction, making them susceptible to powerful storms.[30] As the 2005 hurricane season dramatically demonstrated, Cozumel needs to become much better prepared to withstand the impacts of hurricanes and tropical storms.

Beach erosion caused by storms and rising sea level is another major concern for the cruise tourism industry. Since many tourists visiting Cozumel are attracted by the white sand beaches, warm blue waters, and coral reefs, the island becomes less attractive when the sand is washed away. On average, sea level in Cozumel rises about 2.0 mm per year.[31] According to Elio Reyes Novelo, the Director of Ecology at Cozumel's municipal government, sea level rise has eroded strips of up to 200 meters of beach.[32] In an interview, the port's manager noted that years ago, Cozumel had a lively downtown beach area just a few steps from the island's ferry pier. However, the area has since been adversely impacted by storms and strong currents.[33]

Climate change is already bringing increased costs for both governments and the tourism industry. According to a study by the InterAmerican Development Bank, "Climate change will have an impact on the operating costs of tourism operators, such as insurance, heating and cooling costs, pest management, and the need to augment the water supply for drinking and irrigation needs." The study continues, "Of significant importance to tourism will be the effects of extreme events on infrastructure and insurance costs. The Association of British Insurers suggests that insurance premiums for the Caribbean region could increase by 20–80 percent by mid-century. Private sector insurance coverage may no longer be available in particularly high-risk areas."[34]

Mitigation and Adaptation

In their attempts to keep customers, Cozumel hotel managers have undertaken beach replenishment and restoration, sometimes without the permission of government authorities like SEMARNAT (Environmental and Natural Resources Ministry) and the PROFEPA (Federal Environmental Protection Office). Previous municipal governments have tried to restore the area: in 2009 and 2010, for example, the government carried out beach restoration and maintenance in Cozumel, Playa del Carmen, and Cancun.[35] The project was, however, highly criticized by some environmentalists for harming and destroying coral reefs. A local newspaper reported that Cozumel divers, accompanied by biologists and members of the Department of Civil Defense, obtained photographs and videos of the damage caused by dredging for sand on the north bank. The article stated that the "images revealed the destruction of coral, conch, and oysters, and that the sand had been taken down to the sandstone substrate. Uprooted coral and sponges were covered with crushed conch and shells, and coral beds were covered with sand."[36] The north bank is one of the last sanctuaries of the endangered queen conch, and the divers reported finding only shell remnants and no live conch. They estimated that it would take 10 years to restore the area to its original condition and to repopulate it with queen conch.

In 2013, another beach restoration project was launched by the Municipal Department of Public Works, National Polytecnic's research center (CINESTAV or Centro de Investigaciones y Estudios Avanzados del Politécnico Nacional), and ZOFEMAT (Federal Terrestrial Marine Zone) to restore the downtown zone.[37] The project entailed bringing in 33,000 cubic meters of sand from the northern end of the island to Playa Las Casitas. Seeking to improve on previous projects, the Beach Restoration and Maintenance Trust (Fideicomiso para la Restauración, Sostenimiento y Mantenimiento de la Zona Federal Marítimo Terrestre de Quintana Roo) managed to restore an additional 1.5 kilometers of beach in Cozumel.[38]

Another issue is that most hotels and other tourism structures on the island are built in front of the sand dune, and within Mexico's maritime zone (see Image 4.3.4). In Mexico, the Federal Terrestrial Marine Zone is defined as a strip 20 meters wide above the high tide mark.[39] In other Caribbean countries, the maritime zone ranges from 5 to 152 meters.[40] Based on projections published in an article by the Union of Concerned Scientists, some 90 percent of major tourism resorts in Cozumel could be damaged or destroyed by a combination of 1–2 meters of sea level rise (SLR), storm surges, and SLR-enhanced erosion.[41] Recent studies have shown that the average storm surge during hurricanes in the Mexican Caribbean is now 0.89 to 1.3 meters above sea level.[42] If scientific predictions are accurate, it is clear that adaptation strategies to mitigate these projections are urgently required.

Image 4.3.4 View of Cozumel from the cruise ship pier[43]

The Way Forward: Resilience Strategies for Cozumel

There are no shortcuts or silver bullets for addressing climate change, just a suite of good practices developed over several decades through careful research and experimentation. The range of climate change mitigation and adaptation strategies that Cozumel should consider include hurricane shelters (emergency evacuation centers); improved design of piers, marinas and boatyard infrastructure; and setting dry docks and other facilities back from the coastline. Additionally, the local government needs to update its environmental policies and strictly enforce design and building regulations covering building height limits, installation of alternative sources of energy for generators and other important equipment, safe storage of harmful or hazardous substances, and appropriate design and siting of waste treatment plants.[44]

One of Cozumel's primary challenges is to collect adequate and specific meteorological data that can assist in planning and forecasting climate-related occurrences. However, discussions with municipal authorities, hotel managers, representatives of tourism associations, residents, and cruise travelers revealed that they are not sufficiently aware of the potential impacts from climate change on the island's tourism businesses, including the cruise sector.[45] Based on interviews with local officials and experts, and a review of regional and local development plans,[46] it is evident that most key government agencies involved in tourism regulation and development are not even using the information available on climate change for planning purposes. For instance, local government officials in charge of environmental issues at the Municipal Council of Cozumel are not familiar with climate projections made by regional researchers,[47] or the storm surge atlases and climate change risk atlases produced for most destinations by CARIBSAVE.[48] This information is particularly important for land use planning and for regulation of new tourism development projects. In addition, there are no signs of federal and local governments preparing climate change adaptation and mitigation measures targeted for the tourism industry. Rather, key government agencies have issued broad statements with little detail on how Cozumel and other destinations will overcome potential climate-related challenges.[49]

For planning and forecasting purposes, consolidated, harmonized, and accurate climate information is crucial to both cruise business operators and cruise travelers, as well as government agencies and tourism businesses in Cozumel. Cozumel needs to establish a meteorological center, or improve the accuracy and efficiency in existing climate recording stations. Telecommunications infrastructure needs to be strengthened so that the island can transmit and receive data on climate through satellite links. Given the importance of Cozumel to the cruise industry, and vice versa, Cozumel's municipal authorities might approach the cruise lines to help fund such data collection facilities.

Another critical mitigation strategy for Cozumel is to build human capacity and systems for emergency management, disaster planning, and preparedness. Destination disaster management agencies should be adequately equipped to handle hurricanes as destructive as Wilma, and planning and policy making for disaster management should be based on scientifically rigorous vulnerability studies. Both the OAS[50] and the Pan American Development Foundation (PADF)[51] have longstanding disaster response and preparedness programs that work with communities, governments, and the private sector in the Caribbean to address climate change impacts. Some important cruise destinations such as Puerto Rico have already undertaken climate-related disaster preparation and training.[52]

Dr. Alejandro Palafox Muñoz, a professor of tourism at Quintana Roo University who has done extensive research on cruise tourism, has proposed a Climate Change Management Unit (CCMU) or Coastal Zone Management Unit (CZMU) for Cozumel, with scientists, planners, and adequate budgetary allocation from the local government.[53] As a model, Cuba has succeeded in integrating coastal tourism management with climate change mitigation strategies.[54] Cuba has teams of technicians, scientists, and environmentalists dedicated to management and monitoring of the country's 3,000 miles of coastline. It has also committed resources to create the appropriate legal, institutional, and political frameworks to forecast and mitigate impacts associated with climate change.

Shoreline protection and beach improvement based on environmentally sensitive and successful techniques (See Chapter 2 in *Coastal Tourism, Sustainability, and Climate Change in the Caribbean, Volume 1:*

Beaches and Hotels) are required in Cozumel, and will become more critical in the next 20 years.[55] Ideally, the cost of protecting private property—both hotels and cruise tourism infrastructure—would be borne by companies, and the burden for protecting beaches and other public spaces would be the responsibility of the government. A good example of a destination that has significantly invested in coastal management and protection is Barbados.[56] Since 1983, the government there has invested over US$17.1 million in feasibility and planning studies and beach improvement plans. Another US$28 million has been committed for about seven major beach and shoreline improvement projects.[57] Cozumel should establish a Coastal Risk Assessment and Management Program similar to the one in Barbados to ensure a healthy environment and continued economic development through improved management and conservation/protection of the coastal zone. The program should include a range of coastal management activities related to the following main objectives: shoreline stabilization and erosion control; restoration of coastal habitats; improvement of public coastal access; and institutional strengthening for coastal management.

Addressing impacts of climate change is critical to the future of cruise destinations such as Cozumel, since the industry depends on attractive and healthy coastal marine resources, as well as adequate tourism infrastructure in ports. This requires a holistic integrated management plan involving public and private sectors as well as host communities at the destination. Cruise lines need to invest in and promote climate change research and impact mitigation techniques. Additionally, local and federal governments need to demonstrate political will to safeguard Cozumel from potential impacts of climate change that may affect the most important economic activity for the island.

Notes

1. Universidad de Quintana Roo, SECTUR, and Gobierno del Estado de Quintana Roo. (December 2013). *Agendas de Competitividad de los Destinos Turisticos de Mexico: Estudio de Competitividad Turística del Destino Cozumel.* www.sectur.gob.mx/wp-content/uploads/2015/02/PDF-Cozumel.pdf

2. Ibid.
3. Corey Balazowich, Creative Commons: https://creativecommons. org/licenses/by-nd/2.0/legalcode
4. National System of Statistical Information for the Mexican Tourism Sector (Sistema Nacional de la Información Estadística del Sector Turismo de México – DATATUR). (2015). "Cruise Tourism Activity." Originally from The General Directorate of Ports (Dirección General de Puertos), Ministry of Communication and Transport (Secretaría de Comunicaciones y Transportes). http://www.datatur. sectur.gob.mx/SitePages/Actividades%20en%20Crucero.aspx
5. Novedades Quintana Roo. (2016). "Cozumel's Tourism Arrival Grows by 16% (Aumenta 16% el Flujo Turístico hacia Cozumel)." http:// sipse.com/novedades/turismo-hacia-cozumel-2015-164585.html
6. Universidad de Quintana Roo, SECTUR, and Gobierno del Estado de Quintana Roo. (December 2013). Op cit., 42.
7. Secretaría de Turismo, Quintana Roo (SEDETUR). *Indicadores Turísticos: Estadísticas.* (January – September 2016). Department of Planning and Development (Dirección de Planeación y Desarrollo). http://sedetur.qroo.gob.mx/estadisticas/indicadores/2017/Indica- dores%20Tur%20-%20Enero%20-%20Septiembre%20%202016. pdf
8. Gabriela Rodríguez. (September 22, 2015). "Cozumel, Looking for a Better Hotel Investment." In *Meetings & Events, Venues Hosted by Exhibitions Cargo.* Originally posted in gruposyconvenciones .info. https://exhibitionscargo.com/2015/09/cozumel-looking-for-a- better-hotel-investment/
9. Alejandro Palafox Muñoz and Adalberto Velázquez Méndez. (2008). "Impactos Económicos Originados por el Huracán Wilma en el Empleo Turístico de la Isla de Cozumel." In *Turismo: Desastres naturales, sociedad y medioambiente.* Universidad de Quintana Roo, Mexico. http://www.academia.edu/7257745/Impac- tos_econ%C3%B3micos_originados_por_el_hurac%C3%A1n_ Wilma_en_el_empleo_tur%C3%ADstico_de_la_isla_de_Cozumel
10. Business Research & Economic Advisors (BREA). (October 2015). *Economic Contribution of Cruise Tourism to the Destination Econo- mies: A Survey-Based Analysis of the Impacts of Passenger, Crew and*

Cruise Line Spending, Volume 1: Aggregate Analysis and *Volume II: Destination Reports*. Prepared for Florida-Caribbean Cruise Association and Participating Destinations. http://www.f-cca.com/downloads/2012-Cruise-Analysis-vol-1.pdf and http://www.f-cca.com/downloads/2015-cruise-analysis-volume-2.pdf.BREA

11. Universidad de Quintana Roo, SECTUR, and Gobierno del Estado de Quintana Roo. (December 2013). Op cit.

12. Secretaría de Turismo, Quintana Roo (SEDETUR). *Indicadores Turísticos: Estadísticas.* (January –September 2016). Op cit.

13. Image Source: Whiskey5jda (Own work). (January 28, 2016). [CC BY-SA 4.0 (http://creativecommons.org/licenses/by-sa/4.0)], via Wikimedia Commons.

14. Ibid.

15. Ibid.

16. Ibid.

17. BREA. (October 2015). *Vol. 11: Destination Reports.*

18. Ibid., 253–57.

19. BREA. (October 2015). *Vol. 1: Aggregate Analysis.* 5–7.

20. BREA (October 2015). *Vol. II: Destination Reports.* "Cozumel," 255–56.

21. Alejandro Palafox Muñoz and Adalberto Velázquez Méndez. (2008). Op cit.

22. Ibid.

23. Grant Thornton. (2005). "El Impacto Economico de los Huracanes Stan y Wilma esta Calculado en Poco Mas de 30,000 Millones de Pesos." *Economía*, 11. http://www.nafin.com.mx/portalnf/get?file=/pdf/herramientas-negocio/Economia1105.pdf

24. John C. Bardi, Bruce I. Ostbo, S. Fenical, and M. Tirindelli. (2007). "Cozumel's International Cruise Terminal: Hurricane Wilma Recovery and Reconstruction." Presented during the *11th Triennial International Conference on Ports.* http://ascelibrary.org/doi/pdf/10.1061/40834%28238%2971

25. *Cozumel Insider.* (2005). "Hurricane Wilma Recovery Update." http://www.cozumelinsider.com/wilma

26. Authors' interviews with government officials, tourism businesses, tourists, and experts. (2016–17). Cozumel, Mexico.

27. Image Source: bato93 [CC BY 2.0 (http://creativecommons.org/licenses/by/2.0)], via Wikimedia Commons.

28. Alejandro Palafox Muñoz and Adalberto Velázquez Méndez. (2008). Op cit.

29. *Cozumel Insider.* (2005). Op cit.

30. Murray Simpson, Daniel Scott, Ulric Trotz. (2011). *Climate Change's Impact on the Caribbean's Ability to Sustain Tourism, Natural Assets and Livelihoods.* Technical Notes No. IDB-TN-238. Environmental Safeguards Unit. Inter-American Development Bank. Washington, D.C., 4. http://www19.iadb.org/intal/intalcdi/PE/2011/07903.pdf. Though the authors do not make any direct reference to Cozumel, their findings offer a valid explanation of the probable causes of the destruction witnessed in the aftermath of Wilma.

31. Z.D. Tessler, C.J. Vörösmarty, M. Grossberg, I. Gladkova, H. Aizenman, J.P.M. Syvitski, E. Foufoula-Georgiou. (August 7, 2015). "Profiling Risk and Sustainability in Coastal Deltas of the World." *Science* 349(6248), 638–43. doi:10.1126/science.aab3574

32. Authors' interviews with government officials, tourism businesses, tourists, and experts. (2016–17). Cozumel, Mexico.

33. Ibid.

34. Murray Simpson, Daniel Scott, Ulric Trotz. (2011). Op cit.

35. Top Mexico. (2008). "Beach Recovery Approved for Cozumel, Playa del Carmen and Cancun." http://www.topmexicorealestate.com/blog/2008/12/beach-recovery-approved-for-cozumel-playa-del-carmen-cancun/

36. POR ESTO Quintana Roo. (2010). "Devastador Dragado de Arena." http://www.poresto.net/ver_nota.php?zona=qroo&idSeccion=2&idTitulo=25842

37. Ayuntamiento del Municipio de Cozumel. (2013). "Cozumel Municipal Development Plan" (Plan Municipal de Desarrollo 2013 - 2016 del Municipio de Cozumel). http://www.islacozumel.gob.mx/uvtaip/pdfs/PMD2013-2016.pdf

38. The Trust was established in 2009 by the Government of Quintana Roo with a budgetary allocation of over a billion pesos; however, its efforts were largely focused on Cancún and Playa del Carmen. Source: Novedades Quintana Roo. (2015). "Restaurarán Fideicomiso de

Mantenimiento de Playas." http://sipse.com/novedades/reestructur-aran-fideicomiso-de-mantenimiento-de-playas-172245.html

39. Alejandro Palafox Muñoz and Adalberto Velázquez Méndez. (2008). Op cit.

40. Judi Clarke. (2017). "Overview—Protecting Shorelines from Impacts of Climate Change." Chapter 2: Beach and Shoreline Projection. In Martha Honey and Samantha Hogenson, eds. *Coastal Tourism, Sustainability, and Climate Change in the Caribbean: Volume 1.*

41. Union of Concerned Scientists. (2011). "Sea-level Rise Threatens Yucatán Peninsula, Cancun, Mexico." Climate Hot Map: Global Warming Effects Around the World. http://www.climatehotmap.org/global-warming-locations/cancun-mexico.html

42. Oscar Frausto Martínez, Thomas Ihl, Justo Rojas López. (2016). "Atlas de Riesgos de la Isla de Cozumel, México." *Teoría y Praxis*, 74–93.

43. Image Source: Kennedy Obombo Magio.

44. Authors' interviews with government officials, tourism businesses, tourists, and experts. (2016–17). Cozumel, Mexico.

45. Ibid.

46. Universidad de Quintana Roo, SECTUR, y Gobierno del Estado de Quintana Roo. (December 2013). Op cit.

47. Oscar Frausto Martínez, Thomas Ihl, Justo Rojas López. (2016).

48. Caribbean Community Climate Change Centre. (2012*). The CARIBSAVE Climate Change Risk Atlas (CCCRA) 2009-2011.* http://www.caribbeanclimate.bz/closed-projects/2009-2011-the-caribsave-climate-change-risk-atlas-cccra.html

49. Official Federal Bulletin – DOF. (2013). *Special Program of Climate Change 2014-2018 (Programa Especial de Cambio Climático –PECC- 2014-2018).* http://www.semarnat.gob.mx/sites/default/files/documentos/transparencia/programa_especial_de_cambio_climatico_2014-2018.pdf

50. Organization of American States. *Risk Management and Adaptation to Climate Change.* http://www.oas.org/en/sedi/dsd/riskmanagement/default.asp

51. Pan American Development Foundation. "Disaster Response and Preparedness." http://www.padf.org/disaster-response-and-preparedness/

52. Jenniffer M. Santos-Hernández, Havidán Rodríguez, and Walter Díaz. (2008). "Disaster Decision Support Tool (DDST): An Additional Step Towards Community Resilience." Disaster Research Center (DRC). University of Delaware and Center for Applied Social Research (CISA), University of Puerto Rico-Mayagüez. http://udspace.udel.edu/bitstream/handle/19716/3253/Misc%2057.pdf;jsessionid=A050DF6CF313D8EA253B5FA49666BFC3?sequence=1

53. Authors' interviews with government officials, tourism businesses, tourists, and experts. (2016–17). Cozumel, Mexico.

54. Alejandro Palafox Muñoz, Arturo Aguilar Aguilar, Julia Sderis Anaya Ortiz. (2015). "Cozumel y la Transformación de su Paisaje por el Turismo de Cruceros." *Revista de Ciencias Sociales (Cr)*, 3(149), 103–15. Universidad de Costa Rica: San José, Costa Rica.

55. María de Jesús Moo Canul, Carlos Alonso Estrella Carrillo, Romano Gino Segrado Pavón, and Lucinda Arroyo Arcos. (December 2015). "Estudio de un Destino de Cruceros a Partir de la Estimación del Efecto Multiplicador: Caso Cozumel (México)." *Études caribéennes*. 31–32. http://etudescaribeennes.revue s.org/7522

56. Coastal Zone Management Unit. (2016). "History of Integrated Coastal Zone Management in Barbados." http://www.coastal.gov.bb/?q=content/history-integrated-coastal-zone-management-barbados

57. Ronald Jackson. (2014). "Building Resilience to Disaster Risk and Climate Change in the Caribbean, Caribbean Disaster Emergency Management Agency." http://eird.org/pr14/panelistas/tematica2/BIO-Tematica-2-Panel1-Ronald-Jackson.pdf

CONCLUSION

Marine Tourism, Climate Change, and the State of the World's Oceans

Mark J. Spalding

To the ancient Greeks, Oceanus was the primordial god of the sea, sometimes seen as an endless river encircling the world, from which the sun rose and set. In this vision, the sense that the human world was encompassed and intertwined with the ocean was absolute.

Today, we know that the ocean is more than just a river encircling the earth, although ocean sunrises and sunsets still call to mind romantic and beautiful images. We know that the ocean covers 70 percent of the planet—and rising, thanks to global warming. We know it is a complex global patchwork of rocky coasts and beach-lined shores, intertidal zones and wetlands, kelp forests and coral reefs, seamounts, deep sea reefs and grottoes, and even the deep abyss, all of which are home to a vast array of fish, mammals, invertebrates, flora, and so much more.

Marine habitats provide critical ecosystem services: providing food and other resources to humans (see Image 5.0.1); helping regulate climate, weather, and temperatures; filtering and breaking down wastes and pollutants; and providing cultural, aesthetic, and recreational services. But these services are in jeopardy. The human relationship with the ocean is not sustainable in its current form. Human activities now affect every drop of the vast, complex, life-giving ocean. Put simply, we take too much good stuff out of the ocean, and put too much bad stuff in.

Image 5.0.1 Well-managed fisheries harvest fish at a sustainable rate[1]

The threats humans pose to the ocean are innumerable. A small sample includes:

- Dumping of toxic wastes, as well as chemical runoff from roads and urban areas.
- Sewage discharge from both onshore and offshore (ship) sources.
- Nutrients from agriculture and sewage that lead to algal blooms and oxygen depletion.
- Discharges from mineral and petroleum extraction and transport, including oil spills.
- Noise pollution from shipping, warfare training, seismic surveys, and communications.
- Intentional or accidental destruction of both nearshore and deepwater coral reefs.
- Acidification of oceans due to rising levels of atmospheric carbon dioxide.
- Destruction of coastal wetlands, mangroves, and other vital ecosystems.
- Overfishing, destructive gear, and other harmful fishing practices, including by-catch.

- Decimation of top ocean predators, including sharks and game fish.
- Illegal whaling, ship strikes, and seismic surveys that kill or injure marine mammals.
- Dumping of garbage including plastics, which can bioaccumulate in the food chain.
- Poorly managed fish farming that leads to increased nutrients and pathogens.

While a range of human activities, including those related to tourism, are negatively impacting the health of oceans, the most significant future threat to the ocean is likely climate change. In conjunction with the local, regional, and global stressors listed above, warming of the global atmosphere and oceans may push many marine ecosystems over the edge.

The Oceans and Climate Change

The ocean is Earth's dominant climate regulator, with ocean waters absorbing most of the sun's radiation. Global warming has raised the average global temperature by about 1.2°F (0.68°C) over the past century.[2] Meanwhile, ocean temperatures have risen, on average, by only about 0.18°F (0.1°C). This shows the ability of this great mass of water to absorb thermal energy. This warming has been highly uneven, however, both regionally and in terms of ocean depth. Most warming has occurred from the surface to a depth of about 2,300 feet (700 meters), where the majority of marine life exists.[3] Changes in sea surface temperatures also show wide geographic variation, with some regions warming by as much as 4°F (2.8°C), and others actually cooling, apparently due to runoff of meltwater from polar glaciers.[4]

Rising surface water temperatures can drastically affect regional and global rainfall patterns, increasing the amount of rainfall and the strength and frequency of tropical storms in some areas, while causing extended droughts in other regions. Changing temperatures can also disrupt ocean currents, including major heat conveyors such as the Gulf Stream, with potentially devastating effects on climate and weather patterns. Changing ocean temperatures can also affect where and how marine life feeds, breeds, and grows, and whether or not marine ecosystems can survive. To add insult to injury, the capacity of the ocean to act as a carbon sink and to mitigate the impacts of our carbon emissions is declining.[5]

In addition to soaking up heat from the sun and the planet's atmosphere, the ocean absorbs an incredible amount of atmospheric carbon dioxide (CO_2), including about one-third of the CO_2 produced from human activities.[6] Absorption of CO_2 in seawater creates carbonic acid, a process occurring faster today than any time in the past 65 million years.[7] As with temperature, ocean life is finely tuned to survival in a specific range of pH, averaging around 8.2 over the past 300 million years.[8] For many marine animals, plants, and even entire ecosystems, seemingly small changes in ocean chemistry can mean big changes for future survival. Ocean pH levels have already dropped 0.1 pH units to around 8.1, representing a 25 percent increase in acidity, with a further 0.5 pH drop projected by the end of this century. This could have devastating effects on calcareous (calcium-based) invertebrates including corals, shellfish, and zooplankton, a basic building block of the marine food web.

Coral reefs, the foundation of much marine life, are especially vulnerable. Increased acidity reduces the rates at which corals grow; warmer seawater contributes to coral bleaching (where corals eject the symbiotic algae that give them their color, and which they need to survive – see Image 5.0.2); and more frequent and severe storms can threaten

Image 5.0.2 Bleached coral[9]

overall coral reef health.[10] Damage to coral reefs impacts fisheries and tourism, and reduces the ability of reefs to protect coasts from ocean storms. The loss of coastal ecosystems including coral reefs, mangroves, seagrasses, and salt marshes reduces coastal resilience to rising sea levels and makes these problems more severe. Small Island Developing States and low-lying coastal areas, including in the Caribbean, are already experiencing increased flooding, coastal inundation, and erosion. This can lead to population displacement, infrastructure damage, and in some cases, political instability.

Warmer ocean waters are also shifting fish populations, in some cases leading to decreased catches and destabilizing fishing industries that have been part of centuries-old ways of life.[11] Many Atlantic species have shifted their ranges considerably over the past few decades, while some have declined in numbers.[12] For example, the lobster industries in Connecticut, Rhode Island, and Massachusetts have suffered with the northward shift of the lobster population. In 2013, the number of adult lobsters in New England south of Cape Cod fell to roughly 10 million, just one-fifth the population in the late 1990s.[13] Increased biological stress, reduced breeding success, and increased mortality from epizootic shell disease (ESD) are all thought to be related to warming waters, a problem that has now spread northward to the Gulf of Maine.[14] And while some fish are moving out of their normal ranges, others, including potentially invasive species such as lionfish and black sea bass, are moving in.[15]

These threats are changing the ocean and the communities that depend on it. Climate change is already damaging coastal livelihoods, infrastructure, ecosystem services, and economic stability. It is within this context that these volumes have examined the role of ocean-based tourism, including the impacts of tourism on marine ecosystems, as well as how changes in these ecosystems could impact local and regional tourism economies.

The Future Status and Role of Marine Tourism

The travel and tourism sector has an annual economic impact of around US$7 trillion worldwide, representing 9.5 percent of global GDP and 5.4 percent of world exports.[16] Estimates of the value of marine tourism vary, but it is clearly in the hundreds of billions of dollars.[17] The total economic contribution of travel and tourism in the Caribbean region was US$51.9 billion in 2014.[18] While this might be small compared to other parts of the world, such as Europe, relative to the size of the region's economy, tourism looms large. Compared to 11 other world regions, Caribbean tourism ranks first in terms of its contribution to GDP (14.6 percent), employment (13 percent), capital investment (12.2 percent), and total exports (17.8 percent).[19] In short, no other region relies as heavily on tourism as the Caribbean. And based on current trends, the region's dependence on tourism, including marine tourism, will only increase over time—assuming there are still things to see and do.

Marine tourism depends on a functioning ocean, including predictable weather patterns, safe transportation routes, healthy fisheries, clean waters, and attractive coral reefs and other sites for recreation. Thanks, in part, to climate change, however, these things are in jeopardy. In terms of weather, shifts in rainfall patterns are causing problems with flooding, droughts, and storms, all of which can increase costs and impact tourism activities. More frequent, severe, and unpredictable tropical cyclones make air and ship transport less reliable, and threaten ports and other transportation infrastructure. Sea level rise and storm surge pose threats to coastal development, including facilities that contribute to island nation tourism revenue.

Other impacts of climate change can affect the activities that tourists want to do, such as diving and snorkeling; the places they want to visit, such as pristine beaches and colorful coral reefs; and the things they want to consume, including fish and other marine foods. Among the most pressing issues is the decline of corals reefs throughout much of the Caribbean, a trend that threatens not only the tourism industry, but the many communities that depend on reefs for food and for protection from storm surges and other environmental hazards. Other imminent threats include the decline of important food and game species of fish; the loss of critical coastal and marine habitats that support these and other creatures; problems with seawater quality that can affect marine recreation; and an increase in nuisance events such as invasions of sargassum seaweed, which chokes beaches and bays, making them virtually unusable for tourism.

While marine tourism is affected by these changes in ocean health, it is also a culprit. The general overdevelopment of many areas, including construction of coastal resorts and other infrastructure, places considerable burden on already stressed ecosystems. Millions of visitors contribute sewage and other waste, use precious fresh water and other resources, and sometimes, engage in destructive practices while recreating (Chapter 2). Their presence can also compel local residents to engage in unsustainable practices, such as overfishing or harvesting reef products to meet tourist demands. Poorly sited or designed marinas (Chapter 3) can destroy important coastal and marine ecosystems including mangroves and seagrass beds, both of which are vital habitat for sea life and provide critical ecosystem services, including protection from storms. The cruise industry (Chapter 4), notorious for lax environmental policies and procedures, impacts water quality and can damage reefs and other critical areas, as well as adding to the environmental burden of port towns and cities. And the tourism industry, as a whole, contributes to carbon emissions and other impacts that add to global warming and other environmental problems.

Linking Marine Tourism with Sustainability

Sustainable tourism centered on marine ecosystems and resources can play a key role in protecting the ocean environment while helping local communities adapt to climate change. Marine protected areas (MPAs), coastal habitat restoration, sustainable fishing and aquaculture, responsible marine recreation, and marine ecotourism, all represent strategies that can increase ocean resilience and help safeguard marine ecosystems from climate change-related impacts.

Engaging tourists in protecting and restoring seagrass meadows (see Image 5.0.3), mangroves, and coral reefs can help provide critical nursery habitat for fish, buffer coasts against storm surges, and sequester carbon from the atmosphere. MPAs, which are often major tourist attractions, can also help preserve endangered species and support larger conservation goals. Sustainable artisanal fishing connects visitors with their environment and contributes to local economies. Local aquaculture, done well, can supply island communities and tourism sites while reducing dependence on imported foods, meaning fewer carbon emissions from transportation.

Image 5.0.3 Seagrass meadows, which are declining worldwide, provide critical functions such as coastline protection and nursery habitat for fish[20]

Responsible and sustainable tourism can empower local communities and protect marine environments through social and environmental best practices. By using local supply chains and guide companies, tourism has the potential to foster local economic growth, rather than marginalize and displace communities. Sustainable tourism also promotes place-based cultural heritage and patrimony, showcasing traditional aesthetics while providing income for local artisans. Sustainable marine recreation, including responsible cruise tourism and yachting, can be important parts of the equation.

If we grow our tourism economy on the back of the ocean, we must create opportunities that help restore the ocean and its balance and take pressure off the commons. We need to develop innovative solutions to address the problems associated with climate change and its impact on the ocean. There is great opportunity for research, innovation, and collaboration—because the ocean and its issues are international in scope, and because they affect billions of people, including residents and visitors alike. The case studies in these volumes have described some of the many steps already being taken by residents, researchers, NGOs, and the tourism industry to respond to the challenges facing marine ecosystems in this era of climate change.

Protecting What Remains: The Time is Now!

We have an unavoidable and undeniable dependence on the ocean. One in seven people rely on the ocean for protein, and seafood is the most traded agricultural product from developing nations.[21] At the same time, global fish stocks are declining, even as more and more people turn to the ocean for food. We need to provide greater food security through sustainable onshore aquaculture, restoration of critical coastal habitat, and protection of smaller-scale, well-managed local fisheries. We must also work to rebuild the ocean's failing ecosystems and better prepare them for the added stresses and risks of climate change, including rising temperatures, sea levels, and acidity. Solutions for a healthy ocean include reducing carbon emissions, enhancing the ocean's ability to sequester carbon, and promoting resilience by addressing the cumulative effects of multiple stressors, from overfishing to pollution, and yes, even tourism.

Because of its intimate connection to the oceans through fishing and other resource-based activities, its economic dependence on marine and coastal tourism, and its long experience in living with the threat of ocean storms, the Caribbean can serve as a model for adaptation to the climate-changed world. Caribbean nations should play a key role in climate resilience efforts by being leaders in energy efficiency and renewable energy; by promoting local organic food production, including aquaculture; by protecting coastal and marine ecosystems, including mangroves, coral reefs, and seagrass meadows; and by applying sustainable planning techniques, including new, innovative and ambitious zoning and coastal development policies.

We are at a critical point for the future of life on earth. We must protect the ocean because it is our life support system, and because it is in danger. The good news is that the ocean is resilient. This means that the ocean and marine-dependent communities have great ability to recover. Our communal work has only just begun.[22]

Notes

1. Image Source: Flickr Creative Commons.
2. National Oceanic and Atmospheric Administration (NOAA). (June 4, 2015). "Science Publishes New NOAA Analysis: Data Show

No Recent Slowdown in Global Warming." http://www.noaanews
.noaa.gov/stories2015/noaa-analysis-journal-science-no-slowdown-
in-global-warming-in-recent-years.html

3. Earth Observatory. (2015). *Global Maps.* National Aeronautics and
Space Administration. http://earthobservatory.nasa.gov/GlobalMaps
/view.php?d1=AMSRE_SSTAn_M&d2=TRMM_3B43M

4. For maps showing global sea surface temperature change, see: U.S.
Environmental Protection Agency (EPA). (2016). Climate Change
Indicators: Sea Surface Indicators. http://www3.epa.gov/climat-
echange/science/indicators/oceans/sea-surface-temp.html

5. M. R. Raupach, M. Gloor, J. L. Sarmiento, J. G. Canadell, T. L.
Frölicher, T. Gasser, R. A. Houghton, C. Le Quéré, and C. M.
Trudinger. (2014). The Declining Uptake Rate of Atmospheric CO_2
by Land and Ocean Sinks. *Biogeosciences*, 11(13), 3453–75.

6. Ocean & Climate Platform. (2016). "17 Ocean and Climate
Scientific Items." http://www.ocean-climate.org/?page_id=1800

7. Mark J. Spalding. (March 2015). The Crisis Upon Us. *The
Environmental Forum*, 32(2), 38–43. https://www.oceanfdn.org
/sites/default/files/Spalding_FORUM_2015_March.pdf

8. National Geographic. (April 27, 2010). "Ocean Acidification."
http://www.nationalgeographic.com/environment/oceans/critical-issues
-ocean-acidification/

9. Image Source: Duke University, with permission from The Ocean
Foundation.

10. O. Hoegh-Guldberg, P. J. Mumby, A. J. Hooten, R. S. Steneck, P. Green-
field, E. Gomez, C. D. Harvell, P. F. Sale, A. J. Edwards, K. Caldeira, N.
Knowlton, C. M. Eakin, R. Iglesias-Prieto, N. Muthiga, R. H. Bradbury,
A. Dubi, M. E. Hatziolos. (2007). Coral Reefs Under Rapid Climate
Change and Ocean Acidification. *Science*, 318(5857), 1737–42.

11. Andrew Freedman. (May 14, 2013). "As Oceans Warm, Fish are Finding
New ZIP Codes." Climate Central. http://www.climatecentral.org
/news/as-seas-warm-fish-need-new-zip-codes-15992

12. Northeast Fisheries Science Center (NEFSC). (November 2, 2009).
North Atlantic Fish Populations Shifting as Ocean Temperatures
Warm. *Science Spotlight,* 16. http://www.nefsc.noaa.gov/press_release
/2009/SciSpot/SS0916/

13. Atlantic States Marine Fisheries Commission. (2015). "American Lobster." http://www.asmfc.org/species/american-lobster

14. University of Maine. (November 13, 2015). "Researchers Study Lobster Shell Disease to Protect Maine's Iconic Industry." UMaine News. https://umaine.edu/news/blog/2015/11/13/researchers-study-lobster-shell-disease-to-protect-maines-iconic-industry/

15. Kip Tabb. (September 10, 2015). "Fish Respond to Warming Ocean." *Coastal Review Online*. http://www.coastalreview.org/2015/09/fish-respond-to-warming-ocean/

16. World Economic Forum. (2015). *The Travel & Tourism Competitiveness Report 2015.* http://reports.weforum.org/travel-and-tourism-competitiveness-report-2015/

17. Phillippe Rekacewicz. (2006). "Benefits of Marine and Coastal Ecosystems to Human Wellbeing." Vital Water Graphics 2. GRID-Arendal. http://www.grida.no/graphicslib/detail/benefits-of-marine-and-coastal-ecosystems-to-human-wellbeing_cc9a#

18. World Travel & Tourism Council. (2015). *Travel and Tourism. Economic Impact 2015. Caribbean.* http://www.wttc.org/-/media/files/reports/economic%20impact%20research/regional%202015/caribbean2015.pdf

19. Ibid.

20. Image source: John Mark Arnold, with permission from The Ocean Foundation.

21. World Health Organization. (2015). *Global and Regional Food Consumption Patterns and Trends.* http://www.who.int/nutrition/topics/3_foodconsumption/en/print.html

Contributing Authors

Elisa Guillén Arguelles

Elisa Guillén Arguelles is a tourism professor at the Technological Institute of Cancún. She holds a PhD in Human Geography from the University of Reading. Her areas of research include environmental auditing and tourism sustainability in the Mexican Caribbean.

Travis Bays

Travis Bays is a founder of Bodhi Surf + Yoga, in Costa Rica. His degrees from the University of San Diego in economics and anthropology, and his passion for surfing, led him to create an environmentally sustainable surf tourism business with positive impacts on the surrounding community. He wears many hats at Bodhi, including surf instructor and coordinator of daily operations.

Esteban Biondi

Esteban L. Biondi is associate principal at Applied Technology & Management, where he provides specialized engineering, environmental, and consulting services for coastal resort projects and marinas. He has engineering degrees from Argentina and the United States and has directed over 100 consulting assignments in 30 countries.

Luke Elder

Luke Elder is a master of environmental management candidate in the Yale School of Forestry at Yale University, where he focuses on corporate social responsibility and private sector solutions to climate change. Previous positions include program associate at The Ocean Foundation and field station manager for The Nature Conservancy.

Kreg Ettenger

Kreg Ettenger is associate professor of anthropology at the University of Maine, where he also directs the Maine Studies Program and Maine Folklife Center. Previously, he was founding chair of the Program in Tourism and Hospitality at the University of Southern Maine. He has a PhD in anthropology from Syracuse University.

Samantha Hogenson

Samantha Hogenson is the managing director of the Center for Responsible Travel. She was one of the first undergraduate students of geotourism and holds a master of tourism administration from The George Washington University, with an emphasis in sustainable tourism management. Samantha resides in Charleston, South Carolina.

Martha Honey

Martha Honey is the cofounder and executive director of the Center for Responsible Travel (CREST). Over the last two decades, Martha has published and lectured widely on ecotourism, Travelers' Philanthropy, cruise and resort tourism, coastal and marine tourism, climate change, and certification issues. She holds a PhD in African history from the University of Dar es Salaam, Tanzania, and an MA in African American history from Syracuse University. She worked as an international journalist for 20 years, based in East Africa and Central America.

Julia Lewis

Julia Lewis holds a master's degree from Duke University's Nicholas School of the Environment. She earned a degree in coastal environmental management and broadly focused her studies on the sustainable development and conservation of marine resources. As an intern with the Environmental Defense Fund, Julia's work was specialized in the environmental impacts of cruise tourism. Previously, Julia worked for the U.S. Department of Agriculture, where she monitored international agricultural development projects around the world.

Rick MacPherson

Rick MacPherson is a marine ecologist, conservationist, and science writer. He has worked worldwide in tropical marine science and coral reef conservation, marine protected area planning and management, and community-based conservation. He owns Pelagia Consulting, an ocean science and conservation consultancy with a mission to improve marine protected area (MPA) effectiveness and community support.

Kennedy Obombo Magio

Kennedy Obombo Magio is a CONACYT Research Fellow at the Technological Institute of Cancún. He is a distinguished member of the National System of Researchers in México (SNI Level 1) and holds a PhD in tourism management from the Universidad de Occidente. He does research on tourism sustainability in the Mexican Caribbean.

Mark J. Spalding

Mark Spalding is president of The Ocean Foundation. He is also advisor to the Rockefeller Ocean Strategy, and designed the first-ever blue carbon offset program, SeaGrass Grow. Mark serves on the Sargasso Sea Commission and is a Senior Fellow at the Center for the Blue Economy, Middlebury Institute of International Studies. He holds a JD from Loyola Law School and a master's in Pacific international affairs from the University of California San Diego.

Robin Swaisland

Robin Swaisland is president of the Marine and Yachting Association of Grenada (MAYAG). Originally from the United Kingdom, he has lived in Grenada since 2003. An experienced professional engineer and project manager, he was part of the team that managed Grenada's recovery from Hurricane Ivan. In 2007, he joined Camper and Nicholsons Marinas as project manager for the construction of Port Louis Marina in St George's.

Shengxiao "Sole" Yu

Shengxiao "Sole" (Sunshine) Yu is originally from Hangzhou, China. She graduated from the University of Chicago with degrees in comparative human development and human rights. As an intern at Bodhi Surf + Yoga, Sole helped design their Travelers' Philanthropy Program. Currently the Director of Partnerships at GlobeMed, she remains connected to Bodhi as a consultant and volunteer.

Index

OTHER TITLES IN TOURISM AND HOSPITALITY MANAGEMENT COLLECTION

Betsy Bender Stringam, *Editor*

- *The Good Company: Sustainability in Hospitality, Tourism and Wine* by Robert Girling
- *Coastal Tourism, Sustainability, and Climate Change in the Caribbean, Volume I: Beaches and Hotels* Edited by Martha Honey with Samantha Hogenson
- *Coastal Tourism, Sustainability, and Climate Change in the Caribbean, Volume II: Supporting Activities* Edited by Martha Honey with Samantha Hogenson
- *Catering and Convention Service Survival Guide in Hotels and Casinos* by Lisa Lynn Backus and Patti J. Shock
- *Marine Tourism, Climate Change, and Resiliency in the Caribbean, Volume I: Ocean Health, Fisheries, and Marine Protected Areas* Edited by Kreg Ettenger with Samantha Hogenson
- *Marketing Essentials for Independent Lodging* by Pamela Lanier and Marie Lanier

Announcing the Business Expert Press Digital Library

Concise e-books business students need for classroom and research

This book can also be purchased in an e-book collection by your library as

- a one-time purchase,
- that is owned forever,
- allows for simultaneous readers,
- has no restrictions on printing, and
- can be downloaded as PDFs from within the library community.

Our digital library collections are a great solution to beat the rising cost of textbooks. E-book scan be loaded into their course management systems or onto students' e-book readers. The **Business Expert Press** digital libraries are very affordable, with no obligation to buy in future years. For more information, please visit **www.businessexpertpress.com/librarians**. To set up a trial in the United States, please email **sales@businessexpertpress.com**.

www.ingramcontent.com/pod-product-compliance
Lightning Source LLC
Chambersburg PA
CBHW071700200326
41519CB00012BA/2576